T0327556

Further praise for Corporate Co-evolution

"Based on a longitudinal, multi-level field study of the co-evolution of the Brazilian telecom-munications company Telemig and its environment, Rodrigues and Child lay the ground-work for a political interest theory of co-evolution. In particular, they elucidate the ideational and material factors that shape the changing distribution of power, and the associated legal and psychological contracts, among organizational interest groups that helps shape organiza-tional evolution over time. Their thoroughly-researched study begins to fill an important lacuna in the growing literature on evolutionary organization theory."
Robert A. Burgelman, Edmund W. Littlefield Professor of Management, Stanford University Graduate School of Business, and author of *Strategy is Destiny: How Strategy-Making Shapes and Organization's Future*, Free Press, 2002

"This book is a masterpiece case study covering over two decades of an organization, carefully conducted and showing that cases are still a major source to look deeply into organizational processes and dynamics."
Carlos Osmar Bertero, São Paulo School of Management/Getúlio Vargas Founda-tion and President of the Brazilian Academy of Management

"Rodrigues and Child demonstrate the power of historical thinking in their richly detailed analysis of how the Brazilian telecommunications company, Telemig. Using archival mater-ials, interviews, and a wealth of other information, they put the transformation of Telemig into historical context, drawing on concepts and principles from the resource dependence and political economy views concerning the relationship between organizations and their environ-ments. Along the way, they have extremely interesting things to say about corporate identity, organizational learning, and organizational legitimacy."
Howard Aldrich, Kenan-Flagler Business School, University of North Carolina, Chapel Hill

"Single theme explanations of the adaptation-selection phenomenon have reached their limit. Researchers have tended not to address the interrelationships between firm-level adaptation and population-level selection. This relevant and timely book is an exception. It advances the theory of co-evolution by incorporating a political dimension of how organizations are transformed into new forms."
Professor Henk W. Volberda, RSM Erasmus University

Corporate Co-evolution

Organization and Strategy
Series editors
John Child and Suzana B. Rodrigues

Corporate
Co-evolution

A POLITICAL PERSPECTIVE

Suzana B. Rodrigues and John Child

John Wiley & Sons, Ltd

Published by   John Wiley & Sons Ltd, The Atrium, Southern Gate, Chichester,
                    West Sussex PO19 8SQ, England

                    Telephone (+44) 1243 779777

Email (for orders and customer service enquiries): cs-books@wiley.co.uk
Visit our Home Page on www.wiley.com

Other Wiley Editorial Offices

John Wiley & Sons Inc., 111 River Street, Hoboken, NJ 07030, USA
Jossey-Bass, 989 Market Street, San Francisco, CA 94103-1741, USA
Wiley-VCH Verlag GmbH, Boschstr. 12, D-69469 Weinheim, Germany
John Wiley & Sons Australia Ltd, 42 McDougall Street, Milton, Queensland 4064, Australia
John Wiley & Sons (Asia) Pte Ltd, 2 Clementi Loop #02-01, Jin Xing Distripark, Singapore 129809
John Wiley & Sons Canada Ltd, 6045 Freemont Blvd, Mississauga, ONT, L5R 4J3, Canada

Wiley also publishes its books in a variety of electronic formats. Some content that appears
in print may not be available in electronic books.

Library of Congress Cataloging-in-Publication Data

Rodrigues, Suzana B.
    Corporate co-evolution : a political perspective/by Suzana B. Rodrigues and John Child.
      p. cm.—(Organization and strategy)
    Includes bibliographical references and index.
    ISBN 978-1-4051-2164-4 (hbk. : alk. paper)
  1. Telemig (Firm)—History.   2. Telephone companies—Brazil—Minas Gerais—History.
  3. Telecommunication—Brazil—Minas Gerais—History.   I. Child, John, 1940– II.   Title.
    HE9050.T455R63 2008
    384.6065'8151—dc22   2007019131

British Library Cataloguing in Publication Data

A catalogue record for this book is available from the British Library

ISBN 978-1-4051-2164-4 (HB)

Typeset in 11/13pt Bembo by Graphicraft Limited, Hong Kong
Printed and bound by CPI Antony Rowe, Eastbourne
This book is printed on acid-free paper responsibly manufactured from sustainable forestry
in which at least two trees are planted for each one used for paper production.

Series Editors' Foreword

Blackwell's Organization and Strategy series publishes works of major scholarship based on case studies. It recognizes that case studies offer a unique opportunity to provide an in-depth and holistic understanding of organization and strategy in its context. They offer this contribution through detailed investigation that is longitudinal and/or closely compares key examples. Longitudinal investigation can uncover the dynamics of change, the way that change pervades different levels of organization, and patterns of emergence. Close comparisons between cases can map in detail the nature of variation within a category of organizations. Both types of investigation can also derive lessons from how organizational and strategic innovations have been introduced and their effects.

In this way, case studies address the problem that Andrew Pettigrew noted in his book *The Awakening Giant* (Blackwell, 1985), namely that the lack of a holistic approach, sensitive to both context and history, has seriously limited our understanding of both organizations and their strategies. It is therefore intended that books in this series adopt a holistic perspective that examines the interplay between a range of salient aspects and from several theoretical perspectives. The books should be contextually embedded and, where appropriate, take account of the relevant historical background. They should make an original contribution to theory and offer implications for policy and practice.

Further details on the requirements for manuscripts to be considered for publication in the Organization and Strategy series are available from the Publisher, Business and Management, at Blackwell Publishing.

John Child and Suzana B. Rodrigues

Preface

Corporate Co-evolution addresses a theme that is currently attracting a great deal of interest for the new insights it promises into the way organizations develop in interaction with their environments. While this book has a strong contemporary appeal, it actually emerges from a very extensive period of preparation. It builds on research undertaken over a time-span of twenty-one years. It also results from a long academic partnership between its two authors, the fruit of which is the distinctively political analysis we apply to co-evolution.

We have accumulated many debts of gratitude during these years both to members of Telemig, the company on which the study focuses, and to colleagues and friends in many countries who have helped us more than they realize with advice, encouragement and the inspiration of their own thinking. In this short Preface, we wish to explain the book's genesis and to acknowledge the support we have received.

The origins of *Corporate Co-evolution* go back to 1986, when Suzana Rodrigues embarked on a study of strategic decision-making within Telemig, then the state-owned telecommunications company for the state of Minas Gerais in Brazil. This study was initially an extension of the doctoral research she had undertaken under David Hickson at the University of Bradford. She conducted the investigation at a time when, following the return of Brazil from military to democratic rule, state-owned enterprises were operating under turbulent conditions. It became clear that in order to understand the process of making strategic decisions within Telemig, account had to be taken of the company's socio-political context as well as its historical origins. As a state-owned company in a highly regulated sector, its institutional environment was of particular significance.

The discovery of Christine Oliver's work enhanced Suzana's awareness of the role of institutions in promoting organizational change and also how organizational leaders can in turn influence institutional policies. She also appreciated from Andrew Pettigrew's work on continuity and change in ICI that one could only make sense of organizational transformation through the adoption of a contextual and historical perspective. A Fulbright Scholarship to the United States in 1985 had offered Suzana the opportunity to become directly acquainted with emerging American thinking on organizational evolution especially that of Aldrich, Freeman and Hannan's work on population ecology, and the institutional perspectives of DiMaggio, Granovetter, Powell and Scott.

Within Brazil, certain scholars were by the late 1980s starting to develop an interest in organization culture, notably M.T. Fleury, M. Mello, C. Bertero and C. Machado. Stimulated by this trend, Suzana's access to Telemig's board allowed her to extend her research to the development of the company's identity and culture. This first period of investigation into Telemig, undertaken between 1986 and 1990, brought together various facets of the company's change, applying a range of theoretical perspectives. It was formally submitted to UFMG [the Federal University of Minas Gerais] in support of a full professorship which was conferred on Suzana in 1990.

From the beginning of the 1990s, John Child became part of the story behind this book. Having, with Chris Smith, just completed a longitudinal study of transformation in Cadbury's, the confectionary company, he was convinced of the special value of carefully conducted longitudinal research for understanding corporate change. He also brought with him the political orientation he had earlier developed in his analysis of strategic choice. John's main contribution at this point was to encourage Suzana to continue engaging with Telemig's evolution and in this way to maintain continuity with her previous work. In 1996, Suzana therefore returned to Telemig together with three of her doctoral students, Augusto Cabral, Alexandre Carrieri and Talita da Luz. They were able to chart the changes had taken place since the 1990s and to extend the range of enquiry to include restructuring, changes in formal and informal employment contracts, the role of organizational learning in restructuring, and the changing images of the company being portrayed by its union through the use of metaphor. This second stage of research was completed in 2000.

From 2001, when Suzana accepted a position at the University of Birmingham, she and John began to work intensively in making sense of the data and in collecting further information for this book. Even though the company had by now lost its own identity, Suzana's contacts with Telemig's former directors, managers and trade union officials facilitated meetings and interviews with them to furnish further information and insight right up until 2006. Our debt of gratitude to these many individuals who gave so generously of their time, records and personal insights is beyond estimation.

Corporate Co-evolution has resulted from the many long discussions we have had about the interactions of Telemig's with its institutional environment and how both company and environment co-evolved. We were particularly seeking to understand the role of managerial intentionality in a highly institutionalized environment. It was natural to espouse the new co-evolutionary perspective as the means of framing these dynamics. Its longitudinal approach together with the study of the recursive loops of interaction between the organizations and its context permits one to see beyond the limits of previous perspectives. Both of us had noted McKelvey's early insistence that all organizational evolution was co-evolution, but we were especially impressed by the systematic insights into co-evolution offered by Arie Lewin and Henk Volberda. They demonstrated the potential power of the co-evolutionary perspective and they mapped out many of its main components. However, both the Telemig case study and our awareness of previous work on organizational power and politics led us to believe that the political aspects of co-evolutionary dynamics continued to be underplayed. We hope that this book may contribute towards remedying this limitation.

As well as those already mentioned, we wish to thank others who have provided valuable comments, ideas and inspiration. Special thanks are due to Max Boisot, Andrew Brown, Stewart Clegg, Hugh Willmott, Pascale Guagliardi, Yves Doz, Neil Fligstein, Christel Lane, Marjorie Lyles, John Meyer, Subi Rangan, Gordon Redding, Oded Shenkar, and Kenneth Tse. We also wish to thank the institutions which provided support to the research as well as to the writing of the book: Cnpq (Brazilian Science Research Council), UFMG (Federal University of Minas Gerais), FUMEC University (Belo Horizonte, Brazil) and the University of Birmingham. Yves Doz and Gordon Redding at INSEAD made possible a wonderful environment for discussion and study during which much of the book was drafted in 2006. Special appreciation is due to Jonathan Michie who, as Director of the Birmingham Business School, has consistently encouraged our work.

Above all, we wish to thank our families for their support and forbearance while we undertook our long journey.

Suzana Rodrigues
John Child
University of Birmingham

Contents

Introduction

CHAPTER ONE

Perspectives on Corporate Co-evolution

Introduction

This book presents a detailed account of how one company, Telemig, evolved over its 27-year life history symbiotically with its environment. Telemig was the provider of telecommunications services for the state of Minas Gerais in Brazil. It was established in 1973 as a state enterprise by Brazil's military government. Telemig began operations under military control and management, with a mission oriented towards the economic and social development of Minas Gerais. It ceased to exist in 2000 when it was absorbed into the Telemar Group. The company was privatized in 1998, and its primary goal had by that time become the creation of shareholder value.

Over its lifetime, Telemig experienced a wholesale transformation of its mission, identity, culture and practices. This transformation passed through several stages of evolution. As a state-owned enterprise for all but two years of its existence, and a provider of infrastructural services, the path of Telemig's development was heavily informed by politics – both the policies of different Brazilian governments and political movements in Brazilian society. Its founding corporate ethos and organization were military, technocratic and paternalistic in character, and this was reflected in appointments to its senior positions. Following a strike in 1979 and the growth of public opposition to Brazil's military government, the company's policies softened to the extent of granting independence to its labour union and a measure of participation to middle management. After the country's return to civilian rule in 1985, a pluralist ethos prevailed, which introduced the criterion of political interest into the company's senior appointments and policy priorities. Subsequently, with the adoption of a neoliberal reform agenda by Brazil's government in the early 1990s, the country's telecommunications market was liberalized. Telemig was exposed for the first time to serious competition and obliged to stand on its own feet as a prelude to privatization. New leaders were appointed to carry out the wholesale changes in the company's culture and practices that the new prevailing ideology required. They introduced an ethos that granted primacy to the delivery of value to shareholders and restructured the company accordingly.

Towards the end of the twentieth century many companies underwent profound changes associated with the liberalization of markets and privatization. Why, then, does a study of Telemig warrant a full-length book? The reason is not that Telemig is particularly exceptional. Indeed, its experience probably has much in common with that of many state companies which have been subject to significant institutional and political influence. Quite a few of these companies have also experienced a transition to private ownership. However, companies like Telemig, operating within a heavily institutionalized context, have received less attention from students of organizational evolution than have companies that do not face such constraints. With the exception of anti-competition legislation, political and regulatory forces may well touch many companies only lightly, and studies of how companies evolve therefore tend to give primacy to their own autonomous strategic initiatives rather than to institutional factors. Burgelman's investigation of how strategy and environment co-evolved in the case of Intel is one such example (Burgelman, 2002a, b). The relative paucity of research into the evolution of institutionally embedded companies like Telemig is therefore a justification for investigating them when the opportunity arises.

There is, however, an even more important consideration. A study of how any corporation has evolved requires the collection of information on an extensive span of its history, information that is also comprehensive enough to permit the various strands in its development to be understood so as to provide a balanced and holistic picture. The opportunity to do this occurs only rarely in business and organizational research. Indeed, one can virtually count the number of such studies on the fingers of one hand: Jacques (1951), Chandler (1962), Pettigrew (1985), Johnson (1987) and Burgelman (2002a), and not many more. By contrast, there are many business histories and biographies of entrepreneurs. Valuable though these are, they do not normally devote much attention to issues of management or organization or offer a contribution to theory. The chief reason, therefore, why the study of Telemig presented in this book is of unusual interest lies in the unique opportunity the authors had to examine the process of the company's evolution comprehensively, in detail and over its total lifespan.

We undertook three rounds of empirical research to build up an understanding of Telemig's evolution. Altogether, these three rounds add up to twelve years of fieldwork, which furnished information on the whole lifespan of the company. We utilized a wide range of sources, including over 200 documents on company policies, practices and organization structure; biographical essays on 25 of the company's founders and leaders in the Brazilian telecommunications sector; every issue of the newspaper produced by Telemig's labour union from its launch in 1980; documents issued by the telecommunications regulatory authority; and 192 interviews at different levels inside and outside the company.

The scope of this investigation enables the present book to contribute in several unusual ways to the understanding of corporate co-evolution with the environment. First, its longitudinal span permits an insight into the dynamics of long-term organizational change and how these pervade different levels of the organization. Second, its comprehensive coverage allows us to examine the interplay of different organizational dimensions that enter into these dynamics – for example, the relation between organizational culture, identity and competencies. Previous studies of organization have generally looked at only one dimension at a time. Third, the book adopts a contextual and historical perspective. Analysis at macro (economy and society), meso (sector) and micro (company) levels provides for a contextual perspective, and the longitudinal time frame enables this perspective to be treated historically. Fourth, and most important of all, we take account of the interest group politics that played such a significant role in the company's co-evolution and in so doing are able to advance co-evolutionary thinking by incorporating a political perspective that has so far been relatively neglected.

As Andrew Pettigrew (1985) argued some time ago in his seminal study of continuity and change in ICI, *The Awakening Giant*, the lack of a holistic approach, sensitive to both context and history, has seriously limited our understanding of organizations. He subsequently elaborated a theory of method for conducting longitudinal field research on change, which we noted carefully in conducting the research reported in this book (Pettigrew, 1990). We have strived as far as possible to overcome some of the limitations of previous work, especially in the way we consciously examine co-evolving and interacting phenomena. Thus we are sensitive to context in regarding corporate evolution as a product of the dynamic arising from the interaction over time of external agencies and events with managerial policies and actions. Networks of power are seen to play an active role in these processes: networks that link individuals and groups within the organization to those holding influential external positions.

Choice of Perspective

The problem that immediately confronts any attempt to marshal information on multiple dimensions of organizational life over a long time span is the lack of a well developed theoretical perspective to guide such an endeavour. Some perspectives offer potential insights into the drivers of corporate evolution, while others are concerned with the evolutionary process itself. As we note later in this chapter, the most satisfactory available perspective, which endeavours to take account of both drivers and processes, is that of co-evolution between organizations and their environments. While this is a new perspective still in its early days of development, it offers the significant advantage of drawing attention to the dynamic confluence and interaction over time of forces stemming from an organization's environment and the capacity of its management, for its part, to respond to these forces and indeed in some measure to shape that environment. In the influential statements of the co-evolutionary perspective offered by Lewin and Volberda (1999) and Lewin et al. (1999), its scope is defined to embrace most of the theories that have hitherto contributed partial insights into corporate evolution. The main distinguishing characteristics of such theories are:

1   The level of analysis on which they focus for purposes of explanation. For example, do they focus on the environment as the main determinant of firm behaviour and performance, or do they focus on attributes of firms themselves as playing a significant determining role? Environmental factors may include the competitive structure and attractiveness of an industry, and the regime of institutional regulation. Attributes of firms themselves may include their corporate governance, their idiosyncratic resources and their dynamic capabilities including the ability to learn and adapt.

2   Related to the first distinction is the contrast among different theories in the level of freedom they allow to the actors in firms to shape events, including environmental conditions. Some theories regard the survival of organizations as depending primarily on the extent to which they are able or willing to adopt industry or other externally specified norms. Other theories allow scope for organizational personnel to negotiate or influence such norms, including the extent to which they should apply to a given organization, through social interaction or networking with persons in the environment.

3   There is a contrast also in the role that different theories ascribe to ideational as opposed to material forces as drivers of corporate evolution. Ideational forces include the influence of political ideology, societal culture and ideas concerning appropriate practices. They consist of values, norms and knowledge. Material forces, by contrast, are seen to act primarily through the resources of finance, technology and human competence that firms require for survival (Child, 2000). They may be secured from markets based on ability to pay or to promise future returns, or from public sources such as subsidies or economic rent obtained through governmental protection. At the macro level ideational forces are most evident in the form of prevailing ideologies, while at the micro level (i.e. the firm) they are evident as corporate cultures and practices. Material forces at a macro level are evident in a country's level of economic growth and health (as indicated, for instance, by its rate of inflation), while at the micro level they take the form of revenues, costs and assets.

4   A fourth distinction is between perspectives that focus on initial conditions for corporate evolution, such as the ownership of a firm or the sector in which it is located, and those that take account of dynamic properties that affect the course of evolution itself, such as organizational learning and the management of organizational change. Doz (1996) was one of the first analysts to incorporate this distinction into his research. Initial conditions shape the ideational and material foundations of a company and may therefore have a residual impact through several subsequent stages in its development (Stinchcombe, 1965).

These distinguishing characteristics point to the different, and potentially complementary, insights that different theoretical perspectives can offer to a study of corporate evolution. All of them can therefore provide analytical guidance and insight, and the challenge is how to apply these in a manner that is sufficiently comprehensive and integrated. With this in mind, the present chapter now reviews major contributing perspectives before proceeding to the more overarching and integrative framework offered by the co-evolutionary approach. The review is organized as follows. We start with perspectives that draw attention to potential drivers for corporate change and evolution. Within this broad category, we first consider approaches that focus on the firm's environment, then those that draw attention to its scope for exercising strategic choice, and then discuss the contrast between ideational and material perspectives. Subsequently, we move on to consider the evolutionary perspective itself.

Potential Drivers for Corporate Evolution

1 Natural selection

The natural selection perspective grants primacy to the environment in which a firm is located as the determinant of its performance and hence its capacity to evolve. While firms have the possibility of moving from one economic environment to another, this is regarded as a costly, difficult to achieve and long-term move. Essentially, firms are seen to be situated in a given environment, which determines their action possibilities and to which they have to accommodate in order to survive. At the same time, a favourable environment can provide a basis for a firm to prosper. Thus the rapid growth of telecommunications markets around the world has provided a favourable basis for telecommunications companies to prosper, though the extent to which they can reap good returns from this environment is tempered by the degree of competition in the sector and the ease of entry to it.

Within the natural selection perspective, industrial organization theory (IO) and population ecology (PE) have been two of the most thoroughly researched approaches (Scherer, 1980; Hannan and Freeman, 1989). According to the structure–conduct–performance paradigm in IO (Bain, 1956), industry conditions, namely market concentration, entry barriers and product differentiation, determine market power and hence both the policy options open to firms and their potential performance. PE also assigns primacy to the environment, asserting that resource scarcity and competition select the organizations that survive ('retention'), leaving little scope for managerial action to affect outcomes. The process of selecting the organizations that are 'fittest' in the sense of best coping with environmental conditions is seen to reduce the variety of organizational strategies and forms that can survive within a given environment. Both IO and PE approaches therefore assign causal primacy to the environment, so that corporate evolution is seen to be a product of environmental evolution rather than allowing for any of the reverse process.

Porter (1990) built on the IO approach to extend the range of environmental influences bearing on a firm by adding the quality of resource provision, the presence of supporting industries and the institutional context. The last of these is particularly important in emerging and transition economies (Peng, 2000). It is also of greater significance to firms that are in public ownership and/or subject to direct regulation, as are many firms offering public services or health-related products.

2 The institutional perspective

The institutional perspective is particularly concerned with the ways in which institutions confer, or withhold, legitimacy on organizations and their actions. Institutions are defined here as collective and regulatory complexes consisting of political and social agencies. Institutions potentially dominate other organizations through the enforcement of laws, rules and norms that constitute both 'formal rules' and 'informal constraints' (North, 1990; Powell and DiMaggio, 1991; Henrique and Sadorsky, 1996; Lu and Lake, 1997). Scott (1995) argues that there are three fundamental 'pillars' through which this process takes place. The regulative pillar entails formal systems of rules and enforcement mechanisms sanctioned by the state. The second normative pillar defines the legitimate means through which socially valued ends can be pursued. The cognitive pillar refers to embedded beliefs and values that are imposed upon, or internalized, by actors in society.

The implication is that governmental and social institutions offer normative guidelines for, and impose regulatory constraints upon, the policies of firms and hence the practices they can realistically espouse. Institutions can also bear upon the ability of different groups in society to mobilize opposition to corporate policies, through the laws and regulations that are enacted governing the rights to organize such opposition. If, for example, employees are protected from intimidation when they join a labour union, and if such unions are given the right to organize industrial action, this introduces an additional potential constraint upon corporate actions. Institutions can therefore impose limits on the policy choices available to firms (North, 1990). The institutional perspective perceives that isomorphism – a correspondence in policy and practice – with laws, courts, regulatory structures, educational systems, awards and certification and accreditation bodies offers a variety of advantages for organizational survival (Powell and DiMaggio, 1991).

Institutions are likely to have particular relevance for the corporate policies and forms adopted by publicly owned companies and how these features evolve over time. This is because the legitimacy enjoyed by such companies derives from their conformity to social expectations expressed as norms and laws. The institutional perspective is particularly concerned with the ways in which institutions confer, or withhold, legitimacy on organizations and their actions (Scott, 1995). This has several implications. One is that social and governmental institutions offer normative guidelines for, and impose regulatory constraints upon, the policies of public sector and public service firms and hence the missions they can realistically espouse (Powell and DiMaggio, 1991). Another is that institutions may further impact on a company by regulating the material resources that allow it to realize a preferred mission and distinctive competence (Parsons, 1956; Pfeffer and Salancik, 1978). Institutions can therefore impose limits on the choices available to corporate leaders (North, 1990).

An element in the successful evolution of any organization is that it develops a configuration of policies and practices, and in so doing establishes an identity, that is compatible with external requirements (Moingeon and Soenen, 2002). Firms that are embedded in an institutional context have to accommodate to political regimes (Clegg and Dunkerley, 1980; Granovetter, 1992; Simons and Paul, 1997). The level of this embeddedness is likely to be greater the more that firms depend on institutions because of public ownership, resource-provision and regulation. This will have consequences for the degree of autonomy they enjoy in the definition of their own policies and practices. Private organizations have more autonomy in defining their combination of mission and distinctive competence. They have more choice between alternatives, and greater freedom to pursue different strategies for securing appropriate resources from the marketplace and satisfying stakeholders. Neoclassical economists have for this reason argued that governmental institutions generate organizational traits that lead to inefficiencies (Friedman, 1962). This rationale implies that, under conditions of state ownership or heavy regulation, an organization's policies and practices could be ill suited to prevailing competitive pressures. It also implies that a transition from being a state-owned non-market organization to being a private market-competitive firm will give rise to a fundamental change of identity, as in the case to be studied (Foreman and Whetten, 2002).

Institutions are also socializing agents that transmit values and ideas to organization members (Hall and Soskice, 2001). They can filter political pressures from governmental or non-governmental agencies (such as NGOs and labour unions) by reconfiguring them in terms of ideology, vision or models of organizing. In so doing, institutions do not necessarily operate at arm's length from organizations. They can influence organizations through specific social arrangements or 'relational frameworks' (Meyer and Scott, 1983), such as joint business–governmental committees, which permit networks or coalitions to form. Such networks are institutionally sanctioned arrangements that connect actors through participation in a common discourse. They cross system levels by involving people who occupy strategic decision-making roles within both institutional agencies and organizations (Castilla et al., 2000). These links can be especially effective in conveying and articulating expectations about the identity of organizations that are highly dependent upon institutional approval and resource-provision because of a regulatory regime and public ownership (Gould, 1993; Mische, 2003).

Relational frameworks are also potentially relevant to the process of accommodation between institutional priorities and firms' preferred strategies. They provide channels through which institutional bodies can express approval or otherwise of particular corporate policies and practices. At the same time, they can also provide a conduit for corporate executives to express their point of view, and through which leading firms may have an opportunity to shape institutional regulations by offering relevant and scarce technical expertise.

Many writers within both the PE and institutional perspectives emphasize the ways in which institutions impose conformity to their norms and rules in a constraining and coercive manner (DiMaggio and Powell, 1991). However, the *interaction* between institutions and leading firms may also encourage normative and mimetic isomorphism on a more cooperative basis. This can be illustrated with reference to corporate policies towards the natural environment. The trend of green strategic change, which usually commences in a particular industrial sector such as chemicals and spreads first among competitors, is a form of normative conformity and mimicry. However, this conformity among firms does not simply arise from external institutional pressures. In the chemicals sector, governments and environmental professionals have long recognized DuPont as a leader, not only in industrial and occupational safety but also in greening – witness the Montreal ozone protocol and the company's new refrigerators. The company has often found itself in a position to establish industrial standards for others to follow, including its competitors. In extreme cases, securing the legitimacy to remain in business may largely depend upon a firm's ability to conform to the superior environmental standards implemented by such leading edge companies (Nehrt, 1998). In emerging economies, where environmental protection is still nascent, governments are known to utilize the environmental protection codes of large, reputable corporations such as Dow Chemical, DuPont and ICI as examples on which to base their regulations (Child and Tsai, 2005). This propagates mimicry and normative conformity even further. The environmental priorities expressed by governments are further expected to induce mimicry among the competitors of leading firms that are seeking to gain greater social legitimacy (Bansal and Roth, 2000). Once a firm conforms to higher environmental standards, it is motivated to support their general enforcement in order to bring its competitors' costs into line (Salop and Scheffman, 1993).

3 Managerial action and strategic choice

The institutional perspective, and the so-called 'new' institutionalism in particular (Powell and DiMaggio, 1991), argues for a deeper understanding of the interaction between institutions and organizations. However, as just illustrated, it tends to convey a sense of corporate passivity that can be quite misleading. Oliver (1991) therefore argued for a combination of the resource dependence and institutional perspectives. This is a significant departure from new institutional theory's failure to recognize proactive organizational behaviour, and from its emphasis on conformity, isomorphism and adherence to norms and values as a condition of organizational survival. For the main focus of the resource dependence perspective is a political one, namely on the power that the availability of key financial, technical and other resources gives either to the people who provide these to organizations or to the organizations themselves that possess such resources (Pfeffer and Salancik, 1978).

The institutional perspective assumes that in seeking social legitimacy, a corporation will abide by external regulations, be they formal such as enacted laws, or informal as in the case of pressures from NGOs' environmental protection demands. The resource dependence perspective, however, points out that organizations may be able to mobilize resources of finance, technology and expertise in order to establish a degree of independence from institutional demands. In emerging economies, leading firms will often be in a position to offer government inducements, such as support for educational and other social programmes, as a *quid pro quo* for negotiating some flexibility in the extent and manner to which regulations are applied to them. Even if institutional constraints are applied strictly, Porter and Linde (1995) note that companies may be able to take adaptive action by being more innovative in all aspects of their operations, including the pursuit of greater resource productivity, in order to reduce the burden of compliance.

Despite acknowledgement by resource dependence theorists that firms may mobilize resources to counteract institutional constraints, they join institutional theorists in tending to assume an asymmetry of power in favour of environmental bodies and against organizations. It is true that 'old' institutional theory did take account of political initiatives by organizational leaders, such as the successful lobbying and co-optation strategies of the Tennessee Valley Authority (Selznick, 1949). Pfeffer and Salancik (1978) also recognized there may be some scope for organizational managers to exercise a degree of strategic choice in negotiation with external resource providers, a possibility to which Pfeffer gives rather more attention in subsequent writing (Pfeffer, 1992). Nevertheless, the discussion of options for organizational leaders to take the initiative in their dealings with environmental bodies is generally underdeveloped within both institutional and resource dependence perspectives. A political perspective, which by definition is concerned with the mobilization and exercise of power, has the potential to make up for this shortfall by drawing attention to ways in which firms may be proactive in their strategic responses to institutional bodies.

Within the broad ambit of a political perspective, two specific theoretical focuses, on 'bargaining power' and 'strategic choice', explicitly draw attention to the need to take account of proactive as well as reactive strategic options. The 'bargaining power' perspective was advanced as a modification to resource dependence theory. It suggests that the bargaining powers and skills of an organization's management may mediate the control implications of resource dependence (Blodgett, 1991). Bargaining power can also be used as a strategic response to institutional pressure. A company may be able to negotiate a more favourable accommodation with institutional regulations through having the resources to exploit legal loopholes, or it may be able to negotiate favourable terms with regulators by offering other valued social benefits such as local employment creation (Leonard, 1988). Alternatively, it may have assets at its command, such as technical expertise, which it is prepared to devote to social improvement in return for securing favourable treatment in support of its own development concerning matters such as business licences, investment incentives or infrastructure provision. Hence, the bargaining power perspective warns against an assumption that the impact of resource dependence is entirely deterministic.

The strategic choice perspective reverses the assumption of environmental determinism by focusing on the role played by managers in shaping conditions and processes both outside and within the firm (Miles and Snow, 1978; Child, 1997). It draws upon the social action approach within sociology (Weber, 1978) and strategic management theory to advance the view that managerial action can impact upon how an organization evolves and even upon its environment. On the one hand, the strategic choice perspective accepts that environments have properties that cannot simply be enacted or negotiated by organizational actors (Child, 1972, 1997). It therefore attaches considerable importance to the question of whether they can select an attractive environment in which to operate. In recognizing this as a distinct possibility, the strategic choice perspective contrasts sharply with the IO approach. Organizational leaders may, for example, consider an attractive environment to be one in which social or political pressures are not as extreme as elsewhere. They may be in a position to threaten to move their capital away from an institutionally hostile environment, and this could cause embarrassment for a country seeking to attract foreign investment. On the other hand, strategic choice analysis also recognizes that it may be possible at least to moderate some external expectations through personal interaction between organizational actors and their external counterparts. Such interaction can include informal exchanges of views and information, lobbying and negotiation. There may even be opportunities for organizational leaders to go further and actually amend external conditions through negotiation and persuasion. In other words, the strategic choice view sees key organizational actors as seeking to realize their goals both through selection *between* environments, and through seeking accommodation with external parties *within* given environments.

Strategy analysts recognize that managers have a potentially wide range of actions available to them (Grant, 2005). Cooperation with other organizations, including institutional agencies, is one of the strategic options available to firms. The possibility of cooperation with external agencies is given rather little attention in the institutional and resource dependence perspectives. Both imply that the leaders of organizations come under pressure to comply with external demands, and hence that the relationship may be one of antagonism and even resentment rather than one of positive cooperation. Game theory (Axelrod, 1984) reminds us that two parties in a continuing relationship will usually in the long term secure their objectives better through cooperation than by attempting to maximize short-term gains at the expense of the other party. Thus the aspirations of governmental policy may be more effectively met through cooperation between regulatory agencies and companies, especially when the latter are, as a result, willing to contribute from their expertise and resources to the attainment of public goals. At the same time the companies are then better able to realize their business objectives in the absence of legal distractions or political pressures.

The theoretical perspectives just reviewed focus on the roles respectively of (a) constraints on firms emanating from the industrial and institutional contexts and (b) the managerial actions and initiatives taken by the leaders of firms. Whereas attention to external constraints lends itself to a view of environmental determinism, attention to managerial action lends itself to a recognition of strategic choice achieved through the negotiation and selection of preferred policies. A number of scholars, however, have argued that both sets of factors are likely to be operative, and that account has therefore to be taken of the relationship and interaction between the two. We shall return to this point when considering the co-evolutionary approach.

4 Material and ideational forces

Max Weber's framework for the analysis of socio-economic development (Schluchter, 1981; Mommsen, 1989) distinguished between the material and ideational forces driving social change. He used this framework to account for the emergence of the western capitalist system as well as its characteristic organizational forms (Gerth and Mills, 1946; Weber, 1964).

According to Weber, there are dynamic material forces of an economic and technological nature that give rise to efficiency-oriented rules and codified knowledge. These forces thus encourage the development of what Weber called 'formal rationality'. Formal rationality concerns literally the form of social arrangements in terms of routines, structures and so forth. As societies 'modernize' their economies and technologies, so they adopt a more complex division of labour and institutional arrangements. This increases their requirement for formal rationality. It is expressed both in legally sanctioned organizational innovations such as the joint-stock company and in more autonomous developments such as hierarchical corporate forms. Although countries vary in their level and form of economic development at any one point in time, an implication of the materialist dynamic is that the organizational structures and processes characterizing industrializing nations will become increasingly similar (Kerr et al., 1960). Such convergence is expected to accelerate as national economic systems become part of the same global economy and as cross-border multinational corporations account for increasing shares of activity in many sectors. It is assumed that the economic and technological material forces bound up with 'globalization' are obliging a convergence in corporations' policies and practices as a condition for their survival. This in turn offers an explanation for the wave of privatization and corporate restructuring in pursuit of shareholder-value that has characterized many previously state-owned and relatively protected companies such as Telemig. The material forces that are expected to impact upon a firm's actions and evolution concern the competitive pressures it faces, the quality of its resources, its form of ownership and the obligations resulting from this, and its distinctive technology.

Second, Weber noted that substantive values and idealism, as expressed for example in Confucianism, the Protestant Ethic or political ideologies, have exercised their own historical influence. They shape 'substantive rationality', which concerns the meaning that people give to social organization and to the processes that take place within it, such as the exercise of authority. Substantive rationality is rather more far-reaching than 'culture', at least in the sense accorded to the latter by organization theory. While it is expressed by cultures, it is also conveyed in ideologies and systems of knowledge that claim an ultimate validity. Various social institutions provide vehicles for the articulation and reproduction of substantive rationality: religions, governments and business schools are among these.

Substantive rationality can impact importantly on the identities and practices of organizations, as well as on how people behave and relate within them. One route, already noted, is through the isomorphic effects of institutions which articulate a society's substantive rationality. A recent example is the way that heightened public concern about the probity of business leaders has given rise to new regulations to enforce better corporate governance as well as professions of reform and a new sense of social responsibility from the leaders themselves. The increasingly popular and largely American-inspired international management education movement is another vehicle for convergence in the substantive rationality of firms, especially around ideas such as shareholder value (Locke, 1989). The substantive rationality informing the actions of a firm is manifest in its proclaimed mission, culture and identity (central and distinctive characteristics).

In Weber's analysis, ideational and material forces have the potential to impact on each other. On the one hand, the Protestant Ethic laid foundations for the spirit of western capitalism, and the Confucian ethic shaped the spirit of Chinese capitalism (Redding, 1990). On the other hand, the material conditions of a capitalist economy – especially its products and modes of employment – themselves have significant impacts on people's values and expectations in areas such as personal fulfilment and lifestyle.

Importantly, however, Weber did not adopt a wholly deterministic view of social development. He allowed for the role of 'social action', which is intentional action oriented towards others. The intention behind such action may be informed by economic calculation, values, emotion or tradition (Weber, 1978). In other words, action may be motivated and guided by material interests, ideals or a combination of both. It is not, however, necessarily a slave to the contextual forces that express materialism or idealism. There is always a possibility for initiative and innovation on the part of those who make or influence decisions on organization. As noted, this insight has more recently been adopted by those who seek to take our understanding of organizations beyond the narrow confines of environmental determinism, be this in the form of natural selection or institutional theory.

The integrative and comprehensive character of the Weberian framework can aid the analysis of corporate evolution in several respects (Child, 2000). First, it encourages a balanced appreciation of the contextual factors impacting upon organizations, balanced in the sense that these are not viewed narrowly within the confines of a single theoretical lens, be this cultural, idealist or materialist. The Weberian framework points to the importance of adopting a holistic perspective on co-evolution. Account needs to be taken of changes in the ideational realm (such as prevailing ideologies towards business and stakeholder expectations) as well as in material factors (such as competition, resources, technologies, practices and performance).

Second, the framework encourages us to take greater care in specifying the contextual location of any given organization with respect to the likely impact upon it of both material forces and the influence of ideas. For instance, the extent to which the policies and practices of a firm continue to be guided by its founding identity may depend on how far it can maintain its autonomy from both new external materialist forces (such as international competition) and new external values (such as those expressed by a new political regime). Third, Weber's recognition that organizational arrangements do not simply reflect the impact of external material or ideational forces, but are also the product of conscious, intentional action, allows us to incorporate strategic choice into the analysis (Child, 1997). His framework permits us to take into account the possibility that not only the contextual location of an organization but also the intentionality and sense-making of its actors will have a bearing on its structure, processes and policies (Weick, 1995; Biggart, 1997). In other words, both strategy and context are likely to shape corporate evolution.

5 Evolutionary and co-evolutionary perspectives

Evolution is a concept imported from biology, where it refers to the development of organisms and species over time from one state to another, usually along a path of increasing complexity and sophistication. The primary focus is on development over many generations, fostered by natural selection among the variety of living beings within a population. Evolution in this Darwinian sense can, of course, be used only as a metaphorical term in the study of management, since companies do not breed genetically. It has nevertheless been argued by population ecology theorists that a Darwinian process takes place in populations of companies (Hannan and Freeman, 1989), since those with the best fit to their environments survive in markets requiring companies with certain characteristics, and those without them go bankrupt. This posits a trend towards isomorphism among companies located in similar environments through a process of economic determinism.

The scientifically discredited Lamarckian variant of evolutionary theory, positing that members of a species can pass on their acquired knowledge to their offspring, actually provides a more useful analogy for the analysis of corporate evolution. For it is perfectly possible to conceive of firms learning, adapting, and then passing on their knowledge or know-how to future generations of managers and staff, thus giving those firms a competitive advantage. This implies that the nature of a firm at any one point in time will be a product of previously prevailing ideas and material factors, as well as of its present situation. It suggests that a firm will be conditioned by a degree of 'path-dependency', while at the same time being responsive to current internal and external circumstances. By allowing for the potential influence of both past and present forces, this perspective treats evolution as a dynamic rather than simply an additive process.

The conjunction of past and present informs the useful distinction between initial conditions and subsequent adaptation in the evolution of companies. Firms are created with a set of initial conditions. Initial conditions can be both ideational, such as a firm's founding corporate mission, and material, such as the competencies with which a firm is endowed. IO theorists, for instance, tend to give primacy to initial conditions by assuming that it is not easy for firms to escape the industries in which they were first established. Thus a firm's initial conditions may be expected to have a significant residual effect on its subsequent evolution. They create a 'heritage' in terms of corporate identity and culture, and a 'legacy' in terms of inherited structures, practices and endowments. A firm's initial conditions, along with its capacity to perform as expected, affect its subsequent evolution. Its capacity to perform well is likely to be affected by a combination of internal factors, such as the rate of organizational learning, and external factors such as the extent to which the firm enjoys autonomy or is subject to external regulation.

As Stinchcombe (1965) illustrated in his seminal essay, organizations can bear the marks of their initial founding conditions for a very long time over the years of their subsequent development. This suggests a number of possibilities. One is that the identity and public image attaching to an organization at its foundation, or formulated in its early stages of development, will continue to be meaningful for both their members and other stakeholders even if conditions subsequently change. Another possibility is that the subsequent success of an organization, including its ability to adapt through learning, will depend importantly on the quality of resources provided, and the appropriateness of the structure laid down for it, at its foundation. Thus initial conditions are likely to exert an influence on the subsequent evolution of an organization, including its ability to incorporate and adjust to learning, even though subsequent decisions and events will also play a part. Doz (1996) concluded from a close study of three international strategic alliances that a combination of initial conditions and subsequent learning produced an evolutionary process leading to success or failure of cooperation.

Insofar as established initial conditions may predispose to the retention of founding ideas and material provisions, whereas subsequent learning provides an impetus toward changing these, their conjunction implies that continuity and change will together characterize organizational evolution. Several previous studies have pointed to the existence of this paradox (e.g. Pettigrew, 1985; Child and Smith, 1987). They indicate that in a study of corporate evolution, it is necessary to be alert to instances of where continuity coexists together with change (discontinuity), and how this coexistence is accommodated. One may postulate that a balance needs to be struck between each aspect if corporate evolution is to be maintained over time. For if there is too much discontinuity, a firm may lose its distinctive competencies and the accumulated knowledge held by persons declared redundant or encapsulated in discarded routines. If there is too much continuity, a firm may fail to adapt to a changing environment.

An Overarching Perspective: Co-evolution

The theoretical perspectives considered thus far in this chapter offer a set of distinctive contributions. They distinguish between levels of analysis – economy and society (macro), sector (meso) and firm (micro). Some emphasize the determination of firm behaviour and change by higher-level variables, while others emphasize the ability of managers to negotiate external conditions. Some, like cultural theorists, concentrate on the relevance of ideas, while others like economists focus their analyses on material factors. Some adopt a relatively static view, emphasizing the power of initial conditions like industry membership, while others adopt a more evolutionary view stressing the role both of changing circumstances and of the ability of organizations to benefit from learning.

Certain of the perspectives we have reviewed, such as the Weberian, offer a quite broad and potentially dynamic approach to the analysis of corporate evolution. Nevertheless, despite their undoubted value, each one on its own contributes only a partial insight. There is a need to bring them together within an overarching perspective that more adequately addresses the dynamics of corporate evolution over time. This is the aim and claim of the so-called 'co-evolutionary' perspective developed in recent years. This perspective is briefly introduced here and then discussed at greater length in Chapter 11 with the benefit of insights from the Telemig case.

The co-evolutionary perspective regards environments and organizations as evolving in relation to each other. It 'considers organizations, their populations, and their environments as the interdependent outcome of managerial actions, institutional influences, and extra-institutional changes (technological, sociopolitical, and other environmental phenomena)' (Lewin et al., 1999, p. 535). It posits a framework of analysis, focusing on firms, in which there are ongoing recursive processes linking the evolution of institutional and extra-institutional environments with that of the firms themselves. These processes are mediated by managerial action, strategic intent, adaptation and performance achievement in each firm, as well as by the competitive dynamics established by the behaviour of all firms in a sector. It is important to note, however, that a co-evolutionary perspective is more encompassing than the focus on strategic evolution adopted by writers such as Burgelman (2002a) and Johnson (1987). Studies of strategic change do, of course, take the environment into account, but they tend to confine themselves to its economic and other material features. They have not generally considered the significance of institutional and political factors, including those that can be conveyed in influential ideas concerning the legitimacy of corporate management and its practices.

A co-evolutionary perspective has the potential to inform any research on organizations that spans levels of analysis and involves adaptation over time (Lewin and Volberda, 1999). By drawing attention to the continuing interdependence between context and organization, the co-evolutionary perspective offers a framework in which the development over time of firms and their populations can be

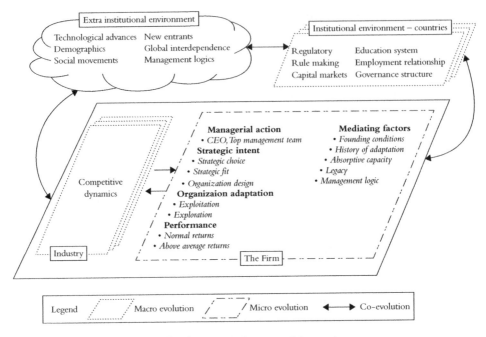

Figure 1.1   Co-evolution of a firm, its industry and its environment.

better understood. It is the framework within which the present study of Telemig will be located. A representation of this framework is given in figure 1.1 (from Lewin et al., 1999, Exhibit 1).

Co-evolution is the most satisfactory available perspective for addressing the question of corporate evolution. It endeavours to take account of both drivers and processes. It also has the significant advantage of drawing attention to the dynamic confluence and interaction over time of forces stemming from an organization's environment and the capacity of its management, for its part, to respond to these forces and indeed in some measure to shape that environment.

While the co-evolutionary perspective has only been developed in a comprehensive form since the mid-1990s, it was foreshadowed in the insights of several scholars who were concerned with the dynamics of organizations' relations with their environments. Selznick's (1949) study of how the Tennessee Valley Authority sought to overcome opposition to its plans under the New Deal was a pioneering analysis of how an organization contributed to the evolution of a community into which it was inserted. Another example is the model of context, structure and process that Pettigrew (1985) developed to interpret his detailed longitudinal study of ICI. Pettigrew was one of the first scholars to argue for longitudinal studies of organizational change within their environments that could advance theorizing on the interactions between context, structure and process. The strategic choice analysis offered by Child (1972) also presaged the co-evolutionary perspective in focusing on the potentially mutual impact that an organization's leading group and parties in the environment could have upon each other. In a later elaboration, Child (1997) distinguished two levels of dynamic interaction in the development of organizations and their environments, through the processes of what he termed inner and outer structuration. Nevertheless, more recent work has for the first time brought together the various theoretical strands informing co-evolution. What still remains as somewhat of a blind spot in co-evolutionary thinking, and provides the leitmotiv of this book, is an analysis of how political interests inform and condition the interplay between organizations and their external worlds.

Limitations of Current Co-evolutionary Theorizing

The co-evolutionary perspective at its current stage of development suffers from a number of limitations, which it is the intention of this book to address. One limitation stems from the infrequent attention that has been given to the evolution of organizations that are subject to a high level of institutional control, through public ownership or through regulation. Most research to date applying the co-evolutionary perspective has examined examples of competitive firms and industries that are not subject to high levels of direct institutional influence (e.g. *Organization Science*, 1999; *Organization Studies*, 2001; *Journal of Management Studies*, 2003). In such less-institutionalized environments, the strategic actions taken by firms themselves are expected to have a significant impact on their subsequent evolution and to some extent that of their environment as well. The co-evolutionary framework allows for the influence of institutional factors, and one of Telemig's key characteristics, as a state-owned telecommunications company for virtually all of its life, was its high embeddedness within an institutional environment. A study of Telemig therefore has the potential to offer a distinctive theoretical contribution within the ambit of co-evolutionary studies.

While the co-evolutionary perspective draws attention primarily to interdependencies between environments and organizations, it has so far had less to say about the processes occurring within each. We shall argue and demonstrate that there are interdependencies between different internal organizational processes and that these interactions are significant for an understanding of how firms evolve. Moreover, the environment may mediate these interactions. For example, the political norms that prevail in the wider society can bear upon the legitimacy of a particular basis for employee compliance with managerial authority (Etzioni, 1961). Early in Telemig's history, compliance was associated with the normative social approval of a military regime that led to acceptance of an authoritarian mode of management. Later on, with the return of democracy to Brazil, militarism lost legitimacy and the basis of compliance with authority became more utilitarian. Consequently, an authoriarian style of management was no longer acceptable. Thus if the social legitimacy enjoyed by a firm's managers declines, goodwill towards them, and even trust in them, may correspondingly reduce with the result that their ability to implement strategy through cooperation from employees is impaired.

The Telemig case leads us to develop a more political perspective on co-evolutionary dynamics than has hitherto typified co-evolutionary thinking. This perspective emerges during the following chapters and is set out more formally in Chapter 11. It regards organizations and their environments as comprising a number of interest groups and hence as arenas of competing interests. The collective expression of these interests may transcend the boundaries of a particular organization, as when the interests of its employees are expressed by a union that is affiliated to a national association and/or a national political party, or when the interests of employers are expressed nationally through an employers' confederation. A co-evolution of national politics and organizational politics can take place though these relational frameworks, which cross different system levels from macro to micro and vice versa. In this respect, organizations, especially those in the public domain, become subject to the evolution of societal politics, while at the same time their members have channels open to them to influence the evolution of policies at a higher level. In these political processes, what Redding (2005) has called ideational and material 'logics' can both play a major role in driving change. Ideational logics, when expressing group interests, take an ideological and normative form, such as the idea of neoliberalism at the societal level and the 'flexible firm' at the organizational level. Material logics typically are expressed with reference to the economic, technological and knowledge-related resources that are crucial for organizations to survive. They can become the vehicles for expressing and enforcing the interests of groups that provide such resources, especially those that are essential to the organization and for which alternative sources cannot readily be found (Hickson et al., 1971; Pfeffer and Salancik, 1978).

Ideas relating to organizations are expressed in discourse and narrative (Heracleous and Barrett, 2001; Chreim, 2005; Suddaby and Greenwood, 2005). Examination of the role played by ideas in the co-evolutionary process therefore requires an understanding of how actors engage in discourses and narratives politically so as to advocate or resist change. This ontological stance requires a hermeneutic approach. A hermeneutic approach is concerned not only with how people interpret discourses but also with situating those discourses in their social and temporal contexts, and understanding the way they form mind sets and shape reality (Heracleous and Barrett, 2001). Discourse will be seen to be important in the evolution of Telemig because it informed and justified political processes and behaviour in an ideological manner. In order to understand the dynamics of evolution, it is necessary to adopt a holistic approach that focuses on different dimensions of the ideational aspects of the evolutionary process, such as organizational culture, identity and strategy, and how they informed each other in the evolution of the whole (Barry and Elmes, 1997).

Hermeneutics on its own is, however, not sufficient for understanding the process of co-evolution. In this book we see co-evolutionary dynamics as resulting from a process in which actors engage in different discourses and narratives associated with political manoeuvres that have particular consequences for organizational constituents and organizational performance. These manoeuvres often related to material factors such as employment, where by the 1990s security versus flexibility (or what the French rightly call 'précarité') was at issue within Telemig. The discourse of flexibility was justified by reference to material changes in the company's environment. The political engagement of actors in particular discourses therefore needs to be understood by examining economic, political and technological changes in a company's context over time. This calls for a much more politically oriented approach to co-evolution than has hitherto be the norm.

Plan of the Book

This book is divided into four parts. Part I provides introductory and background material. The present chapter has introduced the theoretical background to the co-evolutionary perspective we adopt and develop in this book. Chapter 2 presents the economic and political context of the telecommunications sector in Brazil, and briefly the wider global context, within which Telemig's evolution took place. Chapter 3 describes the scope of the study presented in this book and the methodology through which information on the company's co-evolution was accessed and interpreted. The investigations on which this book draws commenced in 1986 and continued until 2006. They addressed circumstances pertaining both within this time period and also retrospectively to the company's foundation. In addition to key events and trends in the company's performance, insight was sought into how these were understood by management and employees, including Telemig's labour union.

Part II treats the historical co-evolution of Telemig and its environment through three principal phases. The first phase is the subject of chapter 4. This examines the formative years of the Telemig company, including the precursors to its formal establishment in 1973. The particular ideational and material characteristics that were laid down for the company in the 1970s provided it with a continuing distinctive competence, especially in technology, and they also persisted as components of the company's identity in the eyes of its members long after. Chapter 5 covers the middle period of Telemig's life from 1985 to 1993. This witnessed the return of Brazil to a civilian government and the intrusion of politics into the direction of state-owned companies such as Telemig. It was a period of economic difficulty and mounting industrial unrest in the country, and one of some turbulence and uncertain development for the company. Chapter 6 is concerned with the final phase of Telemig's evolution from 1993 to 2000. We now enter the period of Brazil's economic reform, which centred on curbing inflation, opening the economy to foreign investment and privatizing state-owned companies. The reform was guided by a neoliberal ideology that denigrated state control and emphasized instead the need for companies like Telemig to stand on their own feet and ultimately to be transferred from the mantle of state sponsorship over to private ownership.

The three chapters in part II treat the various aspects of Telemig's co-evolution together as they occurred historically. This permits an integrated view of how they changed over time and of how interactions between the organization and its environment proceeded. Part III, by contrast, examines four of these aspects as separate issues. Each of its constituent chapters discusses a particular issue within its context in the history of Telemig. These chapters are therefore to a large extent self-contained and they necessarily have to recall certain relevant historical features. Corporate evolution is in this way depicted by analysing different organizational dimensions considered of critical relevance in existing theory, and each of the chapters therefore offers a distinctive contribution to theoretical development. At the same time, we shall demonstrate that an understanding of each issue is enhanced by adopting a politically informed co-evolutionary perspective. Subsequently, in chapter 11, we return to how these issues relate to each other within the process of Telemig's co-evolution. Each chapter in part III therefore offers a theoretical contribution on its particular topic, while at the same time informing the political interest view of co-evolution that is presented at the close of the book in chapter 11.

Chapter 7 focuses on the evolution of Telemig's organizational culture. It analyses how this culture evolved from a condition of integration to one of fragmentation and then differentiation. The chapter identifies the sources of these changes in institutional and political factors, and it proposes a framework for analysing the dynamics of culture change in organizations.

The subject of chapter 8 is corporate identity, defined as the identity of an organization that is articulated and propagated by its leading (corporate) group. It examines how Telemig's corporate identity changed over time and how such change can be accounted for in terms of the legitimacy secured by a given corporate identity and the mobilization of support behind it. These empirical and theoretical foundations allow for a cyclical model of corporate identity construction and deconstruction to be developed.

Chapter 9 examines changes in the use of metaphors applied to management and organization by Telemig's employees and their labour union during the 20 years after 1979 when the union became independent of restrictive regulation. The concept of 'reflective imaging' provides a link between changes in the company's environment and the use of metaphor. Attention to reflective imaging is found to be instructive in revealing the meaning and status of metaphors in an evolving organizational context that presented employees with conditions that were at variance with their expectations and even threatening to their economic livelihood. The chapter indicates that when employees held sufficient collective power, the images of the company that their union formulated had an impact on managerial policy and practice. The chapter also contributes a methodology that permits the multidimensional aspects of metaphors to be demonstrated, and the incidence of different metaphors to be assessed both in a given period and over time.

Chapter 10 continues with an examination of the efforts to redefine the nature of employment and employability in Telemig through programmes of training and learning. These programmes were seen by top management to be a means of developing the competencies considered necessary to support the restructuring of Telemig that was initiated in the 1990s and implemented from 1994 onwards. The chapter indicates that learning within an organization is not necessarily the 'good thing' that it is normally assumed to be. For in the circumstances of Telemig's restructuring, learning could not be regarded simply as an enhancement of capabilities benefiting the collective as a whole. It also had a clearly political purpose as part of a major organizational change that was intended to serve the interests of the new post-privatization shareholders and that was actually very divisive. The chapter develops the perspective of organizational learning as a political initiative within corporate evolution, arguing that the notion of 'contested learning' therefore deserves greater attention.

Chapter 11, the single chapter in part IV, considers the theory development to which the Telemig case study can contribute. This chapter draws together the themes examined in previous chapters, especially chapters 7–10, to indicate their interdependence within the co-evolutionary process. It begins by rehearsing the strengths and limitations of contemporary co-evolutionary thinking, as a basis for indicating how the Telemig case study can inform its further development. It then suggests how the co-evolution of Telemig informs our appreciation of linked evolutionary cycles within the company and its macro and meso environments. The chapter presents a model of these cycles that indicates how co-evolution crosses different system levels – macro, meso and micro – and how its various ideational and material elements are co-related. The primary dynamic behind the process of co-evolution within a highly institutionalized environment is seen to be that between purposive actions taken by external actors and those within the company. This dynamic is evident in the analyses of organizational culture, corporate identity, reflective imaging and learning presented in the previous four chapters. We argue that these phenomena can only be understood if account is taken of the political interests that were at play. They speak for the incorporation of a political interest perspective as the next step forward in co-evolutionary analysis, and chapter 11 closes by outlining the theoretical dynamics this involves.

References

Axelrod, R. (1984) *The Evolution of Co-operation.* New York: Basic Books.

Bain, J. S. (1956) *Barriers to New Competition.* Cambridge, MA: Harvard University Press.

Bansal, P. and Roth, K. (2000) Why companies go green: a model of ecological responsiveness. *Academy of Management Journal,* 43, 717–36.

Barry, D. and Elmes, M. (1997) Strategy retold: toward a narrative view of strategic discourse. *Academy of Management Review,* 22, 429–52.

Biggart, N. W. (1997) Explaining Asian economic organization: toward a Weberian institutional perspective. In M. Orru, N.W. Biggart and G. G. Hamilton (eds), *The Economic Organization of East Asian Capitalism.* Thousand Oaks, CA: Sage, pp. 3–32.

Blodgett, L. L. (1991) Partner contributions as predictors of equity share in international joint ventures. *Journal of International Business Studies,* 22, 63–78.

Burgelman, R. A. (2002a) *Strategy is Destiny: How Strategy-making Shapes a Company's Future*. New York: Free Press.

Burgelman, R. A. (2002b) Strategy as vector and the inertia of coevolutionary lock-in. *Administrative Science Quarterly*, 47, 325–57.

Castilla E., Hwang, H., Granovetter, E. and Granovetter, M. (2000) Social networks in the Valley. In W. Miller, H. Rowen, C. Lee and M. Hancock (eds), *How Silicon Valley Works*. Stanford, CA: Stanford University Press, pp. 218–47.

Chandler, A. D. Jr (1962) *Strategy and Structure*. Cambridge, MA: MIT Press.

Child, J. (1972) Organizational structure, environment and performance: the role of strategic choice. *Sociology*, 6, 1–22.

Child, J. (1997) Strategic choice in the analysis of action, structure, organizations and environment: retrospect and prospect. *Organization Studies*, 18, 43–76.

Child, J. (2000) Theorizing about organization cross-nationally. *Advances in International Comparative Management*, 13, 27–76.

Child, J. and Smith, C. (1987) The context and process of organizational transformation: Cadbury Limited in its sector. *Journal of Management Studies*, 24, 565–93.

Child, J. and Tsai, T. (2005) The dynamic between firms' environmental strategies and institutional constraints in emerging economies: evidence from China and Taiwan. *Journal of Management Studies*, 42, 95–125.

Chreim, S. (2005) The continuity–change duality in narrative texts of organizational identity. *Journal of Management Studies*, 42, 566–93.

Clegg, S. R. and Dunkerley, D. (1980) *Organization Class and Control*. London: Routledge & Kegan Paul.

DiMaggio, P. J. and Powell, W. W. 1991. The iron cage revisited: institutional isomorphism and collective rationality. In W. W. Powell and P. J. DiMaggio (eds), *The New Institutionalism in Organizational Analysis*. Chicago: University of Chicago Press, pp. 63–82.

Doz, Y. L. (1996) The evolution of cooperation in strategic alliances: initial conditions or learning processes? *Strategic Management Journal*, 17, 55–83.

Etzioni, A. (1961) *A Comparative Analysis of Complex Organizations*. Glencoe, IL: Free Press.

Foreman, P. and Whetten, D. A. 2002. Members' identification with multiple-identity organizations. *Organization Science*, 13, 618–635.

Friedman, M. (1962) *Capitalism and Freedom*. Chicago: University of Chicago Press.

Gerth, H. H. and Mills, C. W. (eds) (1946) *From Max Weber: Essays in Sociology*. New York: Oxford University Press.

Gould, R. (1993) Collective action and network structure. *American Sociological Review*, 58, 182–96.

Granovetter, M. (1992) Economic action and social structure. In M. Granovetter and R. Swedberg (eds), *The Sociology of Economic Life*. Boulder, CO: Westview Press, pp. 53–84.

Grant, R. M. (2005) *Contemporary Strategy Analysis*, 5th edn. Malden, MA: Blackwell.

Hall, P. A. and Soskice, D. (2001) *Varieties of Capitalism*. New York: Oxford University Press.

Hannan, M. T. and Freeman, J. H. (1989) *Organizational Ecology*. Cambridge, MA: Harvard University Press.

Heracleous, L. and Barrett, M. (2001) Organizational change as discourse: communicative actions and deep structures in the context of information technology implementation. *Academy of Management Journal*, 44, 735–78.

Henrique, I. and Sadorsky, P. (1996). The determinants of an environmentally responsive firm: an empirical approach. *Journal of Environmental Economics and Management*, 30, 381–95.

Hickson, D. J., Hinings, C. R., Lee, C. A., Schneck, R. E. and Pennings, J. M. (1971) A strategic contingencies theory of intraorganizational power. *Administrative Science Quarterly*, 16, 216–29.

Jacques, E. (1951) *The Changing Culture of a Factory*. London: Routledge.

Johnson, G. (1987) *Strategic Change and the Management Process*. Oxford: Blackwell.

Journal of Management Studies (2003). Special research symposium. Beyond adaptation vs selection research: organizing self-renewal in co-evolving environments. *Journal of Management Studies*, 40(8).

Kerr, C., Dunlop, J. T., Harbison, F. and Myers, C. A. (1960) *Industrialism and Industrial Man*. Cambridge, MA: Harvard University Press.

Leonard, H. J. (1988) *Pollution and the Struggle for World Product*. Cambridge: Cambridge University Press.

Lewin, A. Y., Long, C. P. and Carroll, T. N. (1999) The coevolution of new organizational forms. *Organization Science*, 10, 535–50.

Lewin, A. Y. and Volberda, H. (1999) Prolegomena on coevolution: a framework for research on strategy and new organizational forms. *Organization Science*, 10, 519–34.

Locke, R. R. (1989) *Management and Higher Education since 1940: The Influence of America and Japan on West Germany, Great Britain and France*. Cambridge: Cambridge University Press.

Lu, Y. and Lake, D. (1997) Managing international joint ventures: an institutional approach. In P. W. Beamish and J. P. Killing (eds), *Corporate Strategies: European Perspectives*. San Francisco: The New Lexington Press, pp. 74–99.

Meyer, J. W. and Scott, W. R. (1983) *Organizational Environments: Ritual and Rationality*. Beverly Hills, CA: Sage.

Miles, R. E. and Snow, C. C. (1978) *Organizational Strategy, Structure and Process*. New York: McGraw-Hill.

Mische, A. (2003) Cross-talk in movements: rethinking the culture–network link. In M. Diani and D. McAdam (eds), *Social Movements and Networks: Relational Approaches to Collective Action*. New York: Oxford University Press, pp. 258–80.

Moingeon, B. and Soenen, G. (eds) (2002) *Corporate and Organizational Identities*. London: Routledge.

Mommsen, W. J. (1989) The two dimensions of social change in Max Weber's sociological theory. In W. J. Mommsen, *The Political and Social Theory of Max Weber: Collected Essays*. Cambridge: Polity Press, pp. 145–65.

Nehrt, C. (1998) Maintainability of first mover advantages when environmental regulations differ between countries. *Academy of Management Review*, 23, 77–97.

North, D. C. (1990). *Institutions, Institutional Change and Economic Performance*. Cambridge: Cambridge University Press.

Oliver, C. (1991) Strategic responses to institutional processes. *Academy of Management Review*, 16, 145–79.

Organization Science (1999) Focused issue on 'Coevolution of strategy and new organizational forms'. *Organization Science*, 10(5).

Organization Studies (2001) Special issue on 'Multi-level analysis and co-evolution'. *Organization Studies*, 22(6).

Parsons, T. (1956) Suggestions for a sociological approach to the theory of organizations – I. *Administrative Science Quarterly*, 1, 63–85.

Peng, M. W. (2000) *Business Strategies in Transition Economies*. Thousand Oaks, CA: Sage.

Pettigrew, A. M. (1985) *The Awakening Giant*. Oxford: Blackwell.

Pettigrew, A. M. (1990) Longitudinal field research on change: theory and practice. *Organization Science*, 1, 267–92.

Pfeffer, J. (1992) *Managing with Power*. Boston, MA: Harvard Business School Press.

Pfeffer, J. and Salancik, G. R. (1978) *The External Control of Organizations: A Resource Dependence Perspective*. New York: Harper and Row.

Porter, M. E. (1990) *The Competitive Advantage of Nations*. New York: Free Press.

Porter, M. and Linde, C. (1995) Green and competitive: ending the stalemate. *Harvard Business Review*, September/October, 120–34.

Powell, W. W. and DiMaggio, P. J. (eds) (1991) *The New Institutionalism in Organizational Analysis*. Chicago: University of Chicago Press.

Redding, S. G. (1990) *The Spirit of Chinese Capitalism*. Berlin: De Gruyter.

Redding, S. G. (2005) The thick description and comparison of societal systems of capitalism. *Journal of International Business Studies*, 36, 123–55.

Salop, S. C. and Scheffman, D. T. (1993) Raising rival's cost. Papers and proceedings of the ninety-fifth annual meeting of the American Economic Association. *American Economic Review*, 73, 267–71.

Scherer, F. M. (1980). *Industrial Market Structure and Economic Performance*. Chicago: Rand McNally, 2nd edn.

Schluchter, W. (1981). *The Rise of Western Rationalism: Max Weber's Developmental History*. Berkeley: University of California Press.

Scott, W. R. (1995) *Institutions and Organizations*. Thousand Oaks, CA: Sage.

Selznick, P. (1949) *TVA and the Grass Roots*. Berkeley: University of California Press.

Simons, T. and Paul, I. (1997) Organization and ideology: kibbutzim and hired labor, 1951–1965. *Administrative Science Quarterly*, 42, 784–814.

Stinchcombe, A. L. (1965) Social structure and organizations. In J. G. March (ed.), *Handbook of Organizations*. Chicago: Rand McNally, pp. 142–93.

Suddaby, R. and Greenwood, R. (2005) Rhetorical strategies of legitimacy. *Administrative Science Quarterly*, 50, 35–67.

Weber, M. (1964) *The Theory of Social and Economic Organization* (trans. A. M. Henderson and T. Parsons). New York: Free Press.

Weber, M. (1978) *Economy and Society* (ed. and trans. G. Roth and C. Wittich). Berkeley: University of California Press.

Weick, K. E. (1995) *Sensemaking in Organizations*. Thousand Oaks, CA: Sage.

CHAPTER TWO

The Economic and Political Context of Telecommunications in Brazil

Introduction

This chapter describes the context of Telemig's evolution within the telecommunications sector. The more general developments that took place in Brazil's economy and society during Telemig's lifetime between 1973 and 2000, and that related to the phases of its evolution, are examined in chapters 4 to 6. Telemig's evolution was importantly shaped by developments in its sector. As a result of its embeddedness in the state enterprise system, many of Telemig's internal changes were constrained or triggered by the prevailing conditions of Brazil's political economy and its corresponding institutional apparatus. Some of these conditions were material forces, such as the development of new technologies and the growth of competition in the sector. Others were ideational, reflecting changes in political ideology and new conceptions of how telecommunications companies should be organized and governed. This chapter describes how such forces affected the development of the telecommunications sector in Brazil, and provides the context for Telemig's evolution.

The Foundations of the Industry in Brazil: 1950–1972

In the 1950s and 1960s Brazil's telecommunications sector was in the hands of private companies, some multinational corporations (MNCs), some domestic. The sector was highly fragmented with the players providing an inefficient service. Foreign companies were only interested in serving the large markets of big cities, neglecting smaller cities and the countryside. Their equipment was obsolete, and their focus on the more profitable markets created a large gap in service provision between large urban cities and the interior of the country. In 1957, Brazil had a telephone density of 1.3 per 100 inhabitants, a little more than a third of the then world average of 3.7. In 1960 there were around 1 million telephones for 70 million people, most of them in the states of Rio de Janeiro and São Paulo (Botelho et al., 1998). The market in large cities was dominated by CTB (Companhia Telefonica Brasileira), a subsidiary of the Canadian Traction Light and Power Company. CTB dominated the Brazilian market at the end of the 1960s, but it did not invest in broadening services or in modernization. The system as a whole resembled different communications islands, with around 1,200 telephone companies in the country, of which only 800 served the countryside (Wholers de Almeida and Crossetti, 1997). By the end of the 1960s it became evident that the system of private telecommunications was highly unsatisfactory. Brazil had at the time 1.7 telephones per 100 inhabitants (Novaes, 1999), which was very low in comparison with international standards.

After 1958, Brazil's rate of GDP growth dropped sharply, from an average of 10 per cent down to 0.6 per cent in 1963 (Resende, 1989). This drop in growth together with hyperinflation (around 80 per cent per year) and an inclination of the current government towards the left encouraged the military to take over power in 1964. This political event had important implications for the telecommunications sector. The government went for a nationalizing solution by bringing 27 fixed line companies under the control of Telebrás, which reported to the ministry of telecommunications, responsible for the sector's development and regulation. Telebrás was laterally linked to Embratel, the company in charge of international and interregional operations.

The military regime regarded the telecommunications sector as ideologically and economically strategic. Some authors suggest that its interest in telecommunications was associated with the military ideas of nation building and national integration (Fadul, 1989; Hunter, 1997). Developing telecommunications was consistent with the military's ambitions to centralize economic and political power. It was viewed as strategic for the consolidation of the regime and improving its mechanisms of societal control. Controlling the sector was essential to national security, as a means of integrating remote areas of the country and helping to forestall public uprising against the government.

The regime's intentions were to develop the necessary engineering capability to build a national telecoms equipment industry, and to foster the development of Brazilian industry in general (Straubhaar and Horak, 1997; Wohlers de Almeida and Crossetti, 1997). The first telecommunications plan was viewed at the time as one of the largest investments in communications in the world. In 1976 the government created the Brazilian Telecommunications Research Centre (CPqD). CPqD was reasonably successful in developing commercially and technically competitive technologies, either independently or in collaboration with other companies. Its innovations included a card system for payphones based on an electric technology that was more cost-effective than that in other countries, and new modes of voice and data transmission (Schjolden, 1999). By the end of the 1970s, CPqD had managed to develop highly sophisticated services and to reduce dependence on foreign equipment suppliers.

Import control was viewed as a mechanism to foster the development of a national innovation system. The government's import substitution policy reflected its nationalist tendencies through an application of various control measures such as regulation of equipment imports, centralization of purchasing, reduction in the number of suppliers and standardization requirements (Straubhaar and Horak, 1997). Equipment imports had to be authorized by Telebrás, the new national holding company, which also had the responsibility of promoting a national industry for telecoms equipment. Some MNCs that were already operating in Brazil, such as Ericson, Siemens and NEC, were allowed to remain. They could not procure more than 10 per cent of equipment from international sources. If they formed alliances with Brazilian companies, they were limited to a minority equity share and forwent any voting rights (Straubhaar and Horak, 1997).

Telecommunications was of strategic importance in the governments' development plan. This plan was implemented through three measures, which involved funding, central organization and control of the system. The first measure was the creation of the FNT (a national fund for the development of telecommunications) and the second was the establishment of a system of self-financing, which later on constituted the main source of revenue for FNT. Basically, this involved the consumers paying a surcharge that was subsequently devolved in terms of share rights. The third measure was the national amalgamation of 27 fixed line companies under the control of Telebrás.

The late 1960s and the 1970s are known as the golden age of Brazil's economy, the longest period of sustained growth in the country's history. The economy bloomed with record levels of investment funded by the government, foreign investors and private Brazilian capital (Evans, 1979). From the mid-1970s to 1980, the Telebrás system expanded at a rate of 18 per cent a year, with its local production capacity reaching 1.1 million lines in 1980. In 1982 Telebrás comprised 36 companies. The number of independent private service providers, about 1,000 in 1972, had been reduced to 150, and accounted for 250,000 telephones (Botelho et al., 1998). The number of new lines installed increased progressively until 1978, after which it became impossible to sustain the same level of growth as previously. As table 2.1 indicates, across the sector as a whole telephone density doubled and the number of locations with telephones increased by 50 per cent from 1973 to 1979. From 1974 to 1979, the return on investment rose by 44 per cent on an increase in investment of nearly 71 per cent.

At the end of the 1970s the oil crisis began to hit Brazil hard. Inflation again got out of control. These developments had brought serious consequences for the telecommunications sector. After 1985, the return on investment of telecommunications companies declined substantially in comparison with previous years (see table 2.1). There was a significant drop in investment in 1983, which largely depended on funds provided by FNT through the system of surtaxes on telecom services. FNT was terminated in 1982, after being gradually run down through transfers of funds to other government programmes and departments. By that time,

Table 2.1   Telebras performance indicators, 1973–1997

	Telephone density (telephones per 100 inhabitants)	Locations (thousands)	Number of employees per 1000 terminals installed	Annual investment (US$ million)	Return on investment (%)	Terminals installed (millions)
1973	2.5[a]	2.2	35.0	n.a.	n.a.	1.6
1974	2.7[a]	2.6	34.0	796	4.5	1.9
1975	3.0[a]	2.7	33.6	1,220	8.8	2.2
1976	3.5[a]	2.9	27.0	1,648	8.2	2.9
1977	4.1[b]	3.0	22.0	1,566	11.0	3.6
1978	4.9[b]	3.1	21.0	1,454	7.1	4.2
1979	5.4[b]	3.3	18.9	1,358	6.5	4.7
1980	4.6	3.8	18.0	932	8.9	5.1
1981	4.8	4.7	17.0	1,330	8.9	5.4
1982	5.0	6.1	16.2	1,523	7.7	5.8
1983	5.3	7.1	15.3	992	6.7	6.2
1984	5.6	8.0	14.0	864	6.7	6.7
1985	5.7	8.5	14.0	918	6.1	7.0
1986	5.9	8.8	13.2	1,245	3.4	7.3
1987	6.1	11.4	12.8	1,448	3.6	7.7
1988	6.4	11.9	11.9	1,977	5.6	8.2
1989	6.7	12.8	11.1	2,559	−13.4	8.8
1990	7.0	13.9	10.0	2,121	3.8	9.3
1991	7.2	14.5	9.1	2,311	−1.4	9.8
1992	7.6	15.4	8.4	3,054	2.3	10.6
1993	8.0	16.1	8.3	3,027	5.7	11.3
1994	8.4	17.5	7.9	3,362	2.6	12.0
1995	9.2	18.9	6.9	4,218	3.7	13.3
1996	10.2	20.6	6.0	6,793	9.6	14.9
1997	11.5	n.a.	n.a.	7,584	n.a.	17.0

Source: Telebrás in <www.sinttel.org.br>. [a]Secretaria de Estado do Planejamento e Coordenação Geral. Suplan/Sei.
[b]Telebrás, O Sistema Telebrás e a evolução das telecomunicações brasileiras.

the profitability of state enterprises was declining and their capacity to finance further investment was threatened (Resende, 1989). A large part of Brazil's balance of payment deficit was attributed to state enterprise deficits, as these depended on foreign borrowing. One of the main problems was that the government started to divert state enterprises' funds to resource its negative external account.

As the economic situation worsened, the military regime began to lose the legitimacy it had enjoyed during the economic miracle. With the government's announcement of its intention to hand over power to the civilians at the end of this decade, pressures for civilian participation and voice in the country's affairs began to rise. Public discontent with the regime grew and labour unrest spread throughout the country.

The Politicization of the Industry: 1985–1993

In 1985 the military handed over power to the civilians. To the dismay of the Brazilian population, its elected president died on the very day of his inauguration. Vice-president Sarney, a member of the old coalition centre right that had supported the military, then assumed office. Sarney managed to get the economy growing in the first year, and to reduce inflation from 250 per cent in 1985 to 57 per cent in 1986, but during the following years of his office the economy deteriorated again. In 1990 the rate of inflation reached 1,000 per cent and the growth rate became negative (minus 4.18), the second largest decline in 47 years. The external debt reached US$123,611 million in that year (Instituto de Pesquisa Econômica Aplicada [IPEA], 2001). The inflow of FDI reduced from US$3,069 million in 1982 to US$1,086 million in 1986 (Barros, 1993). It was also during this period that Brazil suffered an unprecedented repatriation of foreign investment, scared by threats to impose an external debt moratorium, which in the end took place in 1987. During this period the foreign investment rate dropped from 24 per cent as a proportion of GDP in 1977 to 16 per cent in 1990 (Barros, 1993). In an attempt to curb inflation, the government introduced eight different economic packages, 54 regulations for controlling prices and 15 wage policies – none of which had much success. From 1978 to 1991 Brazil had nine different economic ministers (Ferraz et al., 1992)

No wonder this period was called the 'lost decade'. Towards the end of the 1980s poor economic performance encouraged the growth of militant unionism. Before the 1980s, the government had succeeded in suppressing civil liberty movements and trade union activities by controlling the appointment of union officials and making union membership compulsory for all employees. However, between 1978 and 1980 Brazil witnessed an upsurge of union mobilization. Antunes (1994) indicates that the statistics provided by the Departamento Intersindical de Estatística e Estudos Sócio-Econômicos (DIEESE) for 1980 show half a million strikers in 1978 and a total of 3.2 million in 1979 (Antunes, 1994, p. 25). Though the strikes had the objective of fighting against the oppression of the military regime and the exploitation of workers, the main actors of the union movement also had political ambitions through association with the Central Workers Union (Central Unica dos Trabalhadores, CUT) and the Workers' Party (Partido dos Trabalhadores, PT). This allowed trade unions, including those in telecommunications, to develop inter-organizational links across different occupations at local and national levels. CUT's strategy together with the rapid devaluation of real wages led to a spread of strikes across the country, with varying levels of effectiveness. In two different studies Noronha (1989, 1994) indicates that labour unrest had been growing since the end of the 1970s, and that it continued into the 1990s, but with declining levels of intensity. The estimated number of strikes rose from 500 in 1983 to 4,000 in 1990 (Noronha, 1994).

During Sarney's term of office, from 1985 to 1990, the government suffered from a lack of legitimacy, primarily because of its incapacity to keep old institutions functioning under a democratic regime. Sarney also made alliances with populist forces, which in the view of many, used state enterprises to advance their political intentions and careers (Hunter, 1997). Populism brought implications for the telecommunications sector and the way in which the companies were managed. In Telebrás, government political appointees took positions that once were assigned to professionals with experience in the sector. Ostensibly in order to prevent an endemic clientelism in state enterprises, the transition government introduced a series of rules that imposed additional procedures that, paradoxically, immobilized the system. Thus Telebrás became a hostage of clientelism, and was submerged by bureaucratic rigidities that distorted important processes such as recruitment (Botelho et al., 1998).

The first national development plan of Sarney's government emphasized the use of telecommunications for social purposes. It criticized the approach of the military government for its focus on national security matters and for increasing the gap between the privileged sectors of the urban centres and the rural areas. This plan differed from previous policy in its emphasis on the democratization of services through the installation of public and semi-public telephones for the poor. Instead of integration, the plan mentioned interiorization, which meant offering telephone lines beyond the boundaries of inner cities, and the need to improve long distance services (Straubhaar and Horak, 1997).

However, this stated mission could not be achieved under the ownership regime that then prevailed. By the end of the 1980s, the state sector was highly indebted and could not afford new investment to meet increasing demand and the need for technological innovation. It was common for the government to use state enterprises' funds in other programmes (Trebat, 1983). To fight rampant inflation, the government controlled telephone charges, which then lagged behind market prices, with negative consequences for investment. Prices for services remained substantially lower than international prices (Botelho et al., 1998). In addition the government was unable to find sources of alternative funding for the sector. The self-financing strategy, considered an innovation in the 1970s, led to distortions in prices, with services becoming inaccessible to the lower and even middle classes. Lack of investment also encouraged the growth of a speculative market, which added to social discontent.

Under the Sarney regime, Brazil's telephone service deteriorated significantly. In the mid-1980s, Telebrás experienced its lowest growth rate in return on investment. It was also unable to keep up with demand and with new technologies that improved the quality of services (see table 2.1). Although the annual rate of line connections had increased from 16 per cent in 1984 to 31 per cent in 1989 (Wohlers de Almeida and Crossetti, 1997), the percentage of failed local calls and crossed lines was much higher than the international standard. At the end of 1990, 30 per cent of calls between Rio de Janeiro and São Paulo were not successfully connected and the costs of setting up lines were excessively high compared with international competitors (Botelho et al., 1998).

On the global front, telecommunications was experiencing radical changes in technology as well as in industry structure. The change of the basic technology from an analogue system (based on electrical signals) to the digital system (based on optical fibre pulses and the use of satellites) represented a leap forward in telecommunications systems. Besides adding speed it opened up alternative modes of mass communication and transmission, and possibilities for combining and integrating technologies from other industries such as software and media into telecommunications. Global competition was already intensifying alongside the industry's restructuring, which had began in the 1980s with the break-up of AT&T and the privatization of British Telecom. The Brazilian telecommunications sector was therefore about to miss the two radical changes that elsewhere were beginning to reshape the sector in the 1980s: (a) the convergence of different electronic technologies, which changed the frontier between telecommunications and other sectors, such as media and software; (b) the opening up of new business in countries that had introduced deregulation and privatization, like Japan and the Anglo-Saxon countries.

According to Wohlers de Almeida and Crossetti (1997), several factors contributed to the low dynamism of the sector in Brazil at the end of the 1980s: (a) the lack of consistent long-term planning; (b) insufficient and irregular investment; for example, from 1982 to 1986, the annual average rate of investment declined from US$1.5 million to US$0.9 million; (c) the absence of a regulatory regime that would encourage investment by the private sector. These factors among others were responsible for the low performance of Brazilian telecommunications. The number of installations did not meet public expectations as the waiting list for business and residential lines reached 2.5 million, half of the total number of lines in operation at that time according to estimates (Straubhaar and Horak, 1997, p. 180). The growth in the density rate and in the number of cities connected, as shown in table 2.1, was not enough to meet the demands of the population. As this table also indicates, the return on investment was erratic and well below the international ideal norm, which was over 12 per cent (Wohlers de Almeida and Crossetti, 1997).

The contrast between state telecommunications in Brazil and rapid developments abroad also helped to build a consensus in favour of privatization. Discussions about privatizing the sector began during Sarney's rule, though his presidency did not show any enthusiasm for the idea. During his regime, privatization was not included formally in development programmes. The National Bank for Economic and Social Development (BNDES), held some preliminary discussions about the different possibilities for privatization, but its chief preoccupation was to solve the problem of indebtedness of state enterprises to the bank. Though there were pressures for privatization emanating from global players and from national private groups, and a growing sympathy for ideas about deregulation, privatization and liberalization at the end of Sarney's government, not much was done (Velasco, 1997). At that time public opinion did not view privatization as the best solution for the sector, and the trade union was fiercely opposed to it. If it had not been for the pressures that Fittel (the national telecoms union) and CUT placed on Brazilian congressmen, Embratel (the long-distance carrier subsidiary) would have ended up in private hands as early as 1987.

During the 1990s Brazil had three different presidents. Collor was in office from 1990 to 1992, when he was impeached. Franco replaced him until 1994, followed by Cardoso, who held office from 1994 to 2002. When Collor took office in 1990, the weakness of the prevailing developmental model, based on a closed economy and interventionist state, had became evident and it was inconsistent with an international context of increasing liberalization and globalization. Collor's development plans were conceived within a liberal perspective, and included the privatization of key sectors such as telecommunications. However, these plans were not well worked out and they lacked legal and public support. Collor also faced serious governance problems. During his brief regime there were as many as 295 provisional measures that bypassed Congress. The country's economic performance remained poor. GDP continued to fall, inflation remained very high, and despite attempts to open up the economy, FDI failed to rise (Ferraz et al., 1992). The combination of poor economic performance and autocratic government generated popular impatience, which together with corruption charges led to Collor's impeachment at the end of 1992. Though his government lasted for only two years, Collor nonetheless succeeded in obtaining approval for 16 measures of privatization (Velasco, 1997).

While the interim government that replaced Collor did not openly declared its preference for a more liberal approach, it was relatively successful in its privatization programme. Franco's government achieved a record of privatizing 17 state enterprises, to the value of US$4.7 billion (Velasco, 1997). An important barrier to privatization at the time lay in the lack of popular support for the reform, which was linked to a lack of trust in the government's real intentions. The press expressed fears of a surrender to pressure from the multinationals because of corruption in the Collor regime, the lack of adequate planning and a legal framework for privatization. These events, however, did not prevent connections being formed between Brazilian interests and foreign firms mainly in the mobile phone area, once Telebrás declared its intention of not being involved in this type of business. Thus, the conditions of regulation and competition in telecommunications began to change in the early 1990s. The emergence of the mobile business brought new possibilities, including alliances between multinational equipment manufacturers and Telebrás and Embratel. New service areas were deregulated.

The Reconstitution of the Industry: 1994–2000

Privatization was undertaken in a more planned and systematic manner under Cardoso's government, and the whole programme from 1990 to 1998 managed to transfer US$85 billion to the private sector (CEPAL, 1998; Pinheiro et al., 1999). A new general law on telecommunications was passed by the Congress in 1997. One of the main objectives of the government was to open the sector to large international operators by defining the parameters for competition. By 1998, the plan for privatization had been specified in terms of four main steps. The first step was the separation of companies in the Telebrás system into fixed and mobile businesses. The second step was to restructure the Telebrás system into three operators for the fixed business, nine operators for the mobile business and Embratel (for long distance services). The third step occurred on 29 July 1998 with the formation of regional companies for fixed subscriber telephone services, companies for mobile subscriber services and one company for international and national long distance services. The fourth important step, in 1999, involved measures to increase competition between the long distance companies and those in the regional fixed segment, and to provide concessions for competitors from each mode to enter the market.

The telecommunications sector was privatized in July 1998 when the government ended the state monopoly by selling most of its shares in Telebrás to private operators and investors. The government had considered two options. The first involved the retention of some participation and control by the state. The second simply involved maximization of financial revenues. Due to the financial crisis, the government opted for the second alternative, generating a total of US$20 billion. The logic behind privatization involved the creation of a competitive environment, including the creation of a duopoly for both the fixed and mobile businesses. This has not been achieved for the fixed business. Four years after privatization, competitors had secured less than 5 per cent of the market. (Szapiro and Cassiolato, 2003).

Before privatization, Telebrás comprised eight regional companies for wireless communications, three for fixed communications and one for the long-distance service. It also included Embratel, which was responsible for long distance calls and interconnected Brazilian capitals. Embratel in addition managed projects and investments in satellites, data communications and optical fibre. With privatization, the 27 fixed line companies that belonged to the state monopoly were broken down into three different companies, which represented the division of the Brazilian market into different regions. The centre-south of Brazil went to Telecom Italia, and to Brazilian pension funds and banks, São Paulo state went to Telefonica de España, to Bilbao Viscava and other investors, and the north, centre and south-east went to Telemar – Telemig's holding – the only Brazilian group, which was composed of investors with no experience in telecommunications, such as pension funds, banks and venture capitalists. The long distance carrier Embratel was acquired by the American MCI.

In the 1990s, the international telecommunications sector began to achieve growth rates that were superior to the general rate of global economic growth. Thus between 1992 and 2003 the sector registered an annual growth of 8.2 per cent in revenue by comparison with the 3.5 per cent observed for annual global economic growth. A study of the transformation of the telecommunications sector indicates that there were two significant periods of change in its evolution (CNI/SENAE, 2005). The first period, from 1992 to 2000, witnessed high rates of growth. This expansion has been attributed to a series of factors, such as the expansion of the American economy, the institutional ownership reforms in emerging economies and

Table 2.2   Structure of the world telecommunications services market, 1992–2003

	1992	1994	1996	1998	2000	2002	2003
Global market (%)	100.0	100.0	100.0	100.0	100.0	100.0	100.0
Fixed-line telephones (%)	80.0	76.8	68.6	62.2	54.8	48.9	46.0
Mobile services (%)	5.3	8.9	15.7	20.9	28.4	33.6	36.4
Other services (%)	14.7	14.4	15.7	16.9	16.8	17.5	17.6

Source: CNI/SENAI Setor de Telecomunicações 2005. Estudos Setoriais 4. Brasília.

innovation leading to a convergence in technology (integration of voice, text and image). In the second period (2001–3), the rate of revenue growth declined to 5 per cent a year. According to the study, this reduction in the sector's expansion reveals differences in the dynamics of different types of business. So, while the fixed line segment accounted for 46 per cent of the telecommunications market in 2003, the growth of its market share has been much less impressive than for the mobile business (see table 2.2).

The international market for telecommunications has completely changed since the 1990s. Innovation in telecommunications and the formation of international networks led many countries to deregulate their markets and open them to competition. These factors have led to the development of new infrastructure options through cable, satellite and wireless networks, providing diverse alternatives for the supply and demand of services. The transformation of the sector since then has been frenetic and subject to frequent reconfiguration through mergers and acquisitions, the formation of global networks, alliances, the splitting up of businesses, divestments and other forms of organizational restructuring. MNCs have split into smaller companies, and some have overinvested to prevent incoming competition from players alien to the sector, such as electricity and gas distributors, and even from small companies (ILO, 2000). Technological convergence and industry integration through mergers and acquisitions added value to services and improved the speed, facility, reliability and diversity of the services offered with lower costs. Telecommunications became one of the most dynamic industries in the world, which resulted in an enhancement of industry competitiveness and profitability. At the end of 2003, the sector achieved a revenue growth of U$1,137 billion worldwide.

In contrast to these international developments, Brazil was in the 1990s still struggling with a unified monopoly, with the universalization[1] of basic services and with improving productivity. Although some Brazilian telecommunications companies managed to introduce new technologies, the sector was generally outdated, with most of the industry still using the analogue system, in which the equipment on the customer's premises is produced and combined to form and use telecoms networks. Nevertheless, the performance of Brazil's telecommunications sector gradually improved during the 1990s, especially once privatization became a serious prospect.

The plan to modernize the telecoms system – PASTE – injected a substantial amount of resources into the sector to make companies more attractive to private capital. Total annual new investment reached almost US$8 billion in 1997. The sector's degree of indebtedness fell from 40 per cent of total assets in 1992 to 23 per cent in 1996 (Wohlers and Crossetti, 1997, p. 41).

In the five years preceding privatization, return on investment improved, as did other indicators, including density in terms of telephones per 100 inhabitants and the number of locations served. As table 2.1 indicates, in 1996 the sector's return on investment more than doubled in comparison with the previous year. Other indicators also registered an improvement: density in terms of telephones per 100 inhabitants increased from 9.2 in 1995 to 11.5 in 1997, and the number of locations reached rose from 17,500 in 1994 to 20,600 in 1996. The improvement of the sector's performance in the middle of the decade suggests that it benefited from cost reductions, measures to improve productivity and the upward revision of tariffs.

With privatization and changes in industrial structure, it became impossible to compare the sector's performance on the basis of the same indicators as before. Nevertheless, a report by BNDES in 2002 indicated that there were positive changes in the sector after privatization. Data comparing the performance of the sector from July 1998 to November 1999 indicate that the number of fixed-line terminals increased by 34 per cent from 20.2 million to 27.0 million. The digitalization of the network increased from 67.5 to 82.3 per cent. Telephone density improved from 11.8 to 15 per cent. On the other hand, the number of lines in service per employee did not change significantly (BNDES, 2002).

Sector Reconfiguration Following Privatization

Privatization in Brazil brought with it immediate consequences for the sector, in the availability of services to the Brazilian population and in levels of productivity. Table 2.3 presents some performance indicators for the major fixed line operators in Brazil. The table shows an improvement after privatization of financial indicators, such as net profit and sales. The large improvements in productivity reflect a downsizing in the number of employees, which is particularly noticeable for Telemar. Over the period 1999–2002, there was a significant rise in the numbers of lines in service, around 55 per cent for Telemar and Telefonica, and 101 per cent for Brasil Telecom. As table 2.3 indicates, Telemar's net profit increased dramatically in the first two years of its existence, but became negative in 2002.

However, a study comparing the global performance of the telecommunications sector with that of Brazil suggests that the Brazilian market registered lower growth rates than the international market post-privatization (CNI/SENAI, 2005). Although the industry exhibited growth rates comparable to international rates of 11 per cent a year between 1999 and 2001, from 2002 to 2003 these slowed to only 5 per cent. More specifically, the telecommunications sector in Brazil

Table 2.3 Performance indicators for fixed telephone companies in Brazil (financial figures are in thousands of Brazilian reals)

Companies and indicators	1999	2000	2001	2002	Change 1999–2002 (%)
Telemar					
Sales/service revenue	6,215	8,120	10,103	11,874	91.1
Employee expenses	721.5	731.0	906.0	801.0	11.1
Net profit	95.7	709.4	140.4	−415.6	−
Number of lines in service (thousands)	9,723	11,819	14,816	15,100	55.3
Lines in service/employee	396	560	984	1,599	274.5
Number of employees	24,563	21,090	15,056	9,441	−160.1
Brasil Telecom					
Sales/service revenue	3,058	4,510	6,158	7,071	133.2
Employee expenses	482.2	451.4	474.3	402.7	−16.5
Net profit	218.0	409.6	261.0	443.0	103.2
Number of lines in service	4,718	7,446	8,638	9,465	100.6
Lines in service/employee	471	700	1,095	1,699	260.7
Number of employees	10,016	10,642	7,890	5,571	−44.4
Telefonica (TELESP)					
Sales/service revenue	5,295	7,310	8,983	10,088	90.5
Employee expenses	116.9	164.8	139.9	124.7	6.9
Net profit	735.8	1,470	1,576	1,076	46.3
Number of lines in service	8,049	10,331	12,283	12,551	55.9
Lines in service/employee	567	770	1,166	1,314	131.7
Number of employees	14,196	13,414	10,529	9,516	−32.9

Source: Companies' annual reports, results 31 December 2002. Adapted from Larangeira (2003).

registered revenue growth rates of 17 per cent from 1999 to 2003 in comparison with the 24 per cent worldwide. The relatively poor performance of the sector has been attributed to the low growth of the Brazilian economy and rising unemployment. The growth of the fixed business was disappointing, reaching merely 3.4 per cent from 1999 to 2003, while the growth of mobile business in this same period of 22 per cent did not compensate for this (CNI/SENAI, 2005). The disappointing performance of the sector following privatization can also be attributed to the low levels of investment of the industry. As table 2.4 indicates, the level of investment by fixed-line operators declined from R$23.7 million in 2001 to R$4.7 million in 2003. The performance of the mobile business also showed a similar tendency, in which investment decreased from R$8.1 million in 2001 to R$5.2 million in 2003.

Privatization had other important consequences for the sector and for the national system of innovation in telecommunications. The Brazilian innovation system was

Table 2.4 Investments in Brazil's telecommunications sector, 1999–2003 (in Brazilian reals at 2003 values, expressed in real terms)

Segment	1999	2000	2001	2002	2003
Fixed-line operators[a]	12,952,946	18,006,391	23,741,104	6,209,349	4,749,804
Growth rate (%)	–	39.0	31.8	−73.8	−23.5
Mobile operators	7,728,886	6,300,138	8,137,454	4,440,388	5,156,629
Growth rate (%)	–	−18.5	29.2	−45.4	16.1
Total	20,681,832	24,306,530	31,878,558	10,649,738	9,906,433
Growth rate (%)	–	17.5	31.2	−66.6	−7.0

[a]Includes data investments.
Source: Balanço das Empresas, Relatório Teleco Telefonia Celular no Brasil.

established with a view to producing indigenous technology in telecommunications. It started with the creation of CPqD in the early 1970s, which evolved through links between companies and universities and with multinational equipment manufactories. By the beginning of the 1980s there were around 120 local suppliers responsible for 17 per cent of the market (Szapiro and Cassiolato, 2003). CPqD was successful in creating technologies appropriate to a tropical climate, using optical fibre and superior telephone cards. Since the 1990s, the sector has gradually declined in its capacity to innovate, with consequences for the whole system of innovation. One of the results of market liberalization in the 1990s was the increasing growth of the market share served by multinationals and the number of partnerships between foreign and national firms. R&D and the source of technology became increasingly foreign. The MNCs installed in Brazil shifted towards adaptation of foreign technology at the expense of new local technology development (Schjolden, 1999). Many national firms undertook restructuring, which further reduced their innovation capacity (Cassiolato et al., 2002).

Privatization has resulted in even deeper consequences for CPqD and the network around it. There has been a reduction of links with research centres and between the MNCs' subsidiaries and local firms. MNCs in Brazil nowadays engage less in research and more in licensing from their own parent company. CPqD itself has witnessed a reduction of its relevance as it has shifted its activities to technological services, consultancy and education. Many small firms have been acquired by MNCs, leading to a decline in research-intensive activities, while others now produce components with reduced value-added (Schjolden, 1999; Cassiolato et al., 2002; Szapiro and Cassiolato, 2003).

Worldwide, privatization in the telecommunications sector has had at least two important consequences for its constituent organizations. The first is a change in the governance system and culture. The second is restructuring. Research on acquisitions and privatization suggests that restructuring is one of the first steps taken by organizations following a change of ownership (Blair, 1995; Cascio, 2002; Börsch, 2004). The motivation for restructuring usually comes from pressures by new owners to create value. This happens more frequently when the organization is acquired by institutional investors, who are primarily interested in return on investment. As institutional investors are under pressure to maximize profits and share price, they expect the company to 'downsize and distribute' additional cash flow to shareholders (Lazonick and O'Sullivan, 2000).

Some studies have suggested that the so-called shareholder value model of organization focuses on downsizing and restructuring. It concentrates on core markets, outsourcing business that is seen as marginal, strict cost control and selling units that do not achieve targets (Börsch, 2004, p. 366). Restructuring on the other hand has been associated with moves towards an employment contract that is consistent with entering a competitive global environment, and that incorporates provisions based on personal self-reliance and temporary employment with no expectations of mutual loyalty (Robinson and Rousseau, 1994). Companies that opt for restructuring tend to emphasize employability as it frees them from the obligation to provide long-term employment (Fligstein and Shin, 2005).

In the case of the telecommunications sector, it has been suggested that its dynamic innovative environment has been responsible for transforming its structure and for giving rise to new organization formats with consequences for employees and labour unions (Katz and Darbishire, 2000; Batt et al., 2004). Telecomunications firms have changed from traditional bureaucracies to incorporate a combination of flexible production and the differentiation of services into separate businesses (Katz, 1997; Larangeira, 2003; Batt et al., 2004). As companies became organized in terms of customer markets (Katz, 1997; Batt et al., 2004), this practice required different types of skills and knowledge to meet the different levels of product complexity and demands of each segment. Market segmentation of telecommunications services therefore led to a concomitant division in labour provision. More specifically, the division was between those employees providing services to corporate clients and creating new services and employees in the retail business responsible for standardized services with low value-added. Market segmentation also encouraged outsourcing and the creation of small companies providing services externally. These outsourcing providers usually recruit young employees who view their employment as a first, temporary job. While the work of those in charge of high value-added activities is characterized by creative activities and autonomy, the work of those performing outsourced activities is characterized by routine activities, low wages and a lack of voice (Larangeira, 2003; Batt et al., 2004). Some authors suggest that telecommunications firms are now converging onto an organizational format in which strategic choice combines different added value activities into diverse types of business, with a work organization that combines lean production with the outsourcing of low value adding activities (Katz and Darbishire, 2000) – characteristics that fit the shareholder model of governance (Börsch, 2004).

These developments have had important consequences for the segmentation of the labour force and for trade unions. Telecommunications trade unions in particular have witnessed a reduction in membership and their bargaining power worldwide.

Studies of the USA have indicated that AT&T's union density has significantly reduced in recent years, from 56 per cent in 1983 to 24 per cent in 2002 (Katz et al., 2003, p. 576). The authors suggest that if the current trend were to continue it would be difficult to find a unionized worker in AT&T. The decline of union membership in this case has also been attributed to a new configuration of industry with a multitude of small players and alliances with MNCs. While in the old system employees were unified within a same industry and a monopolistic centralized structure, more recently trade unions have to struggle to recruit heterogeneous workers from diverse types of firms and industry (Larangeira, 2003).

In Brazil, privatization had an enormous impact on the telecommunications trade union and its capacity to attract and retain members. During the military period, it was attractive to belong to the union because of its provision of health and recreational assistance to members, rather than because of its capacity to mobilize in the employees' interest. Under the military regime, union officials had links to or were appointed by the government. Membership was patronized by the central government, which assured membership through compulsorily deducting union fees from workers' pay slips. From 1985, with Brazil returning to democracy, union membership declined over the years, particularly after the government's announcement of its intention to privatize the sector and even more so following privatization itself.

From 1979 to the beginning of the 1990s the power of trade unions in Brazil grew steadily thanks to their ability to identify with the interests of state companies and their national alliances with political parties (Workers' Party, PT) and with the Unified Centre of Brazilian Workers (CUT). Historically trade unions had a greater presence in state enterprises. This has been attributed to the politicization of industrial relations in sectors such as telecommunications in the 1980s. Until privatization, employment contracts in state enterprises had guaranteed many benefits such as stability, career mobility based on seniority, re-education opportunities, higher wages and fringe benefits. It is no surprise that during the 1990s trade unions concentrated their efforts on preventing privatization. However, opposition to privatization not only involved political action against changes in the employment contract, but also reflected a struggle to maintain their role in representing workers in collective bargaining and to remain as an important player in Brazilian politics. Far from being effective agents for the workers, unions became preoccupied with maintaining their organizational identity (Ferraz, 2005).

With privatization at the end of the 1990s, the restructuring of the sector led to dispersion of employees throughout different industries, including newly set up call centres, with implications for employment. Table 2.5 shows the change of employment in the telecommunications sector from 2000 to 2003. As the table indicates, employment in the sector has reduced for the mobile segment and more significantly for the fixed line area. This has been attributed to the reduction of investment and market retraction in Brazil. Table 2.3 indicates that among the main fixed line providers between 1999 and 2002, Telemar decreased its workforce by 160.1 per cent while Brazil Telecom and Telefonica reduced theirs by 44.4 and

Table 2.5 Employees in mobile and fixed-line operators, Brazil

	2000	2001	2002	2003
Fixed-line operators	54,182	41,859	32,962	29,240
Rate of decline (%)	–	−22.7	−21.3	−11.3
Mobile operators	21,554	21,404	21,845	20,331
Rate of decline (%)	–	−0.7	2.1	−6.8
Total	75,736	63,263	54,807	49,571
Rate of decline (%)	–	−16.5	−13.4	−9.6

Source: Balanços das Empresas, Relatório Teleco Telefonia Celular no Brasil (2004).

32.9 per cent respectively. This situation has affected union membership significantly. The reduction in membership in recent years led to a reduction in union subscription income by 40 per cent (Larangeira, 2003). These changes have encouraged the introduction of the so called Participação Referente ao Lucro (PRL, Employee Profit-sharing Scheme), which linked payment to performance. In most cases PRL was negotiated locally, with no involvement of the national unions and with negative consequences for the trade unions' capacity to aggregate categories with differential needs, and therefore their ability to attract and retain members. Negotiations now occur locally on a company basis rather than a national basis (Ferraz, 2005). In the case of Brazil, the role of the national union for telecommunications (FITTEL) has been substantially eroded.

Conclusion

This chapter has provided a description of the forces that affected the development of Brazil's telecommunications sector since it was first consolidated through nationalization in 1973. Since then, the sector has been affected by cycles of economic growth and decline and by the political instability that accompanied economic downturns. Under the military government up to 1985, and also during Cardoso's presidency from 1995 to 2003, telecommunications was viewed as an important engine of economic growth. In the former period, this mission was seen to require state ownership and hands-on involvement in setting policies for the telecommunications companies, whereas in the latter period it was seen to be appropriate for the state to disengage from ownership and to leave corporate adjustment to market forces. The militarism of the 1970s and neoliberalism of the 1990s were important ideological drivers that informed policies for the sector.

During the 1980s, because of Telebrás' embeddedness in the state system, it was particularly sensitive to the problems of the state itself, such as Brazil's external deficit, its political governance and institutional constraints. The evolution and performance of the telecommunications sector was heavily influenced by the priority given to it by the government. In the 1990s, with the introduction of neoliberalist policies, the sector began to build its independence from the state, which culminated in privatization. Technological innovation and global competition now became the main drivers towards a reconfiguration and restructuring of the sector.

In the 1980s, the state was the most important stakeholder for telecommunications companies. In the 1990s, neoliberalism became an important justification for globalization and the institutional reform that laid the ground for opening the markets of developing countries to international competition. Economic growth was viewed as largely dependent on a country's capacity to build competitive advantages in a free market environment. The heavy hand of the state was now understood to be an impediment to economic growth. The beginning of the 1990s witnessed the entry of important actors that helped to shape telecommunications strategy, such as the multinational corporations and the national private sector. Progressive liberalization encouraged the formation of a market for telecommunications companies and subsequently their privatization. These events had a significant impact on the innovation capabilities of the sector. Adaptation to the market became more significant at the expense of Brazil's capacity to sustain technological innovation in telecommunications.

While the fall of the military regime in the mid-1980s was assisted by and also facilitated the emergence of strong labour organizations in Brazil, including that of the telecommunications workers, the 1990s witnessed a progressive weakening of trade unions in their capacity to attract and retain members, and thus to mobilize opposition to the new economic policies then being applied to Brazil. During the 1980s, Brazilian trade unions secured a wide legitimacy in Brazil largely based on their capacity to further the interests of public servants and state enterprise employees. The association of the telecommunications unions with CUT helped to institutionalize an environment of free collective bargaining and bottom-up participation. Trade union campaigns in the 1980s focused on maintaining real wages in line with high inflation rates. In the 1990s the 'Real Plan' elaborated by Cardoso dramatically reduced inflation, but the concomitant liberalization of the economy forced companies to initiate restructuring and to adapt strategies to increase productivity at the expense of employment. The mission of the trade unions during this decade therefore shifted to one of protecting job security by opposing the privatization of state companies. These factors together with the public desire for change weakened the legitimacy of mobilization against privatization and of the union as a relevant actor in shaping the telecommunications sector.

Note

1   Universalization represented a government policy to make telecommunications accessible to the population at large, as telecommunications was viewed as a tool of social integration.

References

Antunes, R. (1994) Recent strikes in Brazil: the main tendencies of the strike movement of the 1980s. *Latin American Perspectives*, 21, 24–37.

Banco Nacional de Desenvolvimento Econômico e Social (2002) *Empresas de Telefonia Fixa*. Report by A. B Dores Maria and Jose C. Castro.

Barros, O. (1993) Estudo da competitividade da indústria brasileira: oportunidades abertas para o Brasil face aos fluxos globais de investimento de risco e de capitais financeiros nos anos 90. Campinas, São Paulo: UNICAMP.

Batt, R., Colvin, A., Katz, H. and Keefe, J. (2004) Telecommunications 2004: strategy, human resource practices, and performance. Cornell-Rutgers Telecommunications. Project funded by the Sloan Foundation.

Blair, M. (1995) *Ownership and Control: Rethinking Corporate Governance for the Twenty-first Century*. Washington, DC: The Brookings Institution.

Börsch, A. (2004) Globalization, shareholder value, restructuring: the non-transformation of Siemens. *New Political Economy*, 9, 365–87.

Botelho, A. J., Ferro, J. R., McKnight, L. and Oliveira, A. C. M. (1998) Brazil. In E. M. Noam (ed.), *Telecommunications in Latin America*. New York: Oxford University Press, pp. 227–50.

Cascio, W. F. (2002) *Responsible Restructuring*. San Francisco: Berrett-Koehler.

Cassiolato, J. E., Szapiro, M. H. S. and Lastres, H. M. M. (2002) Local system of innovation under strain: the impacts of structural change in the telecommunications cluster of Campinas, Brazil. *International Journal of Technology Management*, 24, 680–704.

CEPAL (1998) *La inversión extranjera en América Latina y el Caribe*. Santiago de Chile: CEPAL.

CNI/SENAI, Setor de Telecomunicações (2005) Estudos Setoriais 4. Brasília.

Departamento Intersindical de Estatística e Estudos Sócio-Econômicos (1980) Balanço Anual de Greves. São Paulo.

Evans, P. B. (1979) *Dependent Development: The Alliance of Multinational, State and Local Capital in Brazil*. Princeton, NJ: Princeton University Press.

Fadul, A. (1989) Comunicação, cultura e informática no Brasil: desafios atuais. *Intercom Revista Brasileira de Telecomunicação*, 61, 13–32.

Ferraz, A. S. (2005) Privatização e Processo Decisório. Tese de doutorado. Programa de Pós-graduação em Ciência Política da Faculdade de Ciências Humanas da Universidade de São Paulo.

Ferraz, J. C., Rush, H. and Miles, I. (1992) *Development, Technology and Flexibility: Brazil Faces the Industrial Divide*. London: Routledge.

Fligstein N. and Shin, T. (2005) Shareholder value and changes in American industries, 1984–2000. Unpublished paper, Department of Sociology, University of Berkeley.

Hunter, W. 1997. *Eroding Military Influence in Brazil*. Chapel Hill: The University of Carolina Press.

Instituto de Pesquisa Econômica Aplicada (2001) <www.ipea.gov.br>.

International Labour Office (2000) *The WTO Negotiations on Basic Telecommunications*. Geneva: ILO.

Katz, H. (ed.) (1997) *Telecommunications: Restructuring Work and Employment Relations Worldwide*. Ithaca, NY: IRL Press.

Katz, H., Batt, R. and Keefe, J. H. (2003) The revitalization of the CWA: integrating collective bargaining, political action and organizing. *Industrial and Labor Relations Review*, 56, 573–89.

Katz, H. and Darbishire, O. (eds) (2000) *Converging Divergences: Worldwide Changes in Employment Systems.* Ithaca, NY: ILR Press.

Larangeira, S. M. G. (2003) A reestruturação das telecomunicações e os sindicatos. *Revista Brasileira de Ciências Sociais*, 18, 81–103.

Lazonick, W. and O'Sullivan, M. (2000) Maximizing shareholder value: a new ideology for corporate governance. *Economy and Society*, 29, 13–35.

Noronha, E. (ed.) (1989) Relaçoes trabalhistas. In S. M. Draibe (org.), *Brasil 1987 – Relatório sobre a Situação Social do País.* Editora SEADE.

Noronha, E. G. (1994) Greves e estratégias sindicais no Brasil. In C. A. de Oliveira, J. Matoso, S. F. Neto, M. Pochmann and M. A. de Oliveira (eds), *O mundo do trabalho. Crise e mudança no final do século.* São Paulo: Scritta, pp. 323–57.

Novaes, A. (1999) *Privatização do setor de telecomunicações no Brasil.* Rio de Janeiro: BNDES.

Pinheiro, A. C., Giambiagi, F. and Gostkorzewicz, J. (1999) O desempenho macroeconómico do Brasil nos anos 90. In F. Giambiagi and M. M. Moreira (eds), *A economia brasileira nos anos 90.* Rio de Janeiro: BNDES.

Resende, A. L. (1989) Estabilização e reforma: 1964–1967. In M. P. Abreu (ed.), *A ordem do progresso:cem anos de política econômica republicana 1889–1989*, 3rd edn. Rio de Janeiro: Campos, pp. 213–31.

Robinson, S. L. and Rousseau, D. M. (1994) Violating the *psychological contract*: not the exception but the norm. *Journal of Organizational Behavior*, 15, 245–59.

Straubhaar, J. and Horak, C. (1997) The history of privatization and liberalization in Brazilian telecommunications. In D. J. Ryan (ed.), *Privatization and Competition in Telecommunications: International Developments.* Westport, CT: Praeger, pp. 167–90.

Schjolden, A. (1999) Globalization, liberalization and restructuring of the Brazilian telecommunications industry: the end of technological capability? Master's thesis submitted to the Faculty of Geography and Regional Development, University of Arizona.

Szapiro, M. and Cassiolato, J. (2003) Telecommunications system of innovation in Brazil: development and recent challenges. The First Globelics Conference on Innovation Systems and Development Strategies for the Third Millennium, Rio de Janeiro, November.

Trebat, T. J. (1983). *Brazil's State Owned Enterprises.* Cambridge: Cambridge University Press.

Velasco, L. Jr (1997) A economia política das políticas públicas: Fatores que favoreceram as privatizações no período 1985/94. Texto para discussão no. 54. Rio de Janeiro: BNDES.

Wohlers de Almeida, M. and Crossetti, P. (1997) *Infra-estrutura, perspectivas de reorganização: telecomunicações.* Brasília: IPEA.

CHAPTER THREE

Scope and Method

Studies of organizational change have been severely criticized for concentrating too much on episodic snapshot changes, and for not taking account of history and context (Pettigrew, 1985; Pettigrew et al., 2001). The critics argue in favour of a more holistic approach to change that would consider how actors enact and react to external and internal events. They suggest that a holistic approach is possible if a methodology is applied that is capable of capturing different processes that proceed simultaneously over time. This methodology needs to take note of the actors who take part in the processes as well as the contexts in which the processes are situated. As mentioned in chapter 1, this research aims to offer a holistic understanding within a comprehensive co-evolutionary framework. To this end, it applies a range of perspectives to a variety of sources so as to inform change over time. This requires both the application of multiple methods and a longitudinal time frame.

A Longitudinal Approach

Since the aim of this book is to understand corporate co-evolution, a longitudinal case study is an appropriate research design (Yin, 1981; Eisenhardt, 1989). The investigation presented in this book covers Telemig during its lifetime from foundation in 1973 to when it lost its separate status in 2000. Three rounds of fieldwork were undertaken: the first between 1986 and 1990; the second between 1997 and 2000; and the third between 2001 and 2004. This adds up to 12 years of fieldwork spread over almost 20 years. Access to Telemig was first gained in 1985 by Suzana Rodrigues to conduct a study of the company's strategic decision-making in which she also gained access to board meetings. The mutual trust she developed with company personnel led to an unusual level of access and cooperation, which enabled different sources to be tapped at different points in time.

The first round of fieldwork utilized biographies, interviews with directors, managers and engineers, company documents and the Telemig union newspaper, named *O Bode* (*The Goat*) and later *O Bodim* (*The Little Goat*). The second round of fieldwork again used interviews with directors, managers and engineers, together with content from the union newspaper relating to developments during the 1990s. The third round of research involved additional interviews conducted with retired directors and long-serving employees, plus officials from the Telemig trade union who had been active since the 1980s. The purpose of these additional interviews was to complement and check information collected in the two previous rounds, and to update information about the further development of the company, including events following its privatization in 1998. In addition, during the third round of research a complete analysis was undertaken of content from the union newspaper from its first appearance in 1980 to the end of 2000.

Suzana Rodrigues conducted most of the fieldwork in the first round, which concentrated on developments up to 1990. Access was gained again in 1997 to cover changes that were happening in the 1990s. Three additional researchers participated in this second round of fieldwork, which continued until 2000: Talita da Luz, Alexandre Carrieri and Augusto Cabral. The second author of this book, John Child, has been advising this research since the mid-1980s and has actively contributed to its conceptual development. As a study of Telemig's co-evolution, the investigations informing this book examined how different aspects and dimensions of the company changed through time within a changing context, and what the drivers of change were. The principal aspects covered are its strategy and mission, structure and restructuring, corporate identity, culture and the images held of the company by its employees.

Data Sources

Table 3.1 indicates the range of sources used over the three rounds of research. The research used multiple sources of data in order to cover various levels and groups within the organization at different periods of its history: autobiographies, interviews and documents such as company reports and the trade union newspaper. The autobiographical material was accessed during the first round of fieldwork. This consisted of interviews that had been conducted independently with telecommunications sector leaders available in the *Historia Oral das Telecomunicações no Brasil* (*Oral History of Brazil's Telecommunications*). This oral history was constructed using a snowball method in which each interviewee named further people considered to have contributed to the formation of the sector. Examination of this archive material led to the selection of 25 autobiographies (from the 75 available) of the leaders who were personally involved in the foundation and early development of Telemig and Telebrás. These autobiographies with leaders and founders of the sector covered their perceptions of the organization's main characteristics during its early history and its relationships with the state until the mid-1980s. They were

Table 3.1 Sources of data during three rounds of research

Source	First round	Second round	Third round
Autobiographies	25	–	–
Interviews with the company's founders	5		
Interviews with corporate directors	8[a]	6	4
Interviews with managers	35	45	1
Interviews with engineers	25	40	–
Interviews with union officials	4	–	5
Interviews with retired employees	4	8	2
Company reports and organization charts	1973–1990	1991–2000	1991–2000
Other documents	Company philosophy	Telemig's transformation	144 documents on Telebras policies and practices (1973–2000)
	Telemig's history	Minutes of board meetings	10 Anatel (regulatory authority) documents
			Organizational charts (1983–2000)
Telemig's trade union newspaper	There were 1,296 issues of the union newspaper during the period 1980–2000 inclusive. All were examined.		

[a]Including three company founders

particularly relevant to understanding Telemig's formative organizational culture and corporate identity. They expressed the leaders' values, their moral commitment to the mission and priorities of the sector, and their views on Telemig's obligations towards its stakeholders. The autobiographies also provided insights into the 'relational framework' that linked Telemig's founders to its institutional sponsors within the governmental system, especially the Ministry of Telecommunications (Meyer and Scott, 1983). To complement this information, five of these leaders were personally interviewed by Suzana Rodrigues. These interviews included information on each leader's career, and his or her role in the construction of the sector and in the creation of Telemig. Questions were also asked about their views on the company's priorities, its obligations towards different stakeholders and the culture of the telecommunications sector. In addition, they addressed the leaders' understanding of their influence on how the sector was constituted.

The main interview checklist used with top management and other employees is presented in table 3.2. The same questions were asked in the first two rounds of research, with the exception of those where a change is indicated in the table. The response formats were open-ended and interesting points were followed up during the interviews in a free-form manner. Interviews with both groups usually lasted for around 90 minutes and all were tape-recorded. The transcripts amounted to a total of 932,503 words and each ranged from 18 to 21 pages in length.

In order to cover the whole of Telemig's lifespan, the top managers and employees in the first round were asked questions about both the time at which they were interviewed (1986–90) and the previous period, which was defined as 1973–85. Those interviewed in the second round were asked about the period 1990–2000. As a result of privatization in 1998, by the end of 2000 a large number of Telemig's employees had moved to a different company in the new owning group or had left. This is the reason why the interviews undertaken after that date during the third round were conducted in order to clarify and update information. Thus the first round of interviews focused on developments in the 1970s and 1980s, while the second focused on developments since 1990. As already mentioned, the objective of the third round was to complement information on the history of the companies, on anecdotes and on the development of the company after it was privatized.

The first two rounds of data collection (during 1986–90 and 1997–2000) employed the same methodological procedure. The open-ended interviews conducted in the first two rounds of research are the main source of information. The number of interviews and data sources for each period are listed in table 3.1. In total, 192 interviews were conducted over the three periods of data collection. Eighteen directors were interviewed: five directors and the three former directors in the first round, six directors in the second round and four retired directors in the third round.[1] The interviews with the directors covered the principal events in the company's life and their perceptions of its salient characteristics during that history.

Out of the interviews, 146 were conducted over the first two rounds with managers and engineers.[2] We selected those with the longest history of service within the company so as to maximize our access to the collective memory of its members. For the interviews with managers and engineers the company provided a list of employees with their position and years of work in the company. The company informed the employees that a study was being conducted by the Federal University of Minas Gerais (UFMG) with their support, but not for their use and control. Employees were personally contacted by the researcher for interview appointments.[3]

Since it was not possible to interview all employees, analysis of the union newspaper was undertaken in part as a proxy for their perception of the evolution of the company. The newspaper was established in 1980 with just six issues in its first year. It became a monthly publication from 1981 until 1989 when it became a weekly publication. Every issue of this newspaper was consulted, including bulletins and

Table 3.2   Interview checklist for fieldwork round 1 (1986–1990) and round 2 (1996–2000)

Round 1, on Telemig's foundation and history; round 2, on the period 1990–2000

1.1   R1 What were the organization's main characteristics at the time of its foundation?
R2 What were the organization's main characteristics between 1990 and now?
1.2   Briefly describe the circumstances at the time of the company's foundation
1.3   Who were the company's leaders at the time?
1.4   What was their role?
1.5   What were these leaders' values?
1.6   How would you describe the company's mission at the time?
1.7   How would you describe the company's main values at the time?
1.8   For what and for whom did the company stand?
1.9   How did Telemig compare to other companies in the Telebras system?
1.10 Who were considered the company's main stakeholders?
1.11 How would you describe the company's relations to the state, customers, the community, employees and competitors?
1.12 Which were the key groups in the organization?
1.13 Was there any conflict between them?

On change

2.1   R1 How did the company change over time?
R2 How did the company change from 1990 to now?
2.2   In which respects did the company change most obviously?
2.3   When did these changes occur?
2.4   R2 only What you did learn from these changes?
2.5   R2 only What did the company learn from these changes and how?
2.6   What have been the company's key strategies since its foundation?
2.7   R1 Which were the main decisions taken by the company since its creation?
R2 Which were the main decisions taken by the company since 1990?
2.8   Who were the main champions of these decisions?
2.9   Which were the internal and external factors that influenced change?
2.10 Who were the main actors in driving changes?
2.11 How have people and groups reacted to change? Was there any opposition?
2.12 Who were the people or groups opposing change?

On the then current situation

3.1   What are the organization's main characteristics?
3.2   Who are the company's leaders?
3.3   What is their role?
3.4   How would you describe the company's mission?
3.5   What is the company's main strategy?
3.6   How would you describe the company's key values?
3.7   What are the leaders' values?
3.8   For what and for whom does the company stand?
3.9   How does Telemig compare with other companies in the Telebras system?
3.10 Which are the company's main stakeholders?
3.11 How would you describe the company's relations to the state, customers, the community, employees and competitors?
3.12 Who are the key groups in the organization?
3.13 Is there any conflict between them?

additional editions. This newspaper was considered an appropriate representation of employee opinion because it circulated widely within the company and because until the 1990s the union's membership covered over 90 per cent of Telemig employees outside top management.

During the third round of fieldwork, further interviews were conducted up to 2006 with four retired directors, five currently serving trade union officers and two long-serving retired employees, primarily to check information. Over the whole fieldwork period, nine union officers and fourteen retired employees were interviewed. Company reports and organization charts were also inspected during the third round. Triangulation through the collection of data over time, at different organizational levels, and using different methods, enabled us to check data and interpretations at multiple points and periods (Scandura and Williams, 2001). While the study relies primarily on qualitative information provided by the sources mentioned, where possible these have been classified and coded in order to provide a degree of quantification to assist interpretation.

Data Analysis

1 Evolution

In constructing a picture of how the company evolved through its lifespan, we shall report on its different characteristics such as: its mission and strategy, structure and performance; organizational culture; corporate identity; the images held of the company by its employees and their union; and its restructuring and the politics around the learning of new competencies during the 1990s. Some of the characteristics mentioned above were accessed through more than one method, while others were accessed through specific instruments such as selected interview questions or documents such as the union newspaper. The sources of information are now described with reference to each relevant chapter.

2 Strategy, structure and performance (chapters 4, 5, 6 and 8)

The company's mission was assessed by examining documents, such as company reports and the founders' autobiographies, and from interviews with directors, managers and employees. The interview questions on mission and strategy are contained in table 3.2. The autobiographies of the founders and first-generation leaders were particularly useful for understanding the mission and strategy during Telemig's foundation period. Information on changes in the company's organizational structure and board composition was provided by interviews, company reports and documents, such as organizational charts. Company reports were available for most years, and organization charts were available for the years between 1982 and 1997.[4]

Organizational performance was analysed by examining Telemig's company reports and secondary publications on the telecommunications sector's performance.

3 Organizational culture (chapter 7)

Telemig's organizational culture was accessed through interviews with managers and employees and by examining company documents. Documents such as the autobiographies of the founders of the sector were essential for understanding their relevance to the creation of Telemig's culture. Company reports and the trade union newspaper provided key insights in the understanding of the different cultures present within the company. Narratives on the issues arising in the company's history and concerning its corporate identity were also used to inform our analysis of organizational culture.

4 Corporate identity (chapter 8)

Telemig's corporate identity was accessed by examining the claims about, and descriptions of, the company's central characteristics that were present in its leaders' narratives (Humphreys and Brown, 2002; Hardy et al., 2005). Corporate identity was therefore assessed by reference to the autobiographies of telecommunications sector leaders, interviews with Telemig's directors and company reports. The autobiographies produced information on each leader's part in the creation of Telemig and the aspirations he attached to the company.[5] As part of wider questioning on the company's change over time, directors were asked to define the main characteristics of the company, and to describe for what and for whom the company stood both at the time of interview and in its previous history. They were encouraged to elaborate on their answers, which were tape-recorded.

5 Images of the company (chapter 9)

The methodology employed for the analysis of imaging is founded on a grounded iterative approach (Glazer and Strauss, 1965). The relevance of images of the company, expressed through metaphors, became evident during our analysis of the trade union newspaper and also from interviews with employees. This raised the question of how metaphors could arise from reflections on changes in the evolution of the company and the changing context this presented to employees. As described in chapter 9, there was a two-stage iteration between the data and our emerging conceptions of reflection and organizational metaphor. It became clear that in order to understand the logic of the images and metaphors, we needed to relate them to the historical context in which they emerged. This then led us to analyse all the metaphors appearing between 1980 and 2000 through a longitudinal perspective with reference to the evolving situation of the company.

6 Restructuring and the politics of learning new competencies (chapter 10)

In addition to the main body of interviews and documents used for this book, two further sources were employed to investigate and interpret the issues of organizational learning and restructuring during the 1990s. The first consisted of interviews with 52 staff who comprised approximately one-fifth of the managerial hierarchy. The second additional source of information was a structured questionnaire sent by e-mail to everyone holding Telemig's 251 managerial positions in 1999. Forty-eight usable questionnaires were returned, giving a response rate of 19.1 per cent. The questionnaire specifically addressed changes relating to competencies and learning perceived to have occurred since Telemig's privatization in 1998, including organizational learning methods, organizational competencies and individual skills and qualities.

Interpretation and Limitations

The study reported here reveals both the strengths and the limitations of reflexivity (Weick, 1999). Because of the case's longitudinal character, spanning 27 years of a company's life, what we report is heavily interpretive in more than one respect. First, in most instances the information we have accessed comes from our respondents' descriptions of the changes that took place. These necessarily reflect the subjects' own interpretations. Furthermore, many of their accounts are retrospective and therefore subject to post hoc rationalization. This is why triangulation through multiple respondents and multiple types of source is extremely important. Second, the authors have inevitably introduced their own element of interpretation in classifying, selecting and presenting these accounts and the documentary sources used. Another limitation stems from the fact that restrictions of length limit the number of examples from interviews and documents that can be presented. On the other hand, no apology is required for attending to the ways in which key actors interpreted events in and around the company or their role in them. Without accessing such interpretations, much vital understanding would be lost, and it would be impossible to take account of factors such as managerial intentions. The use of multiple methods and sources, and the phasing of the research over time, are also relatively unusual features that contribute their own strengths.

While longitudinal research often has to be conducted retrospectively due to obvious limitations of resources and time, the present study was able to combine elements of real time and retrospective enquiry. A degree of real time investigation was possible because the bulk of the fieldwork was conducted during two different periods of time. Another limitation of the investigation was that it was not feasible to interview workers. However, a proxy for their views was provided by the content of each issue of the Telemig union's newspaper. Until the 1990s, around 90 per cent of employees belonged to the union.

Notes

1 All were executive directors.
2 Engineers fell into two categories: those with university degrees and those with technical qualifications. It was not feasible to gain access to unqualified workers.
3 In general, we shall report quotations from our interviews without revealing the identity of respondents. An exception concerns material on the foundation of the company and the sector because this refers to historical information that is already in the public domain.
4 Following Telemig's privatization in 1998, all its documents were taken to Rio de Janiero and most were destroyed. For this reason, there were some gaps in available materials.
5 All were male.

References

Eisenhardt, K. (1989) Building theories from case study research. *Academy of Management Review*, 14, 532–50.

Glazer, B. and Strauss, A. (1965) Discovery of substantive theory: a basic strategy underlying quantitative research. *American Behavioral Scientist*, 8, 5–12.

Hardy, C., Lawrence, T. B. and Grant, D. (2005) Discourse and collaboration: the role of conversations and collective identity. *Academy of Management Review*, 30, 58–77.

Humphreys, M. and Brown, A. D. (2002) Narratives of organizational identity and identification: a case study of hegemony and resistance. *Organization Studies*, 23, 421–47.

Meyer, J. W. and Scott, W. R. (eds) (1983) *Organizational Environments: Ritual and Rationality*. Beverly Hills, CA: Sage.

Pettigrew, A. (1985) *The Awakening Giant: Continuity and Change in ICI*. Oxford: Blackwell.

Pettigrew, A., Woodman, R. W. and Cameron, K. (2001) Studying organizational change and development: challenges for future research. *Academy of Management Review*, 44, 697–713.

Scandura, T. A. and Williams, E. A. (2001) Research methodology in management: current practices, trends, and implications for future research. *Academy of Management Journal*, 43, 1248–64.

Weick, K. E. (1999) Theory construction as disciplined reflexivity: tradeoffs in the 90s. *Academy of Management Review*, 24, 797–806.

Yin, R. (1981). The case study in crisis: some answers. *Administrative Science Quarterly*, 26, 8–65.

PART II

Historical Co-evolution of Telemig

CHAPTER FOUR

Foundations 1953–1985

This chapter covers the years until 1985, when the end of military rule marked a new phase in Telemig's development. It describes the antecedents to Telemig, the company's foundation and formative years, and the beginnings of change once Brazil's political scene began to transform. The story begins with the CTMG company, which preceded Telemig and passed on to it certain fundamental characteristics. Initiatives taken by a group of institutional entrepreneurs led to the establishment of Telemig in 1973 as part of the construction of a state-owned telecommunications system in Brazil. The company's formative period extended to the late 1970s, under a strong leadership of military officers and technocrats. This established a corporate identity that provided many elements of continuity for the years to come. By the end of the decade, however, changing circumstances were already sowing the seeds of significant discontinuities that became particularly apparent after the end of military rule in 1985.

The chapter is divided into three main sections. The first describes the foundation of Telemig, the role played by telecommunications entrepreneurs, the company's mission and strategy, its organizational culture and performance. The second section describes the company's formative period from 1973 to 1979. The third section examines events from 1979, which drove the company towards changes that took place in the period after 1985. The autobiographies of the sector founders provide valuable source material for the years to 1985, in addition to interviews conducted by the researchers. We shall indicate in this chapter where quotations are drawn from the autobiographies. In subsequent chapters, all quotations are drawn from the researchers' own interviews except where otherwise indicated.

Precursors to Telemig 1954–1973: CTMG

Telemig was created from CTMG, a company that belonged to the CTB, a Brazilian Telephone company with its headquarters located in Rio de Janeiro. The latter was controlled by a Canadian company, Brazilian Traction Light and Power, which together with other foreign companies dominated the Brazilian market at the time. In 1968 the Canadian company controlled 70 per cent of the 1.5 million telephones in the country, and handled 80 per cent of telephone connections (Botelho et al., 1998).

Telemig's antecedents go back to 1953 when a group of entrepreneurs got together with local politicians to improve the telephone system in the state of Minas Gerais (MG). This resulted in the concession for developing telephone services in MG being transferred from CTB, located in Rio de Janeiro, to a new company, Companhia Telefonica de Minas Gerais (CTMG) , based in Belo Horizonte, the state capital of MG. CTB appointed the first board of directors of CTMG: Major Malvino Reis (President), Pedro Renault Castanheira (Vice-President), Galvino Reis Neto, Mário Pires, and Dr Luís Carlos de Portilho (Telemig, 1978).

The Vice-President, Pedro Renault Castanheira, was the effective leader of CTMG, and he was regarded as one of the most influential figures in the development of the Brazilian telecommunications sector. Castanheira's reputation as an entrepreneur comes from two of CTMG's achievements. It was the first company in Brazil to introduce a system of communications through microwaves, the technology of which was later shared with other companies. However, Castanheira was better known for introducing a self-financing scheme that required customers who acquired a telephone to pay a premium in return for an allocation of company shares. This scheme helped to provide funds for expansion and, above all, granted some autonomy to the companies in the securing of resources. His system planted the seeds of autonomy and self-sufficiency for telecommunications, once it became applied to the whole sector.

The self-funding programme was controversial and it generated opposition from the city council of Belo Horizonte. Castanheiras nevertheless managed to introduce the programme to other cities of the state and to other parts of Brazil. Approval to introduce the system to Belo Horizonte was only obtained in 1965, as a result of Castanheira's personal involvement and endless negotiations with both the state government and the city council. Alvim Sobrinho, a former director of Telemig, mentioned that:

> One of the precursors of the telecommunications system in Minas Gerais and Brazil was CTMG's Vice-President, Pedro Renault Castanheira. He was the pioneer, the great believer in building telecommunications through self-financing by share issues. At the time, we undertook a lot of political lobbying to convince local politicians to enact legislation that would allow us to surcharge for telephone connections and transform these payments into company shares. Unfortunately, we were blocked politically from doing this for Belo Horizonte, but the system was introduced into the interior of MG and various other parts of Brazil. (Autobiography)

CTMG did not at first have its own engineers and had to rely heavily on CTB for technological support. However, it gradually began to develop its own competencies. General Siqueira de Meneses described how this happened:

I brought in all the military personnel I could to work with me. It was difficult at that time to find civilians who understood telecommunications. Then I started to recruit from other companies. The main targets were Petrobras, Standard Electric and Ericsson. (Autobiography)

Company accounts of its history (Histórico da Telemig, 1997) suggest that in its first board meeting, directors were already discussing how to expand the network inherited from CTB, including interstate communications. The company's expansion plans prioritized institutions such as hospitals, health and education organizations. The same accounts suggest that CTMG's engineers were motivated by a social mission, that of contributing to the social and economic development of the state. Table 4.1 presents a summary of the key actions and events in CTMG's life. It shows that, as the company expanded externally, it also started to grow internally by departmentalizing support activities. It created personnel, public relations and other departments. The company's history indicates that it became more centralized at the same time as it diversified its internal activities.

The microwave system was recognized at the time as the most ambitious project in the whole telecommunications sector. In the founders' autobiographies there are stories about how the engineers had to improvise by finding sites for transmission towers in geographically inaccessible localities, how they had to use flares to illuminate their work at night and so forth. As Borges de Muros, one of the founders, said:

The introduction of microwave stations required a pioneering spirit, hard work, innovation and courage. Though in some situations Telemig engineers were met by farmers with guns, all the stress and hassle was worthwhile because the company managed to install high-speed communications between Rio de Janeiro and São Paulo. (Autobiography)

Table 4.1   Key actions and events that affected CTMG from 1953 to 1973

Year	Key actions and events
1953	Creation of CTMG, the precursor of Telemig.
1954	Expansion of the number of telephones in the interior of the state; expansion of intercity links; new corporate building.
1955	Expansion of contracts giving concessions in small cities.
1956	Introduction of the self-financing plan in the interior of the state.
1957	Political mobilization for introduction of the self-financing service in the state capital – Beb Horizonte (BH).
1958	Survey in the community to verify the acceptance of self-financing in the capital; further extension of the public telephone network; further expansion of the intercity network; introduction of microwave technology.
1959	Further expansion of microwave technology.

Table 4.1   *(cont'd)*

Year	Key actions and events
1960	Problem of introduction of self-financing in the capital not resolved as it depended on introduction of legislation by the city council.
1961	Extension of the microwave technology to other states in Brazil under the leadership of the company; introduction of new distributing units in the capital and in the interior.
	CTMG expanded its network to the capital of Brazil and transferred the head office to Brasilia; this was a strategic decision that would allow it to lobby the central government for the expansion of its microwave technology to other states.
	Introduction of legislation for regulation of self-financing in the state.
	Creation of a state fund for the expansion of telecommunications in Minas Gerais.
	Introduction of legislation that transferred to the different Brazilian states the responsibility for concessions, organization, supervision and the telephone services; the states were also to be responsible for integrating the telephone services in their territories. This legislation obliged the companies to share interstate traffic.
1962	Introduction of the national telecommunications code, which transferred to the federal government responsibility for control and supervision of telecommunications in the country.
1963	Further expansion of the microwave system to other states.
1964	Expansion of telephone provision in the new capital, Brasília.
1965	Creation of Embratel.
1965	Introduction of the system of self-financing to BH.
1966	Continuing expansion of telephone provision in BH.
1967	Opening of a new building for microwaves technology.
1968	Installation of 30,000 automated telephones in BH; introduction of medical service for the company's employees.
1969	Further expansion in the basic service of telephone provision, representing an increase of 191 per cent in the number of telephones available since 1953; new board took office.
1970	Implementation of DDD (system of direct dialling), which made it possible to make calls without the assistance of telephone operators.
1971	CTMG acquired other independent companies already in operation in the state of Minas Gerais.
	Reorganization with the company becoming further centralized at a higher level, and decentralized operationally; it also became more bureaucratized in terms of expanding its hierarchical levels.
	Introduction of various support departments, such as Personal, Public Relations, Personnel Development, Planning and Communications.
1972	Creation of Telebrás at the federal government level (see chapter 2); a new board took office with the intention of implementing the government's plan to unify Brazil's telecommunications services.

Table 4.2 CTMG growth from 1953 to 1973

Year	Number of telephones (000s)	Growth (1953 = 100)
1953	28.6	100
1954	31.4	109.0
1955	35.8	125.3
1956	37.1	129.6
1957	37.8	132.3
1958	n.a.	–
1959	41.0	143.3
1960	42.3	147.8
1961	44.0	154.0
1962	46.7	163.2
1963	n.a.	–
1964	50.9	177.8
1965	52.4	183.2
1966	53.7	187.9
1967	55.2	193.1
1968	66.9	234.1
1969	83.2	291.1
1970	85.9	300.3
1971	87.3	305.2
1972	n.a.	–

n.a.: not available.

The technological developments achieved by CTMG contributed to the expansion of microwave stations for telecommunications in other parts of the country in the mid-1960s. By 1969 all the major cities in Brazil were connected through a microwave network, including the Amazon region (Botelho et al., 1998). As table 4.2 indicates, CTMG grew by over 300 per cent between 1953 and 1972. By 1972 it had already expanded beyond the borders of MG state by creating a network for long distance communications.

The ownership of CTMG was the subject of dispute between different interest groups. There were stories that its headquarters were transferred to Brasília in order to prevent a takeover by the MG government, which disputed the rights to control telecommunications with the capital's city council. CTMG gradually evolved from a situation in which it had substantial autonomy to one of increasing dependency on the state. The state incrementally emerged as CTMG's main partner. The company had been created with the involvement of MG state, which also participated as a shareholder. Besides creating a fund for expanding the telephone system, the state gradually assumed responsibility for the supervision of services, and later became the main organizer and controller of the telecommunications system. However, difficulties in coordinating the responsibilities of regional states and city councils, together with the need for an integrated and unified telecommunications system, led the federal government to take control of the sector in 1973. When CTMG was transformed into Telemig in 1973 through incorporation within Telebrás, the federal holding company, this was resisted by the governor of MG state.

External Forces

1 Bringing the state back in

The year 1964 was an important one for Brazil. The events of that year were to have a deep impact on the history of telecommunications in general, including CTMG. The country was afflicted by political instability, with an explosion of strikes and riots. These led to a military coup that suppressed civil liberties. At the time, the telecommunications sector was suffering from severe fragmentation and stagnation. There were more than 1000 service providers in Brazil, most of which were providing a poor service. Their technology was obsolete and this limited the services that could be offered. Multinationals and private companies did not see much future in Brazil, as most had contracts that were about to expire with little chance of being renewed. Other companies belonging to local councils did not have the necessary resources for investment. Pires de Albuquerque, a sector founder, said of this period that 'it took people so long to get a telephone that they got their children to put their names down so that they would have a phone when they became adults' (Autobiography). The military regime understood that placing telecommunications under the control of the federal government was crucial to achieving a more efficient coordination of services. It also viewed telecommunications as an instrument to promote national integration, security and economic development.

Even before the military coup in 1964, important steps had already been taken towards forming a national telecommunications sector. In 1962 the government issued a telecommunications code, which included the creation of a national fund for development of the sector. This involved drawing resources from the self-financing scheme to constitute a state fund named FNT (National Fund for Telecommunications). Embratel, the long distance carrier, was created in 1965 as a joint-stock company whose shareholders initially were the federal government and large public enterprises. Embratel was to take responsibility for developing national and international links through a microwave trunk network. Embratel had an immediate impact on the quality of services provided: 'When Embratel was created, it introduced the first efficient system for long distance calls between Brasília and Porto Alegre, and the demand for flights between these two cities fell noticeably' (Palha Neto).

2 Constructing a highly institutionalized environment

During the 1970s, the government established favourable conditions for tele-communications companies to pursue the social and economic mission it set out for them, namely to assist Brazil's economic development and integration. This favourable environment relied on a political consensus between the state and the telecommunications companies. The government provided funds for the sector's expansion and for the development of indigenous technology. It also protected the companies from competition, and adopted measures that discouraged a consumer and employee voice. Customers were considered as users rather than as key players in the market. Employee voice was silenced by management control of union appointments and restrictions on the union's right to take industrial action.

The telecommunications system was organized as follows. Embratel provided the technical and infrastructural resources for the development of a unified national sector. The government created the Centro De Pesquisas e Desenvolvimento (Centre for Research and Development, CPqD) in Campinas with the intention of devel-oping a national system of innovation in telecommunications. This centre under-took collaborative projects with various universities and formed alliances with equipment manufacturers already in Brazil. The government also centralized pro-curement. Provision of equipment had to have approval from Telebrás, which was charged with encouraging national suppliers. Foreign equipment manufacturers still operating in Brazil were permitted to establish joint ventures with national com-panies with the latter holding at least 51 per cent of voting shares (Botelho et al., 1998).

The Formative Period: 1973–1979

In July 1972 the federal government passed a law that all telecommunications con-cessions should be transferred to the government when they expired. This law coincided with the foundation of a national telecommunications holding company, Telebrás, which incorporated the majority of Brazil's telecommunications com-panies. Telemig was one among 27 companies established within Telebrás. The pro-cess of nationalization was already under way as the government had previously authorized the acquisition and incorporation of independent companies in vari-ous states, including those belonging to the Brazilian Traction Light and Power group. When it was privatized in 1998, Telebrás incorporated more than 90 per cent of the telephone companies in Brazil.

Telemig inherited several important characteristics from its precursors. One was technical strength and a strong technocratic ethos. Another was the entrepre-neurial character of its first leading group who created the self-funding scheme, which remained active until 1982. A third characteristic was the increasing institutionalization of telecommunications in Brazil under state direction in line with the definition of the sector as an instrument of national integration and economic development. This institutionalization continued during Telemig's formative period.

1 The founding group

Telemig's first board of directors of Telemig included some new faces. It consisted of General Alencastro (President), Colonel Hélio Gomes do Amaral (Vice-President) and José Leitão Viana (Finance Diretor), in addition to others retained from the previous management such as Dr Mário Pires (Director of Public Relations), Dr Luís Carlos De Portilho (Director of Juridical Department) and Mr Valdemar Pires de Lima (Director of Operations). Alencastro remained as Telemig's CEO for less than two years, when he was promoted to be CEO of Telebrás. At the end of 1974, Brigadier Antonio Kopp came in as CEO, bringing with him Calistrato Borges de Muros as Vice-President, Americo Palha Neto as Technical Director and Hélio Silveira as Director of Public Relations. Valdemar Pires and Leitão Viana were kept as members of the board. Two other changes were relevant. In 1976 Valdemar Pires was replaced by José Jorge Pereira and Luiz Claudio Guimarães replaced Palha Neto, who became Operations Director.

Alencastro enjoyed particular influence in the new company not only as its president, but also because he was the most prominent leader of the telecommunications sector. The positions held by the founders of Telemig and other key builders of Brazil's telecommunications sector, together with their main activities and accomplishments, are summarized in table 4.3.

2 The construction of a collective identity

When analysing Telemig's formative period, it is crucial to consider not only the people who were directly involved with the creation of the state company in 1973, such as the leaders of CTMG who continued to hold leading positions in Telemig, but also those who were involved with the establishment of a unified telecommunications sector. The group that established the national telecommunications system comprised a horizontal and vertical network with strong political ties. It linked the military regime to bureaucrats in government and then via Telebrás to top managers and engineers in the companies themselves. In the early 1970s, the network also included members of the MG state government. Telebrás performed the main coordinative role for this network, evidence for which is contained in the autobiographies of the sector leaders. In these accounts, all 25 leaders involved with Telemig referred to at least two other members of the same group, while there was mutual referencing in the case of 11 of them. These sector leaders also shared much the same educational background. Sixteen of them were educated in

Table 4.3 Actions and achievements of founders of the Brazilian telecommunications sector

Name	Main posts/date	Accomplishments/role
1 Américo Palha Neto	1982–4 Operations Director of TELEMIG 1974–82 Technical Director at TELEMIG 1969–73 Head of Department of Traffic of CETEL	• Pioneering the introduction of Pulse Code Modulation equipments in CETEL • Purchasing of commuting equipment (suppliers: Standard Electric, Siemens, Ericsson) and also purchases of transmission equipment for the microwave routes • Establishment of a technology collaboration link with Engineering Schools in Minas Gerais • Integration of 200 independent telecommunication companies to TELEMIG • Participation in the project for extension of telecommunications infrastructure (e.g. electric energy, road construction and introduction of microwaves) • Introduction of telemarketing • Introduction of telephone line extension in residences
2 Antonio Augusto de Lima Neto	1982 to interview date (1984) Executive Director of the company *Camargo Sistemas e Engenharia* 1955–70 Superintendent General Director of CTMG/TELEMIG n.a. President of TELECENTRO	• Introduction of a link of micros between Belo Horizonte and Rio de Janeiro • Organization of the data processing service in the city hall of Belo Horizonte • Development of the first national microwave equipment with solar energy • Organized the company Prodata Consultancy in Rio de Janeiro • Participation in the project of nationalizing telephone operators in Brazil • Participation in the creation of a national code for telecommunications • Participation in the self-financing project for telecommunications • Introduction of conversion of debentures into shares
3 Antônio Salles Leite	1973–9 Founder and first president of TELESP n.a. Director of CTMG/TELEMIG 1970 Financial Director of CTB	• Plan to install a million telephones in four states of the Federation at CTB • Responsible for the elaboration of a plan to install two million telephones in the state of São Paulo, after TELEST was founded • Participation in the foundation of TELESP • At TELESP, acquisition of a number of small companies, acquisition of the Telephonic Company of Borba Gato, and acquisition of COTESP (from the government of São Paulo) • Participation in planning and implementation of telecommunications expansion in São Paulo

Table 4.3 (cont'd)

Name	Main posts/date	Accomplishments/role
4 Calistrato Borges de Muros	1974–9 Vice-president of TELEMIG	• Organization of CTMG engineering department • Introduction of a network linking various cities in Minas Gerais State • Development of a microwave project connecting Rio de Janeiro and Belo Horizonte • Personal engagement in the construction of telephone lines • Participation in the implementation of the system of self-financing in Minas Gerais • Participation in foundation of the National Institute of Santa Rita do Sapucaí • Foundation of the engineering department at CTMG (Companhia telefônica de Minas Gerais) • Participation in the implementation of expansion plans and incorporation of individual companies into TELEMIG
5 José Alvim Sobrinho	Interview date (1984) Economic and Financial Director of TELEMIG	• International fund-raising • Installation of the first microwave link between Belo Horizonte and Rio de Janeiro • Introduction of a telephonic station in Santana do Riacho, the first city in Minas Gerais to adopt telecommunication services • Participation in the planning of the first self-financing project • Creation of a group of supplier companies for TELEMIG
6 General José Antônio de Alencastro e Silva	1972–4 President of TELEMIG 1974–85 President of TELEBRÁS	• Elaboration of the preliminary project of the Brazilian telecommunications system • Convener of the first Brazilian Congress of Telecommunications • Elaboration of the Telegraphic Postal Plan • Introduction for the first time in Brazil of the multiplex telecommunications system • Planning of telecommunications in Southern Minas • Creation of the Training Centre of TELEBRÁS • Creation of SISTEL, the security fund for TELEBRÁS employees

	Positions	Activities
7 José Leitão Viana	1982 to interview date (1984) Vice-president of TELEMIG 1972–82 Director of CTMG/TELEMIG 1964 Head of Financial Department of CETEL/RJ	• Economic financial studies at CETEL, TELEMIG and other companies in Brazil • Participation in the planning and implementation of expansion plans. • Engagement in political mobilization to gain autonomy from TELEBRÁS • Participation in the project to introduce digital lines
8 General José Siqueira de Menezes	1969–72 Director of CTMG/TELEMIG	• Innovation in radio transmission • Expansion of CTB telephone network • Expansion of the telephone access in São José dos Campos • Coordination of recruitment and education for CTMG • Negotiator of plan to implant a network between the states of Paraná and Rio Grande do Sul with the International Telegraph and Telephone Company • Leadership in the nationalization of CTB (Companhia Telefônica Brasileira) • Participation of a project to integrate inter-state systems of telecommunications
9 Luis Carlos de Portilho	1955–79 Director of CTMG/TELEMIG 1974–6 Juridical consultant of the Ministry of Telecommunications n.a. Executive Superintendent of the Federation of Commerce of Minas Gerais	• Plan for transferring the location of the CTMG headquarters to Brasília • Building microwave link between Belo Horizonte and Rio de Janeiro • Restructuring of CTMG • Participation in the introduction of the self-financing project • Political mobilization to transfer the head office from Belo Horizonte to Brasília • Political mobilization for centralization of telecommunications services into CTMG • Member of the National Council for Imports in Telecommunications

Table 4.3 (*cont'd*)

Name	Main posts/date	Accomplishments/role
10 Brigadier Teobaldo Antonio Kopp	1974–85 President of TELEMIG n.a. Director and president of CETEL (Telecommunications Company of Guanabara)	• Introduction of new technologies at CETEL, such as plastic tubes, and expansion of cross networks • Significant expansion of telephone terminals • Introduction of Pulse Code Modulation (PCM) in the CETEL system • Creation of the department of research and development at TELEMIG • Foundation of CETEL • Expansion of telecommunications system in the state of Minas Gerais
11 Alberto Luís Fava	Interview date (1984) Operations Director of TELEPAR	• Development and implementation of a Programme for Improvement of the External Network proposed by TELEBRÁS • Improvement of consumer services for TELEPAR • Creation of the Council of Users and the Panel of Subscribers • Introduction of the Community Telephonic Central at TELEPAR • Introduction of the National Community Network (RENAC) • Introduction of a national system for quality control in telecommunications
12 Areno Pires	1983 to interview date (1984) Superintendent of an industry of Oscillating Crystals 1974 Management Director of TELEBRÁS (Member of the first board) 1974–9 President of Telephonic Company of Brasília 1979–83 Commercial Director of Indústria EMBRACOM Eletrônica SA	• Integration of companies throughout Brazil • Planning of the first management information systems for telecommunications • Nomination to work with the state governments, congressmen and authorities on regulations of stakes transference from private companies to TELEBRÁS • Acquisition of private companies transferred to TELEBRÁS • Establishment of the first operational norms of service, tariff unification and services at a national level • Substantial expansion of Brasília Telephone Company • Founder of the first manufacturer of optical fibres in Brazil

13 Eduardo Alcoforado Pontual	1983 Director of TELOS 1974–6 Head of the Office of Administrative Planning of EMBRATEL 1972–4 Administrative Director of EMBRATEL	• Founder of TELOS, a foundation created with the specific aim of complementing retirements and pensions of telecommunications companies • Introduction of a long distance system integrating various regions of Brazil
14 Commander Euclídes Quandt de Oliveira	1974–9 Minister of Communications 1965–7 President of CONTEL	• Introduction of norms for the operation of the National Telecommunications System • Participation in the creation of TELEBRÁS • Constitution of EMBRATEL • Establishment of norms for colour television • Consolidation and expiation of TELEBRÁS through incorporation of private companies
15 Francisco dos Santos Pires Albuquerque	1966 Head of the Department of Operations Coordination of EMBRATEL	• EMBRATEL: introduction of the Southern network, São Paulo, Curitiba, Porto Alegre • Elaboration of the operating and maintenance plan of EMBRATEL • Decision to introduce central coordination of radio transmissions • Introduction of television operations • Introduction of private voice channels • Introduction of colour TV in Brazil (1971) • Start of the telex network

Table 4.3 *(cont'd)*

Name	Main posts/date	Accomplishments/role
16 Dr Haroldo Corrêa de Mattos	1979–85 Minister of Communications n.a. President of EMBRATEL n.a. President of the Post and Telegraphs	• Restructuring of the Post and Telegraphs • Utilization of satellites for communications in inner areas of the Brazilian territory (launching of the domestic satellite)
17 Colonel Hygino Caetano Corsetti	1969–74 Minister of Communications 1966–9 Director of Escola de Comunicações de Deodoro	• Introduction of a course in Telecommunications at the Military Academy in Resende (*Academia Militar das Agulhas Negras*) • Policy making on the Army telecommunications • Planning and introduction of TELEBRÁS in 1972 • Introduction of colour television • Introduction of the first submarine cable • Transformation of the Post and Telegraph Department into a public company • Division of the Post and Telegraph Department in four companies: TELERJ, TELESP, TELEMIG and TELEST • Organization of central companies in each State • Proposal of state rules for the sector • Adoption of PAL–M for colour television • Raising of funds to create TELEBRÁS • Introduction of the Telex National System connecting the states and territories in Fernando de Noronha • Restructuring of the post and telegraph

18 Joost Van Damme	1973 to interview date (1985) President of TELPA (Telecommunications of Paraíba)	• Development of projects for the states of Piauí and Alagoas • Introduction of a microwave link in Recife • Analysis of economic and financial viability of different telephone companies in Brazil at DENTEL
	1970 Worked for DENTEL – National Telecommunications Department	• Integration of various telephonic companies in Paraíba by TELEINGRA (Telephonic Company of Campina Grande) • Participation in the initial works of staff and recourses assembly at TELPA
	1969 Manager of the Brazilian Industry of Electricity – INGELSA, in Recife	
19 Jorge Marsiaj Leal	1980 to interview date (1984) Research and Development Director of TELEBRÁS	• Introduction of the first telex centrals in Brazil (Post and Telegraphs) • Planning and introduction of EMBRATEL operations • Organization of the General Office of the Ministry of Telecommunications • Definition of the first guidelines of the National Telecommunications Policy • Organization of three areas in TELEBRÁS: research and development, industrial policies and the management of information systems
	1967–72 Operations Director of EMBRATEL	• Contribution to the formulation of the Law of Brazilian Telecommunications and the Brazilian Telecommunications Code • Creation of the National Fund of Telecommunications
20 José Maria Couto de Oliveira	1967–72, 1979 to interview date (1984) Administrative Director of EMBRATEL	• Broadening the Basic National System (connecting all units of the Federation), the Long-Distance Direct Dialling System and the INTELSÁT Satellite International Telecommunications System • Introduction of the Telex National Network • Expansion Plan of TELERJ
	1974–9 Director of TELERJ	• Introduction of data communication services at EMBRATEL • Negotiations with ATT (from the United States) to grant EMBRATEL exclusivity as explorer and operator of telephonic traffic between Brazil and United States

Table 4.3 (cont'd)

Name	Main posts/date	Accomplishments/role
21 José Paulo de Toledo	1962–82 Head of the Juridical Department of CETEL	• Feasibility study of intervention and deappropriation of CTB by the government of the state of Guanabara • Elaboration of Decree 1544 of 20/02/63/RJ, which delimited the market area of CETEL in the former state of Guanabara • Juridical decisions related to the economic feasibility of CETEL • Legal project on the constitution of CTMG
22 Levy Kaufman	Interview date (1984) Vice-president of TELESP 1973–83/4 Operations Director of TELESP 1954–65 Head of District, Head of Construction, southern Superintendent and General Superintendent of CTB/RJ	• Construction of a new network of ducts, cables and buildings for 200,000 lines at CTB/SP • Installation of the first coaxial rod at CTB • Participation in the project of nationalization of CTB (Brazilian Telephone Company) • Introduction of *cross-bar* technology in the state of São Paulo • Participation in the expansion of telecommunications services in the state of São Paulo
23 Luís Sergio Coelho de Sampaio	1978–84 Vice-president of EMBRATEL 1973–8 Financial Director of EMBRATEL 1973 Financial Director of TELERJ	• Introduction of a planning and control system, systemic analysis, balance and productivity evaluation • Creation of HR programme, aimed at developing the culture of the sector through education • Introduction of RENPAC ('Data communications through commuted network') • Introduction of a national training plan for dissemination of digital technology

24 Sebastião Esteves Alpha	1974–84 President of TELEBAHIA	• Introduction of local centrals in Salvador and microwave networks
		• Extension of simple and low-cost telephonic services in Bahia
	1968 Head of Operations of EMBRATEL in Salvador	• Participation in the plans for integration of the State of Bahia in the national system of telecommunications
		• Expansion of public telephone system in Bahia
25 Raul Antônio Del Fiol	1967–76 TELEPAR	• Led the process of integration and incorporation of telecommunications companies into the TELEBRÁS system
	1971–6 Director of Development of EMBRATEL	• Led the expansion of telecommunications system by TELEBRÁS
		• Championed the vision of orientation towards the market by TELEBRÁS system
	1979–82 Operations Director of TELEBRÁS	
	1983 Marketing Director of TELEBRÁS	

Source: Data extracted from the documents on the Oral History of Telecommunications (1984).

a military engineering school, two graduated in telecommunications engineering
from the Catholic University of Rio de Janeiro – an undergraduate programme
established by the military academy – three received a degree in engineering elsewhere and the remaining four had a degree in law or economics.

Education in telecommunications began during the Second World War in the
Military Institute of Engineering (IME) and the Aeronautics Institute. Subsequently,
the staff of these schools established other telecommunications courses in the country, such as the one in the Catholic University of Rio de Janeiro. The staff and
students of these schools were the first to occupy managerial and technical positions in the sector, both in the companies themselves and in the Ministry of
Telecommunications. Their career moves often crossed levels within the system.
An interview with General Alencastro indicates how the group educated in the
armed forces defined and diffused their corporate identity:

> The people who direct the sector today have their past associated with it. This has
> been the case already for twenty years. We have maintained a managerial continuity
> together with a clear understanding at the national level of the relevance of telecom-
> munications for the political and social integration of Brazil. This understanding came
> from the armed forces and then spread to the civilian environment of the engineering
> schools. It gave rise to an organizational culture that conceived of telecommunications
> as a driver of the country's economic and social development. (General Alencastro)

The following passage from one of the autobiographies indicates how the construction of a common professional identity led to the development of shared
values and motivation that informed a collective entrepreneurship:

> At IME we engineers were mixed together with military people. This helped to
> build a consensus in the sector about the mission and the management of telecom-
> munications companies. We all understood the relevance of telecommunications for
> the unity and development of Brazil and spread our values throughout the country.
> (Autobiography, Paulo de Toledo)

Entrepreneurship was a distinctive quality of the founding group. Right from
the days of CTMG, innovation and entrepreneurship were recognized as one of
its most distinguished characteristics. Telemig inherited this entrepreneurial spirit.
Luiz Carlos de Portilho, one of the CTMG directors who remained with Telemig,
commented that 'Pedro Castanheira [Vice-President of CTMG] was a saviour in
inventing a formula for the development of the telecommunications sector in Brazil'
(Autobiography, Carlos Portilho). The biographical material as well as interviews
with the directors and managers provides rich evidence of the entrepreneurship
of its former leaders and directors. The two extracts below refer to the entrepreneurship of Américo Palha Neto, one of Telemig's first directors:

> Américo developed a methodology for constructing a telephone network which was
> imported from Canada. Our former system was based on procedures developed by

Ericsson. This was a system designed to improve the speed of communications. Ericsson asked for six months to install the system. Américo made some adaptations and achieved it in 15 days. (Brigadier Kopp, former President of Telemig)

The Technical Director in the 1970s was Palha Neto. He was only 26. He had little experience, but incredible energy and a strong entrepreneurial spirit. (Borges de Muros)

As table 4.3 indicates, the achievements of Telemig's founding group involved the application and adaptation of technology to new circumstances, organization building, the establishment of rules and standards and the development of a new mentality. This group defined their collective entrepreneurial qualities in terms of having 'the guts to do something never done before', 'learning on the job', 'risk taking' and 'capacity to develop collective competencies'. They also used terms such as 'sweating their blood' and 'having a strong will' to symbolize their commitment to the social project of developing telecommunications in the country.

The above quotations point not only to the kinds of values held by Telemig's founding group, but also to their moral qualities and the high level of integration between the members of the group. The founders attributed the success of the sector to the personal characteristics of its members, such as their entrepreneurship, their moral attributes such as honesty, their dedication and vision. They described themselves as being 'adventurous' in the sense that they were ready to cope with most of the difficulties that arose.

3 Leadership

General José Antônio de Alencastro e Silva – the first CEO of Telemig – was the most influential leader in shaping Telemig's culture and strategy. Though he was the CEO for only two years, his influence over the company continued to be felt when he was appointed president of Telebrás. He was the primary architect of the national telecommunications system. He negotiated with the state government of MG to have the self-financing system formally approved. He was part of the group that conceived Embratel, the state long distance carrier, and Telebrás. He was personally involved in persuading state governments to accept the incorporation of the regional companies by the federal government. When interviewed, former Telemig directors commented on Alencastro's leadership. For example:

I think that the success of the telecommunications sector in Brazil can be attributed to the fact that we had a great man of vision, dedicated to the cause, who was able to gather and direct resources towards the integration of the sector. Alencastro, along with others such as Commander Quandt, Minister Corsetti and Minister Haroldo, made the sector into a big family. (Autobiography, Luís Carlos de Portilho)

Alencastro was a leader not only of Telemig, but also of the system as a whole. He was respected everywhere, by the boards of all companies. Alencastro never assigned a post to anyone out of friendship. He was a man who recognized the professional value of people. Respect for Alencastro was not statutory; he was simply in command of the telecommunications business. (Palha Neto)

In the interior of Minas Gerais communications were awful. It was quicker to go by car to neighboring cities than to use the telephone. This didn't just apply to Minas; the same could be said about Brazil as a whole. We needed an expansion plan, and General Alencastro worked this out. It was a very ambitious plan. What Alencastro carried out had never been achieved by any company in the Telebras system. At that time we dreamed of making Brazil a 'great country'. (Autobiography, José Leitão Viana)

The members of the leading network believed that a nationally independent telecommunications sector would save the country from fragmentation and backwardness. They formulated the role of telecommunications in Brazilian society: to whom and how it should be accountable, the kind of competencies it should develop and from where the company should draw its resources. The way the founders viewed Telemig and their role reflected a sense of social responsibility imbued in a nationalist ideology. It is evident from the leaders' autobiographies that there was a genuine and shared interest in improving the population's quality of life and contributing to the country's development. This was evident in their perceptions of the role of telecommunications in modern society. When interviewed, General Alencastro looked back on the mission of state enterprises at this time and their impact on Brazilian society:

In my opinion state companies have the vital mission of serving their country. They have done this magnificently in terms of their contribution to society, to the government and to the economy. They have contributed to the common good by integrating different regions.

Telecommunications was regarded as a technology that could make a strategic contribution to achieving social goals and bringing wealth to society. Alencastro in his autobiography also stated that:

Telecommunications implies a circulation of intelligence. It is the cause and consequence of societies' progress. Telecommunications should be understood as being at the service of the individual as a person. It is therefore an agent of economic development. It provides the means for the actions and decisions of economic agents. Telecommunications is the nervous system of a national collectivity. Previous governments have not understood its importance to society, but now telecommunications is viewed as a very powerful tool for improving the quality of life.

4 Founding mission and strategy

Telemig's mission at that time reflected its leading group's commitment to a nationalist ideology, with a primary accountability to the military government. This mission was to assist the government's goal of promoting Brazil's economic and social development in general, and of integrating the country's many scattered communities in particular.

Telemig's close links with the state assured the company's growth and survival, since the expansion of the telecommunications system was a government priority. Interviews with directors and former directors suggest that Telemig's priorities at this time were defined by its obligation to the state and to those employees who contributed the most to the achievement of this objective: the engineers. The achievement of the company's goals was highly dependent on the company's ability to develop an engineering competence in telecommunications.

5 Implementation of the mission and strategy

When Telemig was created in 1973, the plan was that it should acquire control of 220 independent companies in MG state. In 1972 there were about 440 towns in MG without any telephone services. The basis for telephone service provision was precarious, since the majority of the companies were owned by small entrepreneurs and by town councils that did not have the necessary funds to invest. Telemig's mission, therefore, involved making the telephone service available to the population of MG by absorbing and integrating these small and scattered companies.

The responsibility for implementing the acquisition plan was given to the Vice-President, Colonel Hélio Gomes do Amaral. Amaral maintained personal contact with the chief executive of each company on the incorporation list. Some companies wanted immediate transfer of their ownership to the state, while others resisted. Resistance came from state governors who regarded Telemig as subservient to federal control, from town councils and from family businesses (Histórico da Telemig, 1997). Moreover, some of these acquisitions were financially very burdensome to Telemig because of their obsolete technology. This burden was to some extent offset by the acquired companies that were profitable. In some cases it was possible to establish a partnership with the local council for building the necessary infrastructure.

Incorporation began by targeting more profitable companies and those more sympathetic to integration. This required an intensive effort to persuade minority shareholders that their rights would be maintained after the transference of ownership to the federal government. In 1974, Telemig incorporated 48 companies and in 1975, 21 more. In 1976 it incorporated 11 further companies and by then controlled 73 per cent of the telephone terminals in MG. By 1979 the company controlled 81 per cent of the terminals in the state and in that year 27 more companies were incorporated. The results were impressive. Whereas in 1972, 440 towns in the state of MG were without telephone services, 420 of these had already been connected to the network by 1980.

Integrating the companies was not an easy task. The first step General Alencastro took was to draw up an integration plan and to build local competencies. Telemig was still dependent for engineers on the former CTMG, and the first task was to reduce this dependence. One of the Alencastro's first actions was to stop the need for Telemig's engineers to travel to Rio de Janeiro for advice:

> I told Amaral to get the directors together because we should not have people travelling to Rio de Janeiro for technical advice. I discussed with the directors over coffee how we needed to build a Minas company, one that had its own personality. Telemig was born for real from that point onwards. (Autobiography)

The implementation of the mission required building new engineering competencies as well as political skills. Alencastro mentioned that he had to convince MG state governors that the strategy of unifying telecommunications could be a way of addressing 'the state of abandonment of Brazilian people' and it could also contribute to unification of the regions within MG:

> Before we could make progress, we had to persuade the conservative forces – the governor of Minas and the community – that integration under Telemig was the best option for the region. Surprisingly, this suited the political interest of the governor because of his worries about losing the south of Minas to the state of São Paulo. (Autobiography)

While the expansion of the sector and incorporation of the different companies created opportunities for exploration in organizational terms (March, 1991), the kind of technology available at the time did not allow for the diversity of services familiar today. The telephone system was based on large 'exchange equipment', which consumed considerable energy and space. The equipment was inflexible and did not allow for the introduction of new services. In the 1970s, Brazil started to use a more advanced technology based on computers. One of the directors, Palha Neto, mentioned when interviewed in 2003 that:

> In the 1970s Telemig constructed a large building in order to locate 200,000 telephone lines. Today we could locate all the telephone lines in the whole of MG in that building. The space taken up nowadays by telephone equipment is much less and the equipment uses far less energy. In the 1970s when the company acquired a telephone exchange, it took approximately two years to get it ready for use. Putting it into an operational condition required a complex skill and involved a laborious process of assembling the equipment bit by bit. It also needed constant testing. With that type of equipment it was very difficult for the company to respond to an increased demand for services. Consumers had to wait for at least two years for the chance to have a telephone.

6 The entrenchment of technocracy

The literature on technocracy became particularly popular in the 1970s with studies of closed regimes in Europe and in Latin America. The term technocracy has been used in various ways, but primarily to indicate the sources of power in state-owned and public enterprises, and the kind of ethos that technocrats engender in these organizations. Technocrats derive their power from technical knowledge and from holding executive positions in state enterprises. Technocracy can therefore be understood as a regime of governance by experts. Technocracy has also been associated with the behaviour of technical elites, their mind set, their preferences and the kind of ethos they develop in organizations (Pereira, 1972; O'Donnell, 1979; Dreifuss, 1981). Grindle (1977, p. 402) describes the technocratic mind set:

> A technocrat has specialized knowledge, is recruited and advanced in his career through universalistic criteria of evaluation, is apolitical and considers himself to be above politics; makes decisions on the basis of rationality and efficiency, and often tends to underestimate the need to consider questions of human relations and politics in his work.

A technocrat combines two types of virtues, those of engineering and the bureaucrat, according to Coslovsky (2002). Some particular types of organizations like bureaucracies or the army tend to attract professionals with an engineering background. They provide a favourable terrain for the development of this particular mind set, one that encourages rationality in decision-making and avoids conflict (Burris, 1989).

Other studies suggest that technocrats base their power on the neutrality of technical discourse and decision-making. Stanley (1981) has suggested that technocrats emphasize the importance of technical control and technical language in problem-solving. This has implications for the kind of ethos that is developed in an organization dominated by technocrats. These organizations tend to ignore political reason, while elevating technical rationality; politicians are cunning, while engineers are virtuous. Politics is in general considered illegitimate by military regimes: 'it is parochial, divisive and above all it is not based on expertise' (O'Donnell, 1979, p. 81). However, the technocratic argument is far from neutral. Exclusion of politics is a political argument itself and technocrats constitute an interest group themselves (Coslovsky, 2002). By virtue of technocrats' integration in government circles they are able to set out organization priorities and influence institutional agendas. Studies of technocrats in Latin America suggest that they were the main conveyors of the government ideologies and instruments of policy implementation during the military period (O'Donnell, 1979; Dreifuss, 1981). The following quotations suggest how Telemig's mission and goals were identified with those of the state. The company's annual report for 1974 celebrates the company's contribution to the country's developmental goals:

> The progress imposed by the revolution is a driver of growth. We in telecommunications are expected to contribute to the rhythm of the country's development. . . . It is our duty to contribute to improve the country's infrastructure in telecommunications. We are very pleased with the results achieved by Telemig so far.

The view of several employees at that time was that Telemig was a company of engineers for engineers, and this was viewed as only natural because of their participation in the achievement of government goals:

> Telemig was an engineering company. Engineering was the company's breathing function. They were the most powerful lot in the company because they were viewed as essential to the implementation of the company mission and because of their contribution to the country's growth. (Engineer)

The objectives of the telecommunications sector were identified with the objectives of the military: 'Telecommunications was a driver of the army's development. There is no command without telecommunications' (Autobiography, General Siqueira de Meneses). Thus, Telemig's culture and practices partly reflected a combination of the technocratic and military ethos. The literature on the behaviour of technocrats suggest that in their mind set, emotion stands in the way of a rational solution and conflict is dysfunctional (Martins, 1974; O'Donnell, 1979). Telemig's organizational culture and practices in part reflected this statement. For example, emphasis on technical issues led the company to neglect the employee as a person, as an important stakeholder and as a key contributor to the organization's goals. The human resources manager mentioned that:

> Telemig's culture was completely tuned to serve the technocrats. There was no space for feelings and viewing the employee as a human being. The focus was on technical issues. At the end of the 1970s, this started to change with managers being intensively trained to respond to the needs of employees and deal with conflict.

In Telemig the trade union was not recognized as a political institution in the early years of the military regime. Indeed, the union was considered to be at the service of the military. As happened generally in Brazilian society at the time, Telemig's management suppressed internal conflict and dissent. The human resources manager recollected the early days of the military period:

> If there was conflict, it was not visible. The regime did not allow any room for conflict to emerge. The union focused primarily on benefits for employees. People in general took this system for granted. But they were also happy because the company was growing and Brazil was growing. Nobody complained about anything when things were going well.

He went on to describe the company as being very centralized and rigidly controlled:

> At this time managers had a lot of authority. They were never challenged. Everything was very rigid. There was a maxim in the organization: 'In this organization there are only two groups: the first are those who give orders and the second those who obey'. Telemig was like an army. If somebody did not do what he was told, this was viewed as insubordination. (Manager)

The military management insisted on communication being formal, and it had a heavy top-down character. This also served to mask dissent. Thus:

> At that time communications were one-sided. Only managers spoke. There was no confrontation. This gave the impression that there was no conflict in the organization, that everything was normal. If the employee brought a problem, the first thing a manager would do was to consult the manual. He would also resort to the most comfortable answer, which was 'the rules do not allow this', or such and such department says that they cannot do what you want. Employees did not dare to rebel against a rule. Moreover, in the early days of the military regime, the human resources manager stayed in his own office and the employees did not have anyone with whom to talk. (Human Resources Manager)

Illustrating the extreme level of formality during this period, a manager mentioned that:

> During the military, the head of division could only write a letter to another division head. Our shared knowledge was the military manual. If a division head occupied a lower hierarchical position and if you had a matter to sort out with him, you had to write a letter to his superior. The organization was very segmented.

In a meeting with the board, the human resources manager recalled making a presentation in which he warned senior management that a radical change was under way and would soon hit the company. The board, however, merely commented about the quality of his transparencies and paid no attention to the content of his presentation. His reaction was to warn the directors that 'not everything that is still is stable; not everything is under control'.

Other salient characteristics of the corporate culture were its affinity with the culture of private enterprises and entrepreneurship. The quote below from General Alencastro, interviewed in the early 1990s, suggests that a technical and entrepreneurial leadership guided by a private ethos was integral to its formative corporate identity:

> Our success was due to the fact that we behaved as if we were a private firm in the past 20 years. We were driven by the objectives we had traced and our technical culture was essential to achieve those as well as our entrepreneurship. We achieved our targets. These were based on plans that were carefully elaborated and with consultation with our engineers.

Palha Neto also suggested how both the private ethos and entrepreneurship were rooted in a technical culture:

> We replaced the obsolete culture with one that was modern and autonomous from the centre. We invented new forms of doing things and pioneered various procedures. Our management was the same as that of a private company. We had

freedom in procurement and in recruiting personnel, but here we followed technical criteria, not political.

Data from the interviews suggest that the military were very keen to perpetuate the company's technical culture. The human resources manager commented on this:

> When the military regime decided to devolve power to civilians, they formed a commission to formalize all sorts of rules and procedures so as to maintain the technical standards and perpetuate the company's culture. Actually, all they wrote about was the technical culture. I think that they should instead have focused on the norms that the employees considered to be good about the company.

7 Structure

When Telemig was established in 1973, it created divisions for different regions of Minas Gerais. The company's growth led to internal specialization, such as the creation of a data processing centre. By 1983 it already had a marketing section, but this was part of the operations department. Telemig also invested in management education and employee training. Its organizational charts do not show a fully fledged human resources department before 1985. Training was a distinct unit but separated from the personnel section. Both were part of the Department of General Management.

Its organizational structure reflected the company's technocratic culture and practices. A manager pointed out that:

> For 20 years the company was managed by the military and there was no proper human resources function. There was an old-style personnel department. For example, when a manager had to lay off someone the procedure involved only settling the accounts. The main concern was to make sure that the company was keeping to its legal requirements, not with treating the employee as a person.

8 Company performance

According to Alencastro, Telemig in its earlier days grew faster than other companies in the Telebrás system. He related that:

> People did not believe in my project for Minas as people from this state do not like to spend money. I believed in Minas. In 1973 the state had only 100,000 telephones. Now [1983], it has 852,000 telephones. That was a glorious time. Everything was growing in the country. Telecommunications grew 8.5 times in size. When I became president of Telebrás we had around two million telephones, today we have around ten million telephones. For Minas this was fantastic. The city had construction sites everywhere and much of this was due to Telemig's expansion. (Autobiography, Alencastro)

Table 4.4   Telemig's performance 1972–1985

	Employees	Number of terminals installed for fixed telephones (thousands)	Number of cities connected	Density (line per 100 inhabitants)	Net operating profit (US$ million)	Annual investment (US$ million)
1972	3,420	71	123	2.0	1.9	20.6
1973	3,943	104	177	2.0	2.9	32.0
1974	5,300	126	198	2.2	3.4	79.2
1975	6,309	155	244	2.4	3.3	144.5
1976	7,297	254	326	3.0	10.7	179.6
1977	7,224	333	363	3.7	10.6	85.7
1978	7,857	371	396	4.2	31.7	91.4
1979	7,726	398	413	4.7	18.3	67.1
1980	7,671	449	442	5.6	3.3	56.6
1981	7,690	474	501	6.1	0.2	52.8
1982	7,573	501	569	6.6	6.3	72.2
1983	7,543	537	580	6.7	−0.8	41.0
1984	7,701	579	635	7.3	4.7	42.3
1985	7,766	596	634	8.1	1.0	54.7

Source: Telemig company reports; for density, Secretaria de Estado do Planejamento e Coordenação Geral, Suplan/Sei.

The company's performance demonstrated the success of Telemig's exploitation strategy. As table 4.4 indicates, Telemig grew rapidly and profitably until 1979. The number of employees more than doubled, the number of terminals installed increased more than fivefold and the number of cities connected tripled. The density – number of telephone lines per 100 inhabitants – rose from 2.0 in 1973 to 4.7 in 1979. Net operating profit increased from US$1.9 million in 1972 to US$31.7 million in 1978. Telemig's growth was supported by a massive injection of investment in 1975 and 1976.

By 1979, Telemig had already incorporated 81 per cent of the terminals present in MG state, and it grew in terms of both number of employees and profit. In 1973 the company had 3,943 employees, rising to 7,726 by 1979. As table 4.4 indicates, the number of localities served and the increase in density suggest that the company had been fulfilling its mission to contribute to the economic and social development of both MG state and the nation.

In 1976 the central government introduced various measures to curb the import of telecommunications equipment. This had a significant impact on Telemig's capacity to implement its expansion plans and to generate profits. By this time, the government was also beginning to restrict funds for the continued expansion of the telecommunications sector. Telemig therefore began to rely on external borrowing for its investments. Palha Neto explained that:

> Telemig had the same legal status as private companies. It enjoyed a significant level of autonomy concerning borrowing and procurement. It could resort to the market for borrowing, usually from equipment providers. This external source was very important for the growth of companies such as ours. A company that is growing cannot rely just on what it generates in order to sustain growth. When the state introduced restrictions on the import of equipment, it also made it difficult for the companies to borrow at reasonable rates of interest and this impaired their ability to expand.

From the end of the 1970s, Telemig's rate of growth began to decline in terms of employment, new terminals installed and new cities connected. After 1978, the level of new investment as well as the level of operating profit both turned down substantially.

Seeds of Change: 1979–1985

As chapter 2 has indicated, towards the end of the 1970s three factors began to sow the seeds for the changes that took place after 1985. The first was the shock to the Brazilian economy triggered by the 1979 oil crisis, which deepened into a serious recession after 1982. The other two factors were political, namely the decreasing legitimacy of the military government and of the state enterprises it used as agents of its policy, and the emergence of new actors – the trade union and middle managers.

1 Economic crisis

The regime's socio-economic ideology was that development and an equal distribution of income could be achieved only by concentrating economic authority into the hands of an interventionist and entrepreneurial state. The country had to be protected from foreign ideologies that could challenge the current distribution of power and from foreign interests aiming to exploit the country's resources.

Until the late 1970s there was a broad consensus that state enterprises were efficient agents of government policies: they served the purpose of creating an adequate infrastructure to improve industrial capacity, and functioned as regulators of the import substitution policy and prices and, above all, as vehicles to finance development through external loans. However, it was these same government policies that subsequently increased the vulnerability of these companies. The sudden rise in international interest rates in 1979 made it impossible to maintain the strategy of financing the expansion of the telecoms sector through international loans. In a context of high inflation, the use of tariffs on telephone connections as a source of investment also proved unfeasible, because high inflation required the rigid control of prices. The country's economy deteriorated further during the 1980s, which, as noted in chapter 2, have come to be called 'the lost decade'. By the end of the 1980s, Brazil was suffering the consequences of chronic inflation. The inflow of foreign capital fell by 40 per cent from 1980 to 1990 and industry was starved of investment as better profits could be obtained from investing in the financial market (Barros, 1993).

2 Declining legitimacy

DECLINING FUNDS FOR TELECOMMUNICATIONS

In 1975 the Ministry of Communications lost control over the application of the FNT (National Fund for Telecommunications), which was closed in 1982 (Botelho et al., 1998). This led companies like Telemig to turn to foreign equipment manufacturers for loans. However, this source of lending was undermined by Brazil's increasing foreign debt. With the crisis in the balance of payments, more rigid restrictions were imposed on imports, and these jeopardized the financing arrangements with foreign equipment manufacturers. Deteriorating economic performance together with inflationary pressures reduced investment in state enterprises, including those in the telecommunications sector. As table 4.4 indicates, investment in Telemig declined by 38 per cent from 1978 to 1980. In the period 1979–85, performance generally stagnated in both the sector and the company. In 1981 the funds Telemig received from Telebrás were reduced by more than half of the previous year's, with serious consequences for the company's ability to invest. In 1983 Telemig made a loss for the first time, which the company report attributed to the heavy devaluation of the Brazilian currency. In that year, the level of new investment dropped by 43 per cent compared to the previous year.

INTERORGANIZATIONAL FORCES

By the end of the 1970s, the alliance between the military and engineers in state enterprises, and between the military and bureaucrats in government, started to be threatened by the government's inability to maintain economic growth. In 1979, the military regime publicly announced its intention to return power to elected politicians. Foreseeing the possibility that state enterprises could soon become political pawns, the government took measures to tie them more closely to central decision-making in Brasilia. Telemig began to lose autonomy as a business in its own right, and was increasingly treated like any other public bureaucracy. One example was the increasing rigidity in the procedures for recruiting personnel.

3 The emergence of new actors

THE UNION

The public announcement of the military regime's intention to return power to elected politicians led to the emergence of new political actors, notably the Central Unica dos Trabalhadores (CUT, Central Workers Union) and Partido dos Trabalhadores (PT, Workers Party). As public pressure to change the regime grew, the opposition and the unions gained power. Telemig's own union was affiliated to the national union for telecommunications (FITTEL), which in turn was linked to the CUT and PT. These links provided the Telemig union (SINTTEL) with a combative leadership and a political identity.

In the 1980s, the number of strikes organized by Brazilian unions exceeded the level of countries with a longer history of organized labour (Antunes, 1994). The sequence of strikes began in 1978 with 41 days of action by metal workers in São Paulo's ABC industrial region. Prior to 1978, labour mobilization in Brazil was localized and ineffective, as the military strictly controlled mass collective organizations. One of the demands of the strikers was the linking of wage rises to the rate of inflation. However, the union movement also espoused political causes such as protest against the exploitation of workers, repressive legislation and government control of unions.

In 1980 the Telemig union, SINTTEL, launched a newspaper called *O Bode* (*The Goat*), the nickname for an old and very noisy telephone exchange device. At this time Telemig was still subject to a bureaucratic military culture coupled to a benevolent authoritarianism that, for example, provided job security and welfare. The human resources department was scarcely organized as yet, and physical working conditions were poor. The issues most frequently raised by the union newspaper concerned physical working conditions, terms of employment, social benefits and the company's autocratic style of management.

The SINTTEL newspaper began to use cartoons and metaphors to portray high power distance in the company's vertical relationships, as well as the authoritarian style that characterized the organization. These attributes were argued to have directly unfavourable consequences for employees whose voice was not heeded regarding, for example, the poor working conditions that prevailed in the organization. The union's attack intensified in the mid–1980s with the fall of the military regime and rising inflation, the latter leading to an increasing emphasis on levels of pay.

The intensification of union mobilization after the end of the 1970s had important consequences for the internal transformation of Telemig, including its organizational culture and industrial relations. The human resources manager described the change that took place:

> In 1978 things happened very quickly. When the government moved towards political openness, a major strike lasting 40 days exploded in the automotive sector in São Paulo. At that time union officials were changing from *pelegos* [government

supporters] to being combative and confrontational. The government itself facilitated the strengthening of the union movement by forcing company owners and
managers to negotiate with the union and talk to the employees, which had not
been common practice in Brazil for more than 20 years. In Telemig a committee
was formed to negotiate with the company. This committee involved professionals
such as engineers. Members of this committee were later incorporated into the union's
board.

With the support of the national union and party, CUT and PT, the strategy
of SINTTEL was to 'eat round the edges of the regime', in the words of one of
its officials. Its intention was to attack those points at which the company's military management was vulnerable. For example, it did not talk directly to employees.
One of the Telemig union's strategies was to open its own channels of communication with employees. It communicated speedily through bulletins, newslet-
ters and the newspaper, which moved to a more frequent monthly publication in
1984. The union also began to stimulate dissent and non-conformity. By visiting
worksites every day, union officers were able to gain the support of middle and
junior managers. Since the company did not have a well organized human
resources department, the union found spaces in which to build its legitimacy, in
areas management had neglected.

Interviews with managers suggest that these actions caught the company completely unprepared. Management vacillated between giving way to pressures and
maintaining an authoritarian style. This vacillation helped the union to seize the
initiative. One of its tactics was to create chaos by interrupting the flow of work
and disrupting managerial meetings. This union-instigated behaviour left the company paralysed, as management was accustomed to an employee culture of obedi-
ence and conformity. In the view of the human resources manager, Telemig's rigid
structure, founded mainly on formal means of communication, contributed to the
chaos that overtook the company until the end of the 1980s. He attributed this
paralysis to the lack of flexibility of an 'army organization'. One of Telemig's former
directors mentioned that Telemig's military managers found it difficult at this time
to cope with the union pressure and the influence of CUT in the organization:

> The military office-holders in Telemig did not pay due attention to the union and
> employees. Today our union is in the hands of the CUT, which is adopting a rad-
> ical approach. The union is one of the most radical in the whole sector as far as its
> principles and actions are concerned. It is very difficult to negotiate with the union
> nowadays. (Borges de Muros)

According to data provided by SINTTEL, union membership grew substantially
from the end of the 1970s. Although SINTTEL does not have precise historical
information on its total membership, it was able to provide some data on the
numbers registering with the union each year. From 1970 to 1974 the average
number of newly registered members was 358, in comparison with an average of
564 from 1975 to 1979. While this membership growth reflected a substantial increase

in Telemig's employment to 1978, it also suggests that the union enjoyed a growing ability to mobilize.

THE MANAGERIAL COUNCIL

In 1979 it was decided to create a Managerial Council within Telemig, with a membership of senior managers and departmental heads – those below the executive directors. The Managerial Council was established with the intention of giving managers greater knowledge of the company's affairs and to allow them more involvement in the decision-making process. At the same time, Telemig also extended the title of manager to supervisors. This strategy of inclusion was linked to the norm that managers were not allowed to take the union's side in matters of dispute. They were expected to act according to company policy and enforce its rules. This was backed up by an intensive programme of managerial training in the mid-1980s. A further justification for the creation of the managerial council was the unsatisfactory performance of the company and hence the need to improve the decision-making process. 'Centralization prevented the company from making appropriate decisions', argued a former consultant of the company. He added that information on costs was imprecise, and not even considered.

The establishment of the Managerial Council gave a new voice to Telemig's middle managers. It took place within the context of the military government's announcement that it would devolve power to civilians and at a time when the regime began to lose legitimacy. The prospect of having a politician in command of Telemig threatened its military legacy and the company ethos. Concerns had already been expressed that, with the opening of the regime and prospects of devolution of power to civilians, vested interests represented by politicians could misuse the company. Telemig's military top management believed that the creation of a Managerial Council would add weight in favour of retaining policies that reflected the company's founding values and priorities, and strengthen its ability to resist the growing cohesion and power of the union. One manager mentioned that:

> Telemig was a strategic company for the military regime. They felt that the company could be threatened by political interests. They realized that politicians could use it for their own interests. This was already happening with CEMIG [the MG state electricity company]. The military managers were averse to politicians because they would not hesitate to damage the company if that helped them to pursue their own interests. The military then created the Managerial Council.

The persistence of a rigid technical culture within Telemig, together with its managers' incapacity to communicate effectively with employees, strengthened the union's ability to mobilize for change. This mobilization forced the company to turn its attention to internal matters and to reflect on the corporate culture. Management self-reflection was particularly encouraged by two cartoons that appeared in the union newspaper depicting the 'powerful little chief' and the 'the telephonist'. Both cartoons accompanied everyday life stories about the authoritarian relationships between managers and employees (see chapter 9). Managers admitted that these critiques were very effective in changing their communications style and also in shaping the corporate culture in general.

Conclusion

This chapter has illustrated the interplay between internal factors, such as managerial intentionality, and external pressures in Telemig's evolution. Managerial intentionality was an important driver of change in the development of CTMG and subsequently in the creation of Telemig. While individual entrepreneurship had characterized CTMG, in Telemig's founding and formation it was collective. The force of external pressures was felt increasingly at the close of this period as new economic, political and social forces took effect.

During Telemig's formative period, certain characteristics of the company's collective entrepreneurship were consequential for the way it co-evolved with its environment. The company's leaders at the time were entrepreneurial in that they brought together resources to form a new template (Gomez and Volery, 2000). Their entrepreneurship was collective in two main respects. First, Telemig's leadership was a combination of military officers and technocrats, supported by ministry bureaucrats. Second, it had strong connections upwards within the telecommunications system to the national holding company and the ministry. Telemig's corporate leaders belonged to a wider supportive network. Common aims and shared roles helped to maintain cohesion within this network. Its members subscribed to a clear ideology and mission regarding the role telecommunications should play in Brazil's development. They had experienced similar educational and training, and many were either military officers or closely attached to the military. They also rotated between positions at these different levels in the system. The autobiographies of telecommunications sector founders demonstrate their sense of common mission and identity. This was therefore a collective entrepreneurial network by dint of its members' self-reference, shared beliefs and common membership.

Telemig's formative period was one of co-evolution because these entrepreneurs were in a position to initiate changes both in the sector environment and in individual companies that were simultaneous and compatible. These changes were introduced with considerable support from the state in terms of both facilitating amalgamations and investment funding. As a result of this mobilization of resources, Telemig achieved impressive growth and profits. Strong foundations were laid down, which became a historical point of reference in later more difficult times. The company's economic strength, together with the way it was contributing to national development, helped to legitimize the coherent identity that Telemig's leaders formulated for the company. At this time, there was considerable cohesion between the company and its environment, as well as within the company between management and employees. In this sense, the telecommunications system constituted a unified organizational field. It was only later, from the end of the 1970s, that this cohesion began to break down, as the military lost legitimacy as the country's rulers.

The example of collective entrepreneurship offered by Telemig's formative period serves to qualify two tendencies in the literature. First, the mainstream analysis of entrepreneurship tends to perceive it in terms of a set of individual characteristics and behaviours. Second, while entrepreneurship has been linked to the creative–destructive process through which new economic combinations are brought into being (Schumpeter, 1934), its contribution to evolution over time has not often been addressed. This chapter raises the question of how collective entrepreneurship contributes to corporate evolution. It draws attention to the possibility that collective entrepreneurship can facilitate the formation of organizations and their distinctive templates by dint of the relational frameworks with institutional agencies (Scott and Meyer, 1983) into which they enter as part of their network properties. Collective entrepreneurs, like individual entrepreneurs, engage in competence building, marshalling and combining resources. In addition, however, they enjoy access to political arenas, which permit them to co-opt support in shaping the environment. In this way they seem to be able to connect organizations to their environment by influencing the conception of rules conducive to favourable outcomes. In this way, they can build isomorphism and regulate competition, therefore shaping the behaviour of a population.

Thus, there is more to entrepreneurship than simply managerial intentionality. In Telemig's case it involved conceiving and implementing a strategy and simultaneously building a propitious culture through engagement and obtaining political support through negotiations with key stakeholders. In Telemig, a group of people gathered and combined resources to constitute the company within a protected environment that would potentially insulate it from the pressures of evolutionary selection. The entrepreneurs not only created a system that improved organizational capabilities but also constructed the basis for shared understanding and application of common rules across organizations. They undertook exploration (March, 1991) in developing a national system for telecommunications innovation, as well as new competencies and procedures. They also undertook exploitation in expanding the system through acquisitions that rationalized the use of assets and applied common procedures and rules throughout the system

The changes that came to affect Telemig from the later 1970s onward indicate that a collective entrepreneurship based on a network that crosses system levels can be vulnerable to political developments in the wider society. Once the military government began to institute changes that detracted from Telemig's autonomy, funding and performance, and also to legalize organized union opposition, the ability of Telemig's top management to maintain its corporate identity was compromised. It was increasingly unable to secure investment finance adequate to its mission of supporting economic development and integration. The growing need to find alternative sources of finance through addressing the market began to qualify its previously engineering-led philosophy. The relaxation of laws restricting independent union organization and activism threatened the internal consensus that management had previously enjoyed with its employees.

References

Antunes, R. (1994) Recent strikes in Brazil. The main tendencies of the strikes movement of the 1980s. *Latin American Perspectives*, 80, 24–37.

Barros, O. de (1993) *Estudo da competitividade da indústria brasileira: oportunidades abertas para o Brasil face aos fluxos globais de investimento de risco e de capitais financeiros nos anos 90.* Campinas, São Paulo: UNICAMP.

Botelho, A. J., Ferro, J. R., McKnight, L. and Manfredini Oliveira, A. C. (1998) Brazil. In E. Noam (ed.), *Telecommunications in Latin America.* New York: Oxford University Press, pp. 227–50.

Burris, B. H. (1989) Technocratic organization and control. *Organization Studies*, 10, 1–22.

Coslovsky, S. V. (2002) Neoliberalism, populism and presidential impeachment in Latin America. Master's thesis presented to the Fletcher School of Law and Diplomacy, USA.

Dreifuss, R. A. (1981) *A conquista de estado: ação política, poder e golpe de classe.* Petrópolis: Vozes.

Gomez, P.-Y. and Volery, T. (2000) *How Do Organizations Come into Existence? Towards an Evolutionary Theory of Entrepreuership.* Lyon: École de Management.

Grindle, M. S. (1977) Power, expertise and the 'Technico': suggestions from a Mexican case study. *Journal of Politics*, 39, 399–26.

Histórico da Telemig [History of Telemig] (1997) Belo Horizonte: Telemig.

Instituto de Pesquisa Econômica Aplicada (2001) <www.ipea.gov.br>.

March, J. G. (1991) Exploration and exploitation in organizational learning. *Organizational Science*, 2, 71–87.

Martins, C. E. (1974) Technocracia ou technoassessoria? *Revista de Administracao de Empresas*, 10, 39–66.

O'Donnell, G. (1979) *Modernization and Bureaucratic Authoritarism.* Berkeley, CA: Institute of International Studies.

Perreira, L. C. B. (1972) *Tecnoburocracia e Contestação.* Petrópolis: Vozes.

Schumpeter, J. A. (1934) *The Theory of Economic Development.* Cambridge, MA: Harvard University Press.

Scott, W. R. and Meyer, J. W. (1983) The organization of society sectors. In J. W. Meyer and W. R. Scott (eds), *Ritual and Rationality.* Beverly Hills, CA: Sage, pp. 129–54.

Stanley, M. (1981) *The Technological Conscience: Survival of Dignity in an Age of Expertise.* Chicago: Phoenix.

Telemig (1978) *25 anos a serviço do desenvolvimento de Minas.* Company report, December.

CHAPTER FIVE

Politicization 1985–1993

This chapter describes the evolution of Telemig from 1985 to 1993. During this period, three main factors were particularly significant. The first was the country's economic problems, with their consequences for the performance of the telecommunications sector and Telemig. The second factor was the populism of Brazilian politics and the way it infiltrated telecommunications. The third was the emergence of international pressures stemming from technological developments and industrial restructuring. There were three main sets of actors during this period. One comprised the managers and engineers who had developed their careers in Telemig and Telemar. The second were the representatives of populist interests in Brazilian society, some of whom were appointed to Telemig's board of directors. The third was the company's trade union, SINTTEL. This chapter describes the relationship between external pressures, these actors and the internal dynamics of the company, which led to changes in Telemig's structure, strategy and implementation, identity and culture.

The chapter covers a period in which political demands weakened the collective vision and values of Telemig's founders, and led to a growing ambiguity in the company's mission and identity. Telemig ceased to be an instrument for social and economic development, and instead became prey to sectional interests: those of politicians, senior managers and the trade union. Although Telemig grew increasingly dependent on the state for its funding, under the surface the seeds were being sown for the company's eventual uncoupling from the state in the late 1990s.

Escalating External Drivers of Change

Three key events marked this period: in 1985 civil rights were restored when a civilian government again took office; in 1990 the second civilian president – Fernando Collor – introduced neoliberal policies and in 1992 the Brazilian people forced Congress to impeach him for corruption. The period was marked by an increasing invasion of political interests into telecommunications. Together with

Brazil's economic difficulties, this contributed to the stagnation of the telecommunications sector at a time when internationally the dynamism of the industry was increasing with the introduction of new technologies and the spread of globalization.

1 Entrenchment of political interests

The 1980s saw the biggest and longest crisis in the modern history of Brazil. These years have come to be called 'the lost decade'. It was a period marked by political and economic instability and by frustration in terms of lost opportunities for development. The government in office in the 1980s had officially proclaimed its preference for a democratic and market regime which some characterized as dual transition (Coslovsky, 2002). Sarney's government nevertheless did not proceed with the institutional changes that would have put into place a genuinely arm's length market system. In practice, his government still permitted the authoritarianism of the military regime to continue, with implications for political and economic instability.

This was the situation that developed under the Sarney government up to 1990 when President Collar took office. Collor was elected by a new alliance of diverse political groups that rejected the populism of the previous government. Populism was one of the most important drivers of Telemig's evolution. It emerged as an issue in telecommunications when politicians attempted to influence decisions and practices in state enterprises. They tried with some success to influence board appointments, organizational priorities and the use of resources. Although it is defined in different terms, populism has been commonly used to describe a situation in which a political leadership obtains popular support by making unrealistic promises to various interest groups in society (Kauffman and Stallings, 1991). Populist interests can gain access to organizations through clientelism – interpersonal relationships in which political office holders allocate positions in organizations to friends and relatives in exchange for their personal loyalty (Kaufman and Stallings, 1991; Rodrigues, 2002). Such appointees frequently resort to paternalism to gain the sympathy and acceptance of organizational members (Coslovsky, 2002).

2 The entrenchment of populism in the telecommunications sector

Brazil restored a democratic regime after 20 years of military rule on a tragic note. The newly elected president died on the very day of his inauguration. The vice-president, Sarney, took office. His government became known for allowing populist forces to penetrate state enterprises.

Various studies point out that during Sarney's government state enterprises served as targets for the rent-seeking beneficiaries of state protectionism and clientelism (Sandoval, 2001; Schneider, 2004). State enterprises became the 'honey pot' for

sectional interests when Sarney's government began to replace top level professional management with political appointees, in order to gain political support.

Some of Telemig's founders expressed their concern over the consequences of
the clientelism pursued by Sarney's government. One of Telemig's previous directors, Calistrato, said of another Brazilian telecommunications company that 'They
appointed a semi-illiterate in telecommunications to run a good state enterprise.
Now the company is in the red because the board of directors followed political criteria. If the same happens to Telemig this will be a disaster.' In the event,
clientelism did affect telecommunications companies, including Telemig. In their
analysis of the development of the telecommunications sector in Brazil, Botelho
et al. (1998) point out that during Sarney's government, political appointees replaced
professional managers and engineers. The then president of Telebrás commented
on this political interference when interviewed:

> In 1985 we had a return to politics which gave scope for political interference. Personally,
> I think that will be very bad for the country and the sector. In the 1970s we had
> an expansion which responded directly to the needs of the country. The military had
> decision-making and financial power in their hands. Now, the sector has regressed.

In his interview, General Alencastro had also recognized the presence of the same
problem elsewhere in the telecommunications sector:

> In the 1970s telecommunications did not have 'goodies' to give out. After the sec-
> tor's expansion, it became the fourth largest beneficiary from the federal govern-
> ment budget. This attracted the politicians. Telemig was then viewed in terms of
> its political potential. In Rio de Janeiro they told me that the inauguration of a tele-
> phone exchange was a very significant political event in terms of attracting votes.

Alencastro and other founders of Telemig, such as Palha Neto and Calistrato, were
already coming to the conclusion that, despite believing that the state could make
a good job of running telecommunications, political interference was reaching the
point where it impeded the companies' growth and efficiency. In his interview
Alencastro said that 'I have been coined as pro-state, but nowadays, I no longer
believe in the state's capacity to direct telecommunications in this country.' Palha
Neto expressed a similar view in his interview:

> I mentioned to you that Telemig had the ethos of a private company. However, if
> the current system of appointments to key posts continues, with political criteria
> overriding merit and competence, then I will defend the option of privatization because
> this situation is badly affecting the performance of telecoms.

While these comments reflected the thinking of the company's previous leaders,
the following extracts from interviews conducted between 1986 and 1990 suggest
that political interference was now being seen by staff within Telemig to affect its
priorities and practices detrimentally:

Directors come here to make a political career or as part of it. This has transformed the way we make decisions, the way we deal with customers, the company's priorities and our career. Beforehand the president only looked at the technical side of a question. He did not care about politics. (Engineer)

Today there is parachuting. Despite the government's restrictions on recruiting people because of a lack of resources for expansion, management continues to recruit its friends and relatives. When these people come into Telemig, they are given higher salaries and are assigned to key positions. The problem resides in the fact that they know nothing about the job, while we have the experience but don't get the high salary. (Engineer)

After 1985, the recruitment and selection process became the victim of interest groups. Every time one person is dismissed another one comes without going through our normal procedures. (Engineer)

People in this company are resented because of the way in which they are being recruited and promoted. (Manager)

3 Declining government legitimacy: the Collor period

By 1990 the Brazilian people were ready for a change. Collor was elected in 1990 because his discourse directly attacked the Brazilian maladies of the time: populism and an inefficient interventionist state. He proposed to combat these through a neoliberal programme. Neoliberalism is a spin-off of liberal economics that advocates a reduction in the role of the state, and relies on the market for resource allocation and distribution (Chase 2002; Coslovsky, 2002; Harvey, 2005). Neoliberal discourse generally associates inefficiencies of economic performance with state intervention. It opposes the paternalist practices preached by populism. While paternalism requires subsidies and protectionist policies, such as price and competition controls, neoliberalism defends entrepreneurship and a small non-interventionist state. Supported by a neoliberal discourse, Collar began his presidency by openly attacking the state and state owed enterprises. In particular he criticized the employment contract in state companies by depicting their employees as 'maharajas' and declared himself a 'maharaja' hunter. This discourse was viewed as a moral attack on state enterprises and their employees. His approach to change has been described as extremely authoritarian (Coslovsky, 2002). Because his discourse and authoritarian style threatened different kinds of interests, and he made little effort to consult Congress, he became progressively isolated, which culminated in 1992 with his impeachment.

Collor's government coincided with the peak of the crisis that had been developing in Brazil through the 1980s. Like his predecessor, Collor intended to create the conditions for a passage from a state planning system – where the state controlled the terms of market entry and exit through technocratic criteria – to a freer market. However, these plans were regarded as inconsistent and lacking in legitimacy because the country's economic performance remained poor and because his term of office was marked by a growing lack of governability. Congress lost influence, while the technocratic bureaucracy tried to cope with the crisis of legitimacy that had arisen. The combination of poor economic performance and autocratic government gave rise to popular discontent, which together with corruption charges led to Collor's impeachment at the end of 1992, when President Franco took over.

4 *Aborted neoliberalism and privatization*

Neoliberalism, and the policies of deregulation and trade liberalization associated with it, had achieved only limited currency among Brazil's elite at the close of Sarney's term of office in 1990. There were, nevertheless, 17 privatizations during the Sarney period (Velasco, 1997).

By contrast to the Sarney government, under Collor, privatization became part of the government's formal agenda, and it included telecommunications. When in the 1990s Collor took office with his neoliberal agenda, the contrast between the state of Brazil's telecommunications sector and the fast-moving new international developments helped to build a basic consensus in favour of privatization. However, he failed to implement his plans. An important barrier to privatization during Collor's period of office was the lack of popular trust in the government's intentions. The press expressed fears of a surrender to pressures from multinational companies, fears exacerbated by evidence of corruption in the Collar government. It also criticized the lack of adequate planning for privatization and the absence of an appropriate legal framework.

Despite failing in his plans to privatize telecommunications, Collar managed to privatize 16 other state enterprises. He also initiated a process of deregulation in the telecommunications sector (Velasco, 1997). Satellite communications and cellular phones were viewed as primary targets. The emergence of the mobile business opened up new possibilities, including alliances between multinational equipment manufacturers and between Telebrás's companies and the private sector. Collor also managed to abolish restrictions on the list of officially approved suppliers of telecommunications equipment. Since the early 1980s public procurement had been limited to early entrants in the Brazilian market, such as NEC do Brasil, Equitel and Ericsson. Collor's administration encouraged foreign companies to manufacture optical fibres in Brazil, terminating the monopoly of the Telebrás CPqD (R&D centre). He went ahead with a more ambitious reform, which included the restructuring of Telebrás and changes to the areas of geographical coverage by its companies. These reforms did not, however, abolish the state monopoly of basic telephone services.

Franco's government (1992–4) subsequently initiated a more systematic approach to reforming the telecommunications sector. This involved a long-term industrial and technological policy for communications and a new profile for the sector, including plans for duplicating plant. Though Franco did not openly declare a preference for a more liberal approach, he was very successful in his privatization programme. During his short term of office, 17 privatization processes were carried out (Velasco, 1997).

5 Brazil's declining economic performance

Although Sarney managed to stimulate economic growth in his first year, and reduce inflation from 250 per cent in 1985 to 57 per cent in 1986, the subsequent years of his presidency were economically disastrous. Table 5.1 presents data on Brazil's economic performance from 1980 to 1990. Sarney assumed office in 1985 with a balance of payments deficit and galloping inflation. By 1990, the annual inflation rate had reached 1,000 per cent and the growth rate was negative (minus 4.2 per cent), the second largest annual decline in 47 years. The external debt reached US$123,611 million that year. The overall trend of inward FDI was unstable and showed a declining trend dropping from approximately US$1.5 million in 1982 to an insignificant amount in 1990. During this period Brazil also suffered an unprecedented repatriation of foreign funds (Barros, 1993).

Table 5.1 Indicators of the Brazilian economy in the 1980s

Year	GNP at 1999 prices (R$ million)	Growth rate (%)	Inflation (IGP-DI) (%)	Total external debt (1994 US$ million)	Net foreign investment (1994 US$ million)	Balance of trade (1994 US$ million)
1980	658,680	10.18	110.88	64,661.80	2,104.52	−5,298
1981	630,664	−4.25	94.69	74,356.21	2,662.09	2,020
1982	635,931	0.84	104.91	85,685.44	1,535.79	1,209
1983	617,289	−2.93	213.18	93,939.90	991.81	9,664
1984	650,623	5.40	232.14	102,415.63	1,544.92	18,776
1985	701,704	7.85	250.43	105,474.83	997.20	17,293
1986	754,259	7.49	56.98	111,370.70	−350.61	11,070
1987	780,853	3.53	448.54	121,512.38	697.90	14,685
1988	780,379	−0.06	1,203.84	114,708.11	2,866.47	24,226
1989	805,077	3.16	2,270.22	115,728.26	150.88	19,455
1990	771,440	−4.18	1,000.03	123,611.84	0.34	12,340

Note: The 1980s were marked by several unsuccessful attempts to halt inflation. The growth of GNP was very unstable. External debt continued to grow, and in 1984 reached its highest level in relation to GNP. Inward foreign investment was decreasing and became more volatile. The government continued to invest in state companies, though not at the same magnitude as in the preceding decade.
Source: Instituto de Pesquisa Econômica Aplicada <www.ipea.gov.br>, March 2001; Consumer Price Indexes <http://stats.bls.gov/cpihome.htm>, March 2001; net foreign investment, *Conjuntura Econômica*, October 2000.

6 Evolution of technology under continuing protection

In the early 1990s, the trend in telecommunications worldwide towards greater concentration intensified with mergers and acquisitions, and the formation of joint ventures between the large operators. Competition now occurred at the boundaries of markets for the more profitable services such as mobile telephony and data transmission. New options were opened up by cable TV, which offered the possibility of innovation in telephone and data transmission (Pires, 1999). As the market became more competitive and internationalized, some operators around the world abandoned their previous identity as public service providers and began to adopt competitive strategies similar to those pursued by other technology-intensive oligopolies. Technological innovations were already encouraged by the adoption of new business strategies focused on the client, and based on product differentiation. The companies began to access the capital markets for funding heavy new investment, and they also internationalized, often through strategic alliances. This evolution of technology and changing market conditions presented further pressures on companies under state control, such as Telemig, to change.

7 Declining performance of Brazilian telecommunications

Despite these developments in competition and the reshaping of the telecommunications business, clientelism, associated with the financial crisis of the state, led to an increase of bureaucracy in telecommunications companies and growing levels of inefficiency. In addition to the inflow of politics, the fact that the government used earnings generated by the individual telecoms companies to finance deficits in other areas served to reduce the credibility of the governance system for the telecommunications sector. This period was one of decision paralysis in Telebrás, the national holding company.

As table 2.1 indicated, return on investment was erratic and well below the international standard of over 12 per cent. The growth in the density rate and in the number of cities connected was not enough to meet the demands of the population. Nevertheless, by the end of 1992 the plant installed in Brazil had already reached 10.6 million terminals, making it the eleventh largest system in the world. The sector's annual average rate of investment declined from US$1.3 billion during 1974–82 to US$1.1 billion in the period 1983–7.

Telemig's Performance

In line with the performance of the telecommunications sector as a whole, Telemig's performance during this period was mediocre (table 5.2). Its level of annual investment increased from 1985 to 1987, but then stagnated from 1987 to 1990. Net

Table 5.2   Telemig's performance 1985–1993

Year	Employees	Number of terminals installed for fixed telephones (thousands)	Number of cities connected	Density (lines per 100 inhabitants)[a]	Net operating profit (US$ million)	Annual investment (US$ million)
1985	7,766	596	634	8.1	1.0	54.7
1986	7,775	632	633	n.a.	5.7	77.2
1987	8,042	711	661	n.a.	15.4	127.2
1988	7,951	735	662	n.a.	41.4	128.4
1989	7,963	769	662	n.a.	16.1	128.3
1990	7,527	817	662	n.a.	32.3	147.7
1991	7,339	853	662	n.a.	−18.3	121.8
1992	7,204	969	691	n.a.	−7.1	222.0
1993	7,065	1,092	691	n.a.	84.7	279.1

[a]Line density is not comparable after 1985 because the company's concessionary area changed.

Source: Telemig company reports; Secretaria de Estado do Planejamento e Coordenação Geral, Suplan/Sei.

operating profit was variable, and negative in 1991 and 1992. The company's performance reflected the government's inability to manage either the economy or the telecommunications sector. According to one interviewee, the company's disappointing performance resulted from its increasing external debt due to borrowing from the international market. At one time liabilities to creditors were ten times more than the value of its assets. One of the measures taken by the government to reduce inflation was to control the prices charged by public utilities, including telephone tariffs, which were well below international levels prices, albeit high for Brazil's low income groups (Botelho et al., 1998).

Developments within Telemig

1 The board of directors

Telemig was led by a board consisting of a CEO and executive directors. Until 1985, when power was handed over to civilians, the board had been composed primarily of those professionals who helped to found the sector and Telemig.

With the coming of democracy, the influence of technocrats in state enterprises reduced substantially. The Ministry of Telecommunications had very little power to influence senior appointments in comparison with the military era. With a few exceptions, until privatization in 1998 telecommunications company boards were composed of politicians or the favourites of politicians. The larger political parties were allocated with quotas for the 'right' to appoint people to higher posts in state enterprises. Some politicians belonging to the government coalition could also fill these positions or appoint a preferred candidate. In the larger and best companies the senior technical and engineering positions were allocated to career personnel, usually the headships of the technical and operations departments. However, their appointment still had to obtain political support and come from a quota allocated to a political party. In some companies political influence went even further, with various positions being occupied by friends or relatives of state governors (Dalmazo, 1999).

As happened with telecommunications in general, Telemig's board was infused by political interests. These political interests consisted of political parties, those associated with the federal and regional government. The positions of technical or engineering director and operations director were occupied by professionals. They were generally engineers who had built their careers in telecommunications, but who were nevertheless appointees of political parties. In some cases, the CEO, the VP and others had some experience in the management of state enterprises, but many of them were already politicians or intended to develop their political career from their position in state companies. Thus, Telemig's board was the outcome of the conjugation of various political forces, and it was impossible to predict in advance how it would take shape. The resulting board was far from homogeneous in its professional background, knowledge and interest in the company. A position on the board of Telemig was viewed by many as a way to advance their political career. There was little interest in developing a reputation in the telecommunications industry, perhaps with the exception of those who were professionals and had built their careers in the sector.

In 1985 the board was reconstituted with the appointments of Paulo Heslander (CEO), Lourenço Menicucci (Vice-President), Fernando Lúcio Silveira (Director of Human Resources), Otávio Marques de Azevedo (Technical Director), Nestor Francisco de Oliveira (Director of Administration), Júlio Boechat (Director of Operations) and Rosendo (Director of Finance). Menicucci was a political nominee, but did not 'survive' in the company for long because he was a dentist and had no experience in running a company. Boechat and Marques had built their careers in Telemig.

Telemig's board at this time had little continuity, with the CEOs leaving for higher positions to further their political career. From 1991 to 1993, a CEO, Paulo Heslander, left once he was elected a deputy in the federal parliament and Djalma Andrade left to take the position as president of Telebrás. Boechat, then a Director of Operations, took over the position as the company's CEO from 1993 to 1995, when Saulo Coelho, another politician, took over the presidency. Boechat was the one who remained, being a board member from 1985 until 1996 when he retired.

2 Organization structure

Telemig's structure in 1985 reflected its relationships with the state and the new role now played by political interests. It had a VP who was in charge of special

issues, and this involved relationships with the executive power and other state enterprises. The vice-presidency was responsible for coordinating the company's various
projects and activities, as well as for evaluating the performance of the company.
As already mentioned, the person who took the VP office in 1985 was a political
appointee. In 1985 the company created a Human Resources Directorship. The
Human Resources, Administration and Finance Directorships were all political
nominations according to information gleaned from our interviews.

Examination of the organizational charts from 1985 indicates that a significant
restructuring took place in that year. Units such as training and development and
industrial relations, which had previously come under the Administration Department,
were reallocated to the newly created Human Resources Department. The
Technical Department now included an R&D unit. The responsibilities of the VP
were reduced, with the information technology unit now being allocated to the
Administration Department. The most significant of these changes was the creation of a separate HR department which signalled that Telemig's senior management was responding to the rising criticism of the management style and climate
prevailing within the company.

Table 5.3 presents the number of units reporting to each director, comparing
1985 with 1993. With the notable exception of the human resources area, there
is evidence of some rationalization in organization during this period. Examination of the company's organizational charts shows that in the same period the
number of employees dropped by 9 per cent and the company's total number of
units reduced by 22.8 per cent. These are further indications that the company
was moving towards a simplification of its structure. The organization charts show
that in 1993 there was no vice-presidency position. Some of the vice-presidency's
previous functions were transferred to the presidency, which became responsible
for strategic planning, company development and organizational modernization.
This reflected a concentration of managerial drive behind the restructuring, training and other changes about to be introduced. The 1993 organizational chart does
not show three units that existed in 1985: the budgeting department (reporting in
1985 to the VP), the industrial relations unit (under HR) and R&D (under the
technical department). The absence of an industrial relations unit in 1993 was a
sign of the declining relevance of the union. The fact that in 1993 the marketing

Table 5.3   Number of units reporting to directors within Telemig, 1985 and 1993

Functional area	No. of units 1985	No. of units 1993
Administrative	5	3
Finance	5	4
Human resources	3	8
Operations	16	9
Technical	6	3

department continued to be a small unit within the operations directorate also suggests that the company had not yet adopted a significant market orientation.

3 The Managerial Council: an instrument of continuity and change

The Managerial Council was created in 1979. However, it only began to operate fully after 1985 when democracy was reintroduced into Brazil. The Managerial Council consisted of all managers below the directorate and above first-line supervisors, namely heads of departments and units, and the managers of different regions within the state of Minas Gerais. Managers regarded the council as an important defence against external political influence. For example, one said, 'The Managerial Council preserved Telemig's ethics and ethos. It prevented politicians from interfering with the company. It contributed enormously to the management of the company.' Another commented that:

> The Managerial Council was very clear in the way it operated. Its members did not allow anything to be approved without the council's agreement. They used to say: 'It does not matter if some politician wants to get something from the company. We just give them unimportant things and isolate them.' Nothing went ahead in the company without the council's approval.

Interviews with employees suggested that they regarded the Managerial Council as an invisible layer in Telemig. This referred to the way that the council articulated the influence of the telecommunications professionals, 'raised in the telecommunications system', and to the council's role in protecting the company against political interests. A former manager said that:

> The Managerial Council operated like a protective cover. It was like an invisible group that kept the company on the right track. The council was responsible for the budget and everything else of importance in the company. In fact it was the Managerial Council which directed the company. The council indirectly and subtly suggested to top management that they did not really understand the business. (Manager)

The Managerial Council retained considerable power within Telemig until it was abolished in 1996. A manager explained how members maintained the same group in power and thus preserved continuity in the 'way of doing things':

> How did the Managerial Council stay in power for almost 20 years? When a new top management was appointed, the council would agree with a proposed restructuring, but would implement this in its own way. They appointed their members to posts in such a way as to maintain their seats in the council. It was just putting on make up.

However, the price for securing this degree of autonomy from top management was that the Managerial Council enabled the same groups to retain power for an extended period of time. An engineer commented that 'The Managerial Council was a good thing for Telemig because it defended the company against vested interests. However, it also encouraged the formation of fiefdoms inside the company which lasted for 20 years.'

The Managerial Council was also viewed as the body that introduced innovations both in Telemig's orientation towards the customer and in its practices. A former president of the company claimed that:

> The Managerial Council represented an ultra-modern management which was admired by other companies. It extended the channels of communication within the company and it provided the proper environment for the introduction of innovations, such as our programme of total quality in services, which was introduced in 1991. It fostered the culture that the customer was our main stakeholder.

The Managerial Council was also seen as the body that sowed the seeds of privatization. The following extracts from interviews indicate that members of the council saw privatization as a way of securing adequate finance for Telemig while preserving its technical strengths:

> The managers thought that shareholders taking over with privatization would act rationally and would certainly invite those with technical competence to remain. They had this idea that technical knowledge would provide them with eternal power. They thought that privatization was the best option for the company. They were fed up with paying for the state's debts. In their minds, the principals should be the stock market and their responsibility was to do what the stock market wanted. They had the illusion that they could resort to New York to get the money they needed. They also thought that they were going to be promoted and have better salaries. (Supervisor)

> The members of the Managerial Council. They went to the US, to Chile and other countries and longed to have the same system. They thought privatization was ideal for the sector. (Manager)

The Company's Mission and Strategy

During the second half of the 1980s, Telemig's plans continued to be oriented towards developing the interior of MG. This was partly a response to pressures from Telebrás, the holding company. At the same time, the company was now subject to new pressures from more local political interests. The company's report for 1986 mentioned that 'the year was marked by the intensive interaction of the company with city councils and mayors of the state of Minas Gerais'. The 1988 report also indicates that the company was tuned into the local community. It mentions that Telemig was involved with the implementation of its managerial

Table 5.4   Training within Telemig, 1988–1993

Training indicators	1988	1989	1990	1991	1992	1993
No. of employees trained	4,816	10,451	5,686	7,727	13,036	23,519
Training per employee (%)	1.14	1.60	1.30	1.45	2.38	3.66
Training expenses/resources for innovation (%)	0.30	0.20	0.11	0.25	0.40	0.41

Source: Telemig company reports.

philosophy through 'investigation of the needs of the community'. The 1989 report dedicates various paragraphs to the company putting together a strategic plan that aimed to take into account both the economic feasibility of new projects and improvement in the quality of services. According to these company reports, Telemig carried out various developments that had an impact on local communities, such as expanding the public telephone provision to peripheral areas of cities and to the interior of the state. Telemig also began to develop some new services for banks and large customers.

Nevertheless, the reports suggest that most of the company's activities in this period were focused on internal development: that of its management system and its employees. Table 5.4 presents information on the resources allocated to training from 1988 to 1993. The number of employees who received training increased from 4,816 in 1988 to 23,519 in 1993. Other indicators in this table point towards the same trend. Training per employee went up from 1.14 to 3.66 in the same period. Expenditure on training as a proportion of funds allocated to innovation also went up during the period. Though comparative data for previous years are not available, it is clear that the company devoted substantial resources to the training of its employees during these years. It also introduced performance evaluation schemes, formulated a new managerial philosophy and monitored the quality of its internal organization by introducing continuing assessment of its employees' quality of life and of organizational climate.

Telemig's reports indicate that, from 1990 on, its strategic plans became more long term, externally oriented and economically focused. It started to invest in re-engineering by reducing organizational layers and the number of employees. Its strategic planning at the time considered the company's weak and strong points, within an environment of market and technological transformation. From 1990 to 1993 the company introduced discrete services to differentiated clients and innovated on various fronts, such as in graphic software capable of visualizing areas of telecommunications provision and in the introduction of mobile phones. It improved its digital and data commuting network and data transmission services. In 1992, the company obtained an award as the 'premier company in the sector for quality of services'. In that year the company made an initial public offering, returning to the stock market after eight years' absence. A company history mentions that 'The return of Telemig to the stock market in July after eight years was extremely positive. The negotiation of its papers had an immediate impact in demonstrating the company's market credibility' (Histórico da Telemig, 1997). According to the company's 1993 report, the price of the company's ordinary shares rose by 29.9 per cent from 1992 to 1993. The measures taken by the company at the beginning of the 1990s initially contributed to losses in 1991 and 1992, but thereafter led to a substantial improvement in its profit levels.

Two other important steps were taken in this period: the introduction in 1993 of a mobile service for MG, and the introduction of a quality control programme in 1992. Investment in quality control permitted the company to rise from ninth to fifth position in the Telebrás system in 1992 and to reach third position by 1994.

Telemig's Politicization

Interviews with managers and engineers reveal a parallel within Telemig of the conflict that was taking place at the governmental level as populist forces began to dismantle the network that had supported technocracy under the military regime. As already mentioned, with the restoration of democracy in Brazil, populist forces began to interfere in state organizations. Positions in state enterprises became the subject of negotiation with the government's political allies and opponents, and they were distributed among members of the coalition supporting the government (Cardoso and Helwege, 1991). A manager and an engineer respectively described the interference of these political forces within Telemig:

> One of the most serious problems we have to deal with, nowadays, is the following. Because Telemig is a state enterprise it has a large interface with public power. This puts it between *a cruz e a espada* [a rock and a hard place]. Everyone knows how our politicians are. If one of them rings asking to talk to the president of the company and he says he is busy this creates a serious problem.

> Today there is insufficient authority within the company. If you go to talk to the president about a ten-year plan, which has been carefully detailed, he says to you that he cannot approve the plan because he does not know how long he will stay in his post. There is too much uncertainty about how long he can keep the job because of the political instability in the country. Political forces might drive him out. He can only plan for three years. That corresponds to how far he can see his own future. Thus we have to be aware that command in this organization is going to be transitory.

In this period, there was an underlying dispute between engineers and top management, which was fuelled by the engineers' fear of losing power and prestige. With reduced investment coming from the state, new alternatives for expansion lay in innovations in how services were provided. As has been mentioned, the operations and technical departments – regarded as the heart of the company during the military period – became reduced in size. The inflow of political influence particularly affected the interests of the engineers. Political interference threatened the legitimacy of their claim to be the group that understood the business and that had the capacity to manage the company. After all, it was the engineers who had led the company during its period of steady growth.

Rejection of political influence expressed itself through rejection of the board. We have noted how the Managerial Council was used for this purpose. This sentiment was not confined to engineers, but was shared by other staff, as the following extracts show:

> I do not think that the employees thought that the board and others were legitimate. The perception that some directors were illegitimate has caused relations between the company and the employees to worsen. (Engineer)

> There were people who came to this company tainted with the intention to benefit from corruption. This is not an acceptable practice. I think it is valid to listen to politicians, but in their own sphere. I do not agree with people coming here to use the organization for political ends. (Manager)

An engineer said that:

> Today the company board examines not only the technical relevance of a given project, but also how many votes it is going to secure. This is strange to us. Beforehand directors had a technical career that evolved within the telecommunication system and Telebrás. Everything was focused in the same direction. Today the board concerns itself whether a political demand will result in some votes.

Telemig's military managers had adopted a scientific approach to management, which was expressed in decision-making routines as well as rituals. They emphasized technical competence by reassuring the primacy in decision-making of technical criteria over political ones. They established awards for technical inventions and innovations as well as ceremonies for their public delivery. The new management not only ceased some of the organizational rituals such as innovation award ceremonies, but gave priority to demands coming from those stakeholders they most feared – the politicians. In the view of Telemig's existing staff, acceding to political demands would amount to a desecration of the values they had learned to cherish, such as technical rationality and universalism. One of the previous directors suggested that a deprofessionalization of Telemig was under way during this period:

> I do not think that it is necessary to discuss privatization yet. But, if the organization continues to move from its private ethos to become politicized then I see no other choice. In the early days we use to recruit people on the basis of merit. Now new recruits come on the basis of political connection and they have no understanding of engineering.

Table 5.5 Growing industrial unrest in Brazil, 1985–1988

Indicator	1985	1986	1987	1988
Number of strikes	843	1,493	2,259	1,914
Working days lost (millions)[a]	48.8	32.2	59.0	63.5

[a]Number of striking workers multiplied by the average number of days on strike.
Source: Antunes (1994).

The Union as an Emerging Force

The 1980s were a period during which the union movement's capacity to mobilize grew, as did its membership. The unions that belonged to the CUT represented around 12 million workers in 1986. By 1990, 1,117 unions were affiliated to the CUT, with 13 million members. In 1993, the CUT had 2,702 affiliated unions representing over 19 million workers. This amounted to a 38 per cent unionization of all industrial workers in Brazil (Rodrigues, 2004).

The strength of the union movement was sustained not only by the need to maintain the values of incomes at a time of rampant inflation; it was also motivated by a desire to 'develop workers' social consciousness' (Sandoval, 2001). It claimed to be the main force behind the transition to democracy. In step with that transition, the unions began to press for negotiations between management and labour that were free from government interference. As Rodrigues (2004, p. 9) has put it, the union movement of the 1980s intended to develop the workers' ability 'to think about the world of work, about society and politics'. The sponsoring of long and mass strikes was an important strategy through which the trade union movement demonstrated its collective identity to the Brazilian public. Taken from a study by Antunes (1994, p. 27), table 5.5 demonstrates the increasing capacity of the unions to mobilize strike action between 1985 and 1988.

Internally, Telemig's union – SINTTEL – was progressively gaining ground. From 1990 to 1993 there were 17 strikes in the telecommunications sector (DIEESE, 2001). The increasing capability of the union to mobilize stimulated a process of mutual learning in its relations with Telemig management. From 1986 when the new management took office until the early 1990s, the union insistently attacked the company's working conditions and relationships between managers and subordinates. It particularly criticized the lack of communications and management's authoritarian style. Its criticism was expressed primarily in material published by the union newspaper in the form of cartoons, metaphors and stories. These cartoons became the main tool for expression of resistance to authoritarian practices. The stories of the 'Zizi the Telephonist' and the 'Powerful Little Chief' were usually embedded in humour. These forms of expression and their meanings are discussed in detail in chapter 9. The cartoons and the metaphors had a significant impact on the organization and its management style. The following comment suggests that despite their humour, employees and management took these cartoons very seriously:

> I became acquainted with the things done by 'the little chief' through the union newspaper. There were various things that shocked me, such as the manner in which managers related to employees. For example, there was a manager who gave a dismissal notice to an employee because he was caught in a bar outside the building during working hours. It turned out that he was fixing its telephone. (Manager)

Managers recognized that their previous denial of conflict had impaired their ability to listen and negotiate with employees. Union activism left the organization paralysed. The union learned to take advantage of the fact that managers had neglected workers' needs for the previous ten years. It started to take responsibility for sorting employees' problems in the workplace. This involved contesting working conditions and building channels of communications with employees. The following extracts from interviews describe how the employment relations environment had been during the military period:

> The managers had complete authority in the organization. No employee would dare to talk to a manager. Most managers stayed locked in their own room. When I arrived and started to talk to people they were surprised that I exchanged ideas with them. (Manager)

> At that time managers had a lot of authority. They were never challenged. Everything was very rigid. There was a maxim in the organization: 'In this organization there are only two groups: the first are those who give orders and the second those who obey.' Telemig was like an army. If somebody did not do what he was told, this was viewed as insubordination. (Manager)

As Telemig's union's membership began to grow – 2,732 workers joined SINT-TEL from 1978 to 1985 – its capacity to mobilize in support of its demands increased. This encouraged managers to improve working conditions, as well as communications, within the company. In 1985 the company created an integrated and 'fully fledged' Human Resources Department and an industrial relations unit to deal directly with the union. Top management introduced different measures to offset the increasing power of the union. Heads of sections and units were given the title of managers at the same time that the company prohibited managers from joining the trade union. A director explained the thinking behind this policy:

> [The manager] is the spokesman for the company; he represents his director and this is one the fundamental roles of the manager. If he is smart he will perceive that he starts to become an important agent for the shareholders [i.e. the state and individual shareholders]. He becomes an important source of information too. We now realize how important this role is, and so do the managers.

One of the intentions behind the managerial philosophy issued in 1987 was to attract the loyalty of middle and lower-level employees. The document states that it is their responsibility to look after the work environment and create a healthy organizational climate. The same director reinforced this point:

> All managers without exception are expected to be ambassadors of the managerial philosophy. 'Dressing in the company's shirt' implies that managers cannot go on strike or be allied to the union's campaigns. They now represent the company.

The number of items in the trade union newspaper about working conditions had actually reduced substantially by the end of 1990. The following extract suggests that the quality of relationships between superior and subordinate had also improved by then: 'Today I would say that the relationships between superior and subordinates are very open. Today we have various opportunities to exchange ideas with our superiors' (Manager).

The union employed a strategy which they called *Radio Peão* (Workers' Radio). This involved generating rumours about a particular event of interest to employees that were spread throughout the organization by word of mouth. An engineer described the process and its effect in generating a critical awareness about management: 'Most information that comes through *Radio Peão* is distorted. Then you go to your chief just to check on the matter and you find that there was some truth in it.'

Managers recognize that during this time they learned a lot from the union about taking a more flexible approach to hierarchy, communications and negotiations. As three managers commented:

> Managers usually remained in their offices and did not communicate with the employees. Pressures from the union led them to leave their 'pigeon holes' and talk to the employees. Managers are changing their attitudes.

> In the 1970s the company used a structured and formal language. We were not allowed to use slang. But the union used a simple language, similar to the employees'. Ours was the language of the bureaucrat: hierarchical and difficult to understand. We now have learned that we should have multiple channels to communicate with employees and to do so very quickly.

> After being perplexed for a while, we managers are now learning how to deal with conflict. We now consider conflict as natural. We are learning to separate personal issues from company issues. This was not the case during the military period.

In addition, Telemig's management had by the end of the 1980s already begun to introduce measures to reduce the union's capacity to mobilize support. The Human Resources Department learned to develop strategies that enhanced symbolic control over the employee. One of them involved the establishment of the family programme, which an HR manager mentioned in his interview:

It was well known in Brazil that the family was an important element of support of the trade union movement. So we initiated a programme of family visits to the company. This involved explaining to the wives and kids the relevance of the employee's work for the achievement of Telemig's mission. We also showed them the benefits the company provided to the employee in comparison with other companies. By doing this, we intended to neutralize the union's influence.

The HR director explained how the company also established several programmes of direct benefit to employees' families:

We established an interesting programme for the family. This was called a basket of skills and family competences. If the company needed any of the services included in the family portfolio of skills, we would give preference to them. This was our way to enhance a family's income in a situation in which the inflation was eroding the purchasing power of salaries. Another programme for integrating the family was the Arts School, which included clubs to teach crafts and also the company's sport club.

The intention of the Human Resources Department was to change the ideological orientation of SINTTEL, the company union. The HR director mentioned the following:

Our intention is to change the union's approach. CUT and the unions linked to it rely on ideological assumptions. CUT tries to form allies on the basis of worker dissatisfaction, but its real intention is to change the political and economic regime. We counteracted by reducing the levels of employee dissatisfaction with the company. We want a unionism which would be oriented towards results, one that is preoccupied with the company's performance. We aim to change the mentality of employees so that they recognize that making profits creates results which are for their own good.

The Beginnings of Change to the Employment Contract

The concept of a psychological contract was first introduced by Argyris (1960), and later developed by Rousseau (1989) with reference to organizational members' perceptions of mutual obligations in an employment relationship. New conceptual developments consider that perceptions of the organization are in the individuals' mind and may not be related to the formal specifications of the contract. In this book we follow Schein's (1965, p. 11) notion of the psychological contract by suggesting that it refers to perceptions about 'the whole pattern of rights, privileges and obligations between the worker and the organization'. Rights, privileges and obligations are embedded in the organization's governance system and in its organizational culture. An ownership system defines in principle who are the organization's principals and for whom the organization stands. The organizational culture reflects how mutual obligations are reinforced through practices. For example, an organizational culture may be defined as friendly or familial and this may reflect an emphasis on employment security. A breach of the psychological contract may be perceived to amount to a breach of trust if employees perceive that management fails to fulfil its promises and obligations. The perception of breach of trust is subjective and may or may not reflect the actual terms of the contract (Rousseau, 1989; Roehling, 1997).

As we mentioned in chapter 3, we did not set out to assess the psychological contract or a breach of its terms. However, the analysis of the union newspaper and interviews with employees exposed many perceptions that there had been a breach of trust. Our analysis of Telemig suggests that situations of a breach of trust were associated with changes in taken-for-granted conditions that inform employment relationships. These were detected in employees' or union news-paper narratives during the 1980s, which contested and exposed contradictions in management's discourse and practices. For example, the newspaper exposed man-agement policies and practices that contradicted management's implicit promises in the managerial philosophy. Another example came with the downsizing that occurred at the beginning of the 1990s. That took away security of employment for the first time since 1973. Until then state employees, as public functionaries, had been granted security of employment.

One of the main characteristics of Telemig's founding culture was its family ethos. In spite of the authoritarianism in the company, its general climate was con-sidered to be a positive one. Telemig was described as a family, as a mother and as a widow to indicate the prevailance of a protective managerial style that compensated for authoritarian relationships. The paternalistic state and advantageous employ-ment contract that provided employment security and other benefits was a major support for familial values. In 1990, however, the company laid off around 300 employees. Managers decided over a weekend which employees to make redund-ant, so as to avoid getting the union involved in this process. Redundancy was considered as a threat, even a heresy, in a company that had preached employment for life and extolled the virtues of a familial organization. To make matters worse, at the same time as the company justified redundancies in terms of a need to reduce costs, it was still perceived to be taking on new people who were political nom-inees. One manager commented that the 'number of new arrivals almost fill an entire building'. In fact, the company's employment data suggest that this was a significant exaggeration, since overall employment actually reduced by 436 per-sons in 1990.

As will be explained in more detail in chapters 7 and 8, the discourse of the top management which took office in 1985 emphasized its intention to build a more pluralist and open organization. However, during the period 1986–93, the trade union newspaper insistently attacked the company's working conditions and relationships between managers and subordinates. It particularly criticized the lack of communications and management's authoritarian style, and the way these belied the claims being made by Telemig's management. Its criticism was expressed primarily in material published by the union newspaper in the form of cartoons, metaphors and stories, which chapter 9 analyses in detail.

From 1985 to 1993, the union newspaper frequently exposed management's contradiction regarding its intention to improve communications, by saying that the 'open door' policy was simply a case of the company opening its doors to the street, i.e. redundancy. The union newspaper frequently cast doubt on managers' honesty over the open door policy through the use of metaphor. In an interview a union official said:

> The open door policy is a farce. It does not provide opportunities for saying what we think and expressing our reservations about managerial policies. If you talk about certain issues, you can receive a warning. The next step is that you are dismissed. I would not dare to try the open door policy. Imagine what would happened if I bypassed my boss. I would be out. It is possible to break the hierarchical system in theory, but just don't try it in practice.

Conclusion

This chapter has described how Telemig evolved from a period in which it had a clear mission and identity to a period in which its corporate identity was weakened. Back in the 1970s, collective entrepreneurship and a pioneering spirit encouraged a sense of common identity that enabled the fulfilment of the organization's social and economic role. Conflict between management and employees emerged at the end of the 1970s, once the military regime permitted some political expression and independent union organization. In the period from 1985 to 1993, the mission and identity of the company became subject to pressures from society, which set up a tension between external clientelist political demands and the desire of its managers and engineers to preserve Telemig's distinctive technological strengths and ethos. The directors now had to respond to pressures coming from politicians, the union and a management that now used the Managerial Council as an instrument of power within the company. The directors' attempts to cope with these pressures took several forms. One was the expression of a new philosophy to provide a basis for enlisting the loyalty and focusing the commitment of managers and staff. This was supported by significantly increased expenditures on training. New rules were also formulated to support the new values.

The effect of the closure of the self-funding scheme in 1982, in which the government reallocated resources to the companies, together with the country's economic downturn, affected Telemig's performance and led to a dysfunctional evolution in which Telemig became more dependent on the state. The fact that telecommunications was viewed by the government as another public bureaucracy contributed to this dependence and created the conditions for a 'competence trap' in the words of Levinthal and March (1981). While in the previous decade there was some ambiguity as to which organizational identity could be maintained – the private or the state – in this period institutional and political forces imposed a bureaucratic identity on Telemig that was incapable of responding to international market pressures and technological innovation. The entrenchment of the state and its politics generated resistance among long-serving managers who began to search for a new institutional model that could permit an arm's length relationship with the state. The strains in the relationship between the company and the wider polity to which it was beholden provided a platform for a dramatic evolutionary change in the next phase of Telemig's life.

References

Antunes, R. (1994) Recent strikes in Brazil. The main tendencies of the strikes movement of the 1980s. *Latin American Perspectives*, 80, 24–37.

Argyris, C. (1960) *Understanding Organizational Behaviour*. Homewood, IL: Dorsey Press.

Barros, O. de (1993) *Estudo da competitividade da indústria brasileira: oportunidades abertas para o Brasil face aos fluxos globais de investimento de risco e de capitais financeiros nos anos 90*. Campinas, São Paulo: UNICAMP.

Botelho, A., Ferro, J. R., McKnight, L. and Oliveira, A. C. M. (1998) Brazil. In E. Noam (ed.), *Telecommunications in Latin America*. New York: Oxford University Press, pp. 227–50.

Cardoso, E. and Helwege, A. (1991) Populism, profligacy and redistribution. In R. Dornbush and S. Edwards (eds), *The Macro Economics of Populism in Latin America*. Chicago: Chicago University Press, pp. 45–70.

Chase, J. (2002). *The Spaces of Neoliberalism, Land, Place and Family in Latin America*. Bloomfield, CT: Kumarian Press.

Coslovsky, S. V. (2002). Neoliberalism, populism and presidential impeachment in Latin America. Master's thesis presented to the Fletcher School of Law and Diplomacy, USA.

Dalmazo, R. A. (1999) As mediacoes cruciais nas mudancas politico institutioncionais nas telecomunicacoes no Brasil. Doctoral thesis, Universidade Estadual de Campinas.

DIEESE (2001) <www.dieese.org.br>.

Harvey, D. (2005) *A Brief History of Neoliberalism*. Oxford: Oxford University Press.

Histórico da Telemig (History of Telemig) (1997). Belo Horizonte: Telemig.

Kaufman, R. and Stallings, B. (1991) The political economy of Latin American populism. In R. Dornbusch and S. Edwards (eds), *The Macro Economics of Populism in Latin America*. Chicago: University of Chicago Press, pp. 15–45.

Levinthal, D. and March, J. (1981) A model of adaptative organizational search. *Journal of Economics and Organization*, 2, 307–33.

Pires, J. C. L. (1999) Políticas regulatórias no setor de telecomunicações: a experiência internacional e o caso brasileiro. Textos para Discussão no 71. Rio de Janeiro: BNDES.

Rodrigues, I. J. (2004) Crisis of unionism in Latin America? Aspects of the Brazilian experience. Department of Economics, University of São Paulo.

Rodrigues, S. B. (2002) Management in Latin America. In M. Warner (ed.), *Management in the Americas*, 2nd edn. London: Thompson Learning, pp. 3750–64.

Roehling, M. V. (1997) The origins and early development of the psychological contract construct. *Journal of Management History*, 3, 204–17.

Rousseau, D. M. (1989) Psychological and implicit contracts in organizations. *Employee Responsibilities and Rights Journal*, 2, 121–39.

Sandoval, S. A. M. (2001) The crisis of the Brazilian labor movement and workers political consciousness. *Revista Psicologia Política*, 1, 173–95.

Schein, E. H. (1965) *Organizational Psychology*. Englewood Cliffs, NJ: Prentice Hall.

Schneider, B. R. (2004) Organizing interests and coalitions in the politics of market reform in Latin America. *World Politics*, 56, 456–79.

Velasco, L. Jr. (1997) A economia das políticas públicas: fatores que favoreceram as privatizações. BNDES report.

CHAPTER SIX

Reconstruction and Demise
1993–2000

Introduction

This chapter discusses the evolution of Telemig during the period from 1993 to 2000. It describes the preparations for Telemig privatization, the role of different actors in this privatization process and the external and internal forces that culminated with Telemig's demise as a company shortly after it was privatized in 1998. The chapter divides into two main sections. The first section describes the preparations for Telemig's privatization up to 1998. During this period, progressive deregulation led to an increase in management's autonomy and in efforts to develop a market competence. These changes resulted in a significant improvement of the company's performance. The managerial council also played an important role in preparing the company for privatization. The second main section focuses on the events immediately after privatization. Privatization completely changed the company's ownership configuration, with fundamental and wounding consequences for its corporate identity and employment. Restructuring was part of the package of changes brought by the new owners, most of whom were financial and institutional investors. The culture and system of state ownership was replaced by a shareholder value style of management and governance. Telemig's employees experienced this as a breach in their psychological contract with the company. We discuss these issues and their association with the weakening of the trade union as a significant evolutionary force.

Reconstruction: the Context

1 Pressure of international developments

By the 1990s, the introduction of new telecommunications technologies together with deregulation gave rise to innovations and substantial economies of scale in

the global industry. Technological improvements reduced the physical resources necessary to provide connections and also permitted the transmission of large amounts
of data through the same channel. The application of computer technology to
telecommunications permitted the combination of voice, data and multimedia transmission, giving rise to unprecedented service innovations (Shima, 2004). Fransman
(2001) has described how the industry evolved from a stage in which the focus
was on equipment development to a further stage focused on network development, and then to a third stage in which innovation was primarily directed towards
the diversification of services. Integration between different industries encouraged
the creation of hybrid services such as video-conferencing, multimedia and data
transmission. New players entered the sector, including cable TV, electricity
suppliers, computer companies and even transportation and construction firms.
Companies became client-focused, investing heavily in marketing and in the
development of managerial skills (Wohlers and Crossetti, 1997).

These technological developments transformed the way the telecommunications
industry was organized. They permitted the adoption of new business strategies
based on product differentiation and focused on the client. Competition now occurred
at the leading edge of markets in more profitable services such as mobile phones
and data transmission (Pires, 1999). Innovation encouraged new differentiated demands
on the part of customers and created opportunities for companies endowed with
particular capabilities to specialize in particular niches. Market segmentation and
product differentiation in turn encouraged concentration through mergers and acquisitions, as well as the formation of joint ventures between the large operators. These
were motivated by the desire to achieve economies of scale and scope. As the market became more competitive and internationalized, some operators around the
world abandoned their previous public service provider identities, and began
to adopt the competitive strategies common to other science and technology-
intensive oligopolies. These developments in technology and industrial structure
created further pressures on companies, such as Telemig, that remained under
state control.

2 The politics of telecommunications

Changes in the international telecommunications industry began to affect Brazil.
The first step towards privatization was the termination in 1991 of the reserved
market for the computer industry, through which national companies were protected from imports and foreign competition. The end of this market protection
both stimulated and enabled the development of alliances between state enterprises,
MNCs in the electronics industry and equipment manufacturing companies
already in Brazil. During the 1990s, Brazil's telecommunications underwent a radical transformation in terms of technology, services and products, competition, regulation and governance. International equipment manufacturers already in Brazil,
as well as private national firms such as Globo TV, began to establish alliances with

Table 6.1 Key economic indicators, Brazil, 1993–1998

Year	GPD growth		Inflation rate INPC (%)	Real interest rate (%)	External debt (US$ billon)	Domestic debt (% of GDP)
	Total (%)	Industry (%)				
1993	4.9	7.0	2,489.1	7.1	1,143	21.6
1994	5.9	6.7	929.3	24.4	1,197	21.0
1995	4.2	1.9	22.0	38.9	1,293	25.5
1996	2.8	3.7	9.1	23.9	1,441	29.3
1997	3.7	5.5	4.3	42.0	1,678	30.2
1998	−0.1	−1.2	2.5	31.2	2,219	40.4

Source: Boletim do Banco Central do Brasil (1999).

MNCs and lobbied the government to open the market. These developments encouraged the discussions about telecommunications privatization that had already begun.

In 1993, Cardoso, then the Economics Minister in Franco's government, introduced a stabilization programme – the so-called Real Plan. The Real Plan was very successful in controlling inflation. As shown in table 6.1, the annual rate of inflation fell from 929 per cent in 1994 to 22 per cent in 1995, 9.1 per cent in 1996, 4.3 per cent in 1997 and 2.5 per cent in 1998. This was the beginning of a more stable period for Brazil, in both economic and political terms. It witnessed the adoption of neoliberal ideals of development and the country's re-engagement with the global economy. Various reforms were introduced during Cardoso's subsequent presidency (1994–2002). These were intended to stabilize the economy in order to get Brazil on to a path of sustainable development. The government's policies had a profound effect both on Brazil's institutions and on the economy. One of the key changes was the move from a closed to an open economy, and from a state-regulated system to an entrepreneurial one. In 1995 the rate of GDP growth reached 4 per cent. The measures to attract foreign direct investment resulted in Brazil recovering its position as one of the most important hosts of foreign capital in the developing world. FDI increased from US$6 billion in 1992 to US$17 billion in 1993, and peaked in 1998 at US$55 billion, due to the privatization programme.

Cardoso's reforms included a more extensive privatization of state companies. Compared to preceding regimes, his government undertook privatization in a more planned and systematic manner. Between 1990 and 1998, there was a transfer of US$85 billion of assets to private ownership (CEPAL, 1998; Pinheiro et al., 1999). The share of state ownership of business companies dropped from 24 per cent in 1994 to 17 per cent in 1998. Due to the massive purchase of privatized assets by foreign multinationals, the share of private Brazilian ownership declined from 44 to 39 per cent in the same period (Gonçalves, 2000, p. 81).

In contrast to previous governments, which had not enjoyed much public support for privatization, Cardoso's managed to enlist the backing of politicians, private interests and multinationals. His staff drew upon neoliberal ideology to argue for a reduction of the state's role to a minimum. Cardoso's agenda for reform was more successful than his predecessors' because his programme was firmly based on the fundamentals of neoliberalism. These were presented to the nation as being neutral and rooted in theoretical and scientific principles.

As was the case during President Collor's period of office, the government's plans were based on the assumption that state companies were an economic burden, and an obstacle to the achievement of developmental goals. By contrast, the role of private companies and foreign capital was elevated to being agents of development. Similarly, state enterprise employees and civil servants came under sustained criticism from the government and the press for their deficient performance and resistance to change. The Brazilian press, having regarded state enterprises as heroes in the 1970s, now portrayed them as parasites.

Privatization has had an important impact on the governance of telecommunications in Brazil, with the new companies having various types of owners represented on their boards. These owners included companies whose main activity was the provision of telecommunications services, manufacturers of equipment (including some multinationals), civil engineering groups, media and communications companies, banks, institutional investors and financiers.

3 The relational framework: reshaping the telecommunications industry

The plans for privatizing Brazil's telecommunications sector were carried out by a coalition of sector professionals and politicians who supported Cardoso's government. The government created a network of people who were in favour of privatization and able to convey the government's ideas about its benefits to the companies. According to one manager, 'Otavio Azevedo, a former president and engineer of the company, was a very influential professional in establishing links between Brasilia and the company. He had close links with Saulo Coelho, Telemig's CEO at the time.' Another manager explained how this network was created so as to guarantee that the government's plans were carried out:

> Sergio Motta, the Telecommunications Minister, initiated the network that implemented privatization. He could not interfere with the political appointments for the presidency of the companies, but he reserved the right to nominate the vice-president, technical and operations directors. These were to be career people. This was his strategy for large companies. For the smaller companies he kept the appointment of the technical and operations directors in his hands.

The leaders of Telemig had espoused the goal of privatization for a long time. Career engineers and other professionals prominent in the Managerial Council regarded privatization as a panacea for the deficiencies of state ownership. Throughout the 1990s, the key actors in the Managerial Council gradually built a consensus in favour of privatization. This was done largely through visits to other companies abroad and through links with equipment suppliers. Managers visited companies in various parts of the world to see how they functioned. As a former director explained:

> In 1995, I was given the task of transforming the operations department into a services department. This was an important watershed. Following privatization, the services department became a business unit. We believed that privatization was unavoidable. My colleagues and I had worked in international consulting firms and we learned that from them and from our visits to international companies. Then when I came to this department to change it into a business unit the soil had already been prepared and was ready to bear fruit. (Director)

Some managers elaborated further on how foreign contacts influenced the way in which the Managerial Council supported privatization and also predisposed other managers towards this option:

> The leaders of the Managerial Council dreamt of privatization. They went on visits to the largest companies around the world and saw a beautiful picture that it was impossible to copy because of Telemig's ties to the state. Why could they not implement changes? Because they needed a lean company with its excess baggage discarded.

> At the time of privatization one of them [a member of the Managerial Council] visited Chile and came back full of ideas about how telecommunications operated in that country. He organized talks within the company to demonstrate the virtues of the private system.

Telemig was also visited by various MNCs interested in acquiring the company:

> The period of pre-privatization was a very active one. Potential bidders visited Telemig and they admired what has been accomplished in the past few years. They were surprised to see that Brazilians are capable of managing companies effectively, like ours. They were also surprised to see a company with such a good technical capacity and oriented towards the market. They said to us: 'there is no difference between this company and any other private global company'. (Director)

An important element of Telemig's vision for the future involved an attempt to change the nature of its institutional environment. The document *Building Telemig's Transformation*, issued in December 1994, clearly indicates the intention of Telemig's management to work for the transformation not only of the company, but of the sector as a whole. This meant gaining greater autonomy for its constituent companies in respect of tariffs, marketing, competitive strategy and human resource policy, the latter including headcount, salaries and collective agreements.

A manager explains how Telemig's management planned to influence the architects of privatization:

> Sergio Braga was appointed as vice-president and he together with some other managers and engineers were the prime actors in privatization. The members of this group, including Fernando Xavier and Jose Eustaquio Drumond, were the key people participating in meetings in Brasília. They not only defined what was going to happen in Telemig, but also helped to design the future telecommunications sector.

The government's plans to privatize the sector therefore found fertile ground in the company. The Managerial Council articulated the concept of privatization through a discourse that emphasized the virtues of the private organization as opposed to the weakness of state enterprises. New senior appointees initiated a programme of major change to put the company into good shape for privatization and they exercised a direct influence in government circles preparing for privatization.

Internal Political Forces

1 Pro-privatization discourse

The case for privatization was expressed by leaders of the Managerial Council, some of whom went on to occupy key positions in the company after privatization had been introduced. Directors' and managers' narratives from interviews suggest that they viewed it as a growing and inevitable development. There appears to have been a consensus among senior managers that privatization was the most feasible way for the company to gain the freedom to secure its resources and as the means to get rid of political interference in the company. For example:

> The company needed to get rid of the fat which it had accumulated during the years of populism. There was an entire department in Juiz de Fora [a town in the interior of the state of Minas Gerais] that they needed to 'dispose of', since most people in this department had been recruited for political motives. Privatization was viewed as a solution to political interference. (Manager)

Another justification for privatization reflected the dependence of state enterprises on the government and the handicap this imposed on their efficient operation in a hypercompetitive environment:

> The culture of a state enterprise is oriented to the past. The way it was in bondage to the state prevented it from enjoying greater flexibility. Our company had reached international standards, but it could not move because of its ties to the state. The market involves competition. In order to survive we need to win by using our claws

every day. Telemig was an elephant and like all large animals, it found it difficult to move. In our case, we did not change overnight. Opening up people's minds was important. With education, the animal began to see further and realize that it needed to get rid of the bonds that restrained it and run together with the other animals. This is the kind of learning that we want to happen inside the company. Telecoms in Italy, Spain, the UK and the US, they run free. We should do the same as these companies. (Director)

Narratives extolling the virtues of privatization were also evident in the management newsletter, *DDdicas*. For example:

> Privatization will bring advantages for the client, who will benefit from a myriad of differentiated services, with differentiated costs, stimulated by the competition. There will also be advantages for the employees who can be employed by other companies needing their services. (Telemig's CEO reported in *DDdicas*, January 1998)

Another item in the same issue of *DDdicas*, coming from the Finance Department, claimed that 'Privatization will bring freedom to everyone. We will have more autonomy to recruit qualified people, and we will be able to acquire the equipment we need faster. We will have more ability to raise funds from the financial markets' (*DDdicas*, January 1998).

Privatization was primarily regarded as a means to get rid of dependency on the state. It was argued that any innovation the company wanted to make found top management returning empty handed from meetings with the holding company, Telebrás, at which they had sought approval. Nothing could be done to modernize the company. They went off to Brasília 'round and returned a square', one engineer stated. He continued:

> The Managerial Council recognized that we were failing to respond to the pressures of demand. The managers thought that one alternative was to cover the deficit in terminals by raising funds from international companies. But this was vetoed by Telebrás. We became surrounded by a wall. We had no feasible alternative for survival. So managers imagined that privatization could provide the light at the end of the tunnel.

> Every time there was a pressure for cutting costs it was the state enterprises that were expected to do this. Yet, at the same time, the money they generated was being used for supporting other activities. (Manager)

2 The board and leadership

Telemig's board experienced various changes during the years following 1993, partly in response to the recomposition of political alliances in the government, in part because of the Cardoso government's plans to privatize the telecommunications sector. Telemig had five different CEOs during these years. The first was Otavio Marques de Azevedo, who replaced Paulo Heslander when he ran for the post of federal deputy in a by-election; the second was Djalma Andrade, who soon left to become the President of Telebrás; the third was Julio Boechat; the fourth was Saulo Coelho, who left to become Minister of Telecommunications; and the fifth was Ivan Ribeiro.

Julio Boechat was the first CEO with a career inside the company. He took office as the President of Telemig in April 1994 and remained at the head of the company until July 1995. Boechat was an electronics technician with an undergraduate degree in business management. He joined Telemig in 1968 and became Director of Operations twice, from 1985 to 1989 and from 1990 to 1994. He retired in 1998, shortly before privatization. During his mandate as CEO he had as fellow directors Paulo Rabelo Sancho (Administrative Director), Labib Jose Kallas (Director of Finance, Economics, and Market Relations), Luiz Gabriel de Castro (Director of Operations), Roberto Faria de Medeiros (Director of Human Resources) and João Jose Rezende Bronzo (Technical Director).

Some of the managers we interviewed singled out Djalma Andrade as the man who particularly wished to change the company and improve the quality of services. He built a team of long service men to help to rethink Telemig. But he was also seen as someone who was known for the opposition he raised. A manager mentioned that:

> Djalma was a strong leader in the sense that he created a climate that led others to quit the company. At the time Telemig lost some important men, such as Ivan Ribeiro and others. He wished to sort out the huge debt of the company. He was the one who initiated re-engineering. He found a way of raising cash by implementing an expansion plan in collaboration with private investors.

Other managers nevertheless expressed the view that Boechat was the more significant leader of the company during the first half of the 1990s. He led a plan of transforming Telemig from an engineering to a market-focused company. Boechat was the architect of strategies developed by the Managerial Council, such as the redefinition of the company as a service provider, splitting the mobile and fixed-line businesses, and the re-engineering that took place later in the decade. The following statements by various managers and other staff point to Boechat's leading role in the company during the 1990s. As one manager said:

> Various people led the process of change in this company. However, the great champion of change was Julio Boechat. When somebody believes in an idea so strongly and implements it, other people start to believe in the project as well. Everybody believed in what he said. The managers began to believe and influence other people. His energy was transmitted downwards throughout the organization.

Despite his strong leadership and the legitimacy he enjoyed, Julio Boechat's period of service as CEO was short. Political alliances behind the election of Cardoso brought Saulo Coelho, an ally of Itamar Franco (former President of Brazil), to the presidency of the company in 1995. Saulo's board was composed of people from the political world with the exception of those occupying the Engineering and Operations Departments. Sergio Braga, a long-serving Telemig manager, took over the vice-presidency. Julio Boechat accepted the position of Administrative Director, with an option to retire within two years. Other members of the board were Geraldo Pereira Sobrinho (Director of Finance, Economics and Market Relations), Mario Assad Junior (Director of Human Resources), Heleni de Mello Fonseca (Director of Telecommunication Services) and Carlos Alberto Ribeiro de Andrade (Director of Engineering).

Evidence concerning Saulo Coelho's position on privatization is not clear-cut. In fact, it was Sérgio Braga who was appointed by the minister to lead privatization rather than Saulo Coelho. According to convention, the presidency of the board of directors was the most powerful post in Telemig, but in 1995 the vice-president became the person primarily entrusted with the mission of privatization. Specifically assigning special responsibility for the implementation of privatization to the VP granted special legitimacy to the project, as well as the authority to carry it out. The former Human Resources Manager recorded that:

> It was the Minister of Telecommunications [Sérgio Motta] who assigned authority for the implementation of privatization to the vice-president. So it was Sérgio Braga who led the sector's privatization programme at the company level. This move took everyone in Telemig by surprise. But it was in fact very well thought-out and intelligent.

He went on to explain the logic behind this appointment:

> Telebrás took people who were opposed to privatization out of key positions and replaced them with people who supported it. All the VPs were career people and they were the ones with the responsibility for implementing privatization. The VPs were hierarchically subordinate to the President, but functionally they had more power. . . . The government's plan was that the presidency should be a political appointment. The VP should be a career person either from the holding company or from Telemig, or recruited from other telecommunications companies. . . . As a figurehead, the President did not voice his opinion about privatization, even if deep down he disagreed with it.

The government's strategy involved controlling appointments for the presidency of the company and other positions, while reserving the technical directorship and the post of vice-president for career employees. The intention was that these positions should be occupied by people with professional experience in telecommunications and who were in favour of privatization.

In 1998 after the company was privatized, Ivan Ribeiro became Telemig's chief executive. His board members were Edson Jose Vidigal Paulucci (Director of Support), Heleni de Mello Fonseca (Director of Business) and Walkyrio Jose de Faria Tostes

(Director of Network). Ribeiro had been a member of the Managerial Council, but he left the company when negotiations for privatization got under way and returned once it had taken place.

Strategic Developments

A manager, currently director of a competitor, described Telemig's strategy at this time in terms of two different developments. The first, up to 1995, involved an improvement in the quality of Telemig's services in order to have a visible impact in the marketplace, and 'to defend Telemig and people in it'. The second development commenced once the plan to privatize telecommunications was officially announced in 1995. This was intended more specifically to make privatization feasible in such a way that would 'save Telemig and its people's employment'. In describing these two developments, this manager employed the simile of a 'movement' to characterize emerging strategies that prepared the company for privatization. While both 'movements' were described in terms of actions by a group of managers to change the prevailing mentality through persuasion and re-education, each had its own distinct aims. The first one was designed to improve the quality of services through re-engineering.

1 The first strategic movement: re-engineering

Re-engineering can be seen in retrospect as a critical preparation for Telemig's privatization. It was a project that emerged from the grass roots in the early 1990s. It arose from the perception of a group of managers and engineers that the company was locked in an institutional and cultural trap. It was justified as a way of defending Telemig against the threats of an increasingly competitive industry. Its proponents understood that Telemig would not survive if it did not recognize and react to increasing competition. So they urged Telemig to reinvent itself. In their view, a drastic change in the company's culture and processes was needed in order to provide solutions that extended Telemig's strategic choices even in a constrained institutional environment. Senior managers, such as Luiz Gonzaga Leal, Francisco Mendonça, Roberto Machado, Julio Boechat and Sergio Braga led the re-engineering project. Their objective was to create new paradigms and a new mentality. One of them said:

> Re-engineering emerged as a bottom up moment fostered by a group that was interested in defending the company and its people from competitive pressures. This group was sure that the company could not survive under its current model of management and with the mentality then prevailing. There was no consensus about the direction the company should go in, since various interest groups, even directors,

felt threatened by proposals. Thus, some people stressed one direction while others stressed other directions. I knew that the outcome would be the result of the various forces at play. Everything had to be negotiated.

There was a mental blockage in the company. There was a lack of commitment to achieving results. There were too many people, too much structure, and unfocused processes. (Manager)

In order to provide appropriate benchmarks, these senior managers visited various companies, such as Sprint, GTE and Bell Canada. During these visits, they studied the processes in the companies and how they could be applied to Telemig. These were then fed back to the company through presentations to the board and to wider audiences. The group successfully implemented various improvements in the company's processes, and this raised Telemig's national ranking for quality of service provision. However, there was resistance even from directors, because the members of this group were viewed as potential rivals to occupy higher positions in the company as well as in the sector. Moreover, the term re-engineering encouraged resistance because of its association with downsizing. Critics of re-engineering attacked it in the union magazine using mockery.

Thus, under Julio Boechat, the leading group decided in 1994 to drop the term re-engineering and instead to call the project 'Telemig's Transformation'. Their ideas were brought together in a document, *Building Telemig's Transformation 1994*, which articulated the company's mission, strategy and core capabilities. This document played down the notion of Telemig being a missionary organization, an identity that had been given to it during its formative years (see chapter 8). *Building Telemig's Transformation* refers only tangentially to the need to contribute to social and economic development, which contrasts dramatically with the company's goals under the military regime. The document reveals Telemig's intention to dominate its local and national markets, and become an international player.

2 *The second strategic movement: preparing for privatization*

The second movement, however, was of a different nature. It was coordinated from the top through the political link between government and company. It was concerned with preparing the company for privatization. It led to Telemig drawing up its first ever business plan, and to separating the mobile from the fixed-line business. The manager whom we have been quoting as an active participant in both these movements added the following:

With the second movement, our CEO stated, it is a case of take it or leave it. We were all considered agents of privatization. For the first time we had a business plan to guide strategy. This involved separation of the mobile from the fixed-line business. It involved the constitution of a new organization, Telemig Cellular, which is still in the market.

In his view, the re-engineering project was overtaken by that for privatization:

> The cycle of the first movement was short. It was superseded by the second. At that time [1995] the government made clear its intention to privatize the telecommunications companies and this diverted attention away from re-engineering and the quality of services.

At this stage, developing a more profitable company was not a major issue. The second movement involved making privatization work and this involved a series of measures to change mentality, build new competencies, and invest in plant expansion and restructuring, with these measures having consequences for the company's performance in the stock market.

3 Changing the mind set: attending to the market

By contrast with the 1970s when the development of services was promoted by advances in the technology and manufacturing of telephone equipment technology, advances in manufacturing and technology now tended to follow, and be subservient to, market demands. Building new competencies that were responsive to market demands, rather than to technology, required a change in the mentality prevailing within the company. It involved changing the way in which employees perceived the business. As chapter 8 shows, Telemig's top management endeavoured to do this by changing the company's identity.

Managers and other members of the Managerial Council involved themselves in the company's training programme. In their message, they affirmed the need to change the company into a more proactive and fast acting organization that would possess a detailed knowledge of the telecommunications market. Terms like creativity, flexibility, motivation and optimization became part of the company's vocabulary. The most important axiom was that 'the client is always right' (Carrieri, 2001; Luz, 2001). In the document *Building Telemig's Transformation*, management stated that 'the company is breaking with traditional paradigms by giving primacy to the client, and by building up strategic alliances'.

Attention to the market in terms of a network of competition and alliances became part of top management's vision once privatization became imminent. As other directors commented:

> An emphasis on the market meant that it was the client who determined what we had to do and not technology. Our business was directed by market demands. Telemig has always been interested in large clients, but in a timid way. (Director)

> It is the clients who should say how we should conduct the business, not technology. We have to get hold of the technology that meets their needs. (Director)

The following extracts from interviews with two directors reflect the move to change the traditional paradigm that used to orient the company's strategy and priorities. They also point out the intention to redefine Telemig's core business:

> There is no need for the service provider to develop its own technology. First, it is impossible to be competent in the development of all these technologies. A company cannot undertake R&D in all of them. Technology is important of course, but the company does not need to engage in its development. It all depends on your kind of business. We, for example, are a service provider company. We do not need to develop technology. Rather, as a service provider we need to find the best application for a particular technology. One does not need to have innovative technology, but rather the one that is appropriate to the business. (Director)

> One thing employees have to realize is that Telemig is transforming itself into a conveyer of information. We do not install telephones any more. What we sell is services, not telephones. In that case, my operational costs will have to be much lower. I need to respond quickly to the client and I need to anticipate what the client wants. I have to obtain loyalty from the client. (Director)

Interviews with both directors and employees suggest that top management expected to achieve this change of mentality through communication and training, using available media channels. Two other directors said:

> It is not enough to meet everybody and pass on a message from the top. It is not like that. There is a need to change the culture. We have made a video in which our president sends a message to all employees. We had to inform them eye to eye, that the changes which were about to take place would hurt many people. We knew that we were going to affect the power of some people, and of people that were about to retire. (Director)

> We used video-conferencing and started to inform everyone. Our message was that they were free to choose [whether to come on board or to quit]. (Director)

In short, during the mid-1990s the market started to occupy a special place in the discourse of Telemig's top management and it became the major point of reference for the company's strategy and activities. From being just 'users', customers became the *raison d'être* of the company. However, management's idea of the market was incomplete. Though Telemig's elite was aware of the technological and business transformation that had taken place in telecommunications internationally, competition was still seen as a somewhat theoretical concept. Prior to the announcement of privatization, telecommunications in Brazil was a state monopoly, and market competition did not pose a threat to the survival of companies in the sector. The market was regarded merely as equivalent to paying attention to the client, with no real conception that competition for clients could pose a threat.

4 Building a consciousness of accountability

The document *Building Telemig's Transformation* suggested that each employee needed to reflect on his or her role and contribution to the company. Employee behaviour should be characterized by commitment to the organization and his or her team, and by high levels of productivity. Employees should therefore monitor their own conduct by asking themselves the following questions:

- How can I contribute to the success of Telemig's business plans?
- What is my level of commitment to Telemig?
- How can I improve the image of the company?
- How can I improve my skills?
- How can I improve my productivity and that of my team?
- Where do I want to go?

This change of mentality also implied that it was legitimate to make a profit, and controlling costs was considered to be essential:

> An example of a change in mentality was when the company realized that it could make money as a state enterprise and this was considered a right thing to do. Earning money is not anti-ethical. If the market is mine why not take advantage of this? (Manager)

> The culture in Telemig is undergoing a radical change. When we introduced stricter budgetary control this was a shock for the company. (Director)

Improving financial performance was now regarded as an important issue. The manager who had used the notion of strategic movement went on to explain that:

> In the first movement, arriving at a more profitable company was not much of an issue. It fitted the context and interests of the politicians. At that time, we were not worried about EBIDTA.[1] It was enough to achieve a balance or not to incur losses. Image was more important than financial performance. Our ideas involved projecting a better image of Telemig to the external public. For example, improving the company's image was of greater concern than the costs in doing this. What we wanted at that time was to achieve a better coverage, having more cities providing good services. With the second movement, we intended to change the way people considered costs. Our goals were to get them to take costs into account.

5 Expanding the plant

During the three years that preceded privatization, Telemig shifted further from an engineering company to a service providing company. Julio Boechat, then CEO, had begun to expand the plant in 1994. The executive group that succeeded him consolidated the changes he had initiated. In 1996 Telemig's investment rose by

37 per cent. According to the document *Histórico da Telemig 1997*, its plant grew by 27 per cent with the installation of an additional 228,000 terminals. Mobile installations expanded by 160 per cent. The company also diversified and expanded its data transmission services. It formed a corporate virtually integrated network, which offered advantages to customers in terms of data transmission speed. In the same year, the company defined its strategic objectives as: approach the market in a stratified and profitable manner; identify client needs in terms of location, time, price and quality; be the market leader in the mobile business; maximize plant productivity; and invest in high capacity infrastructure.

In 1997, when Brazil's Federal Congress approved the new General Law on Telecommunications, Telemig's mobile business was legally separated from the rest of the company. The 1997 report records 122.8 kilometres of optical fibre lines installed compared with only 12.3 for 1994, a tenfold increase. The same report also reports a 66.5 per cent digitalization of fixed-line equipment and 72.8 per cent of the mobile. The company revised its strategic objectives for 1997 to be: (a) to focus on the client; (b) to achieve management excellence; (c) to improve the effectiveness of investment; and (d) to improve business performance. In order to achieve these objectives, it introduced a myriad of new services that offered specific solutions for clients, with lower costs and higher value.

In February 1998, the mobile business was transformed into an independent company. Telemig invested US$542.4 million in plant modernization, which grew by 1998 to 2.1 million terminals and access points, an increase of 17 per cent over the previous year. The decrease in the level of investment shown in table 6.2 reflects the separation of the mobile business in the second half of this year. While the number of terminals increased, but the number of cities connected did not show an equivalent increase for reasons already mentioned.

Company reports for the period 1994–8 suggest that the expansion of its infra-structural base was a major plank in Telemig's strategy. The company invested quite substantially in expanding its plant, nearly doubling its size from 1.1 million fixed terminals in 1994 to 2.1 million in 1998, most of them digital. The interview data indicate that most of the resources for plant expansion came from partnerships with the private sector.

Building New Competencies

As chapter 10 describes in detail, the aim of new management development pro-grammes was to build the skills necessary for moving the company away from depend-ency on the state and towards securing resources from the marketplace. These competencies involved computer and language skills, and the ability to establish partnerships and to work in teams. One of the directors pointed out that:

> The main force behind Telemig's change is the desire to increase competitiveness rather than privatization. Personal competence is important. For example, today peo-ple have to know English and another language. Computer literacy is fundamental.

Table 6.2   Telemig's Performance, 1993–2000

Year	Employees	Number of terminals installed for fixed telephones (thousands)	Number of cities connected	Net operating profit (US$ million)	Annual investment (US$ million)
1993	7,065	1,092	691	84.7	279.1
1994	7,742	1,145	691	104.3	343.9
1995	7,666	1,262	691	161.4	446.7
1996	7,636	1,490	783	353.7	567.9
1997	7,432	1,807	783	445.5	542.4
1998	5,506	2,121	783	192.8	368.2
1999[a]	5,011	2,490	n.a.	81.9	86.1
2000[a]	4,265	2,895	n.a.	504.5	n.a.

Line density is not applicable because the area of concession changed from 1985. [a]Following its privatization in 1998, Telemig no longer produces its own reports. The performance and financial indicators have changed. Thus data on investment for 2000 are not present in the company's documents. The company that has absorbed Telemig, Telemar, also incorporates 15 other telecommunications operators and its performance does not, therefore, reflect that of Telemig alone.

Source: Telemig company reports; for line density, Secretaria de Estado do Planejamento e Coordenação Geral, Suplan/Sei, 'Comportamento da Economia Mineira: Período 1960–77. Comunicações'.

In terms of attitude people have to be more open so as to have a positive attitude towards change. They have to be able to work in groups, be proactive rather than passive. They have to be connected to world events. . . . We are trying to get people to work in multifunctional teams and to share ideas among themselves. (Director)

In our training course there was quite a lot of talk about the ideal manager. The manager that the company needs is not only the one who has power, but one who is capable of learning new knowledge. He is expected to work in teams and with the client. Process was important and this means working with the client. This was not such an easy change to make, as many people who attended the training came to Telemig in the 1970s. They were accustomed to keeping power in their own hands. At the beginning of the privatization process, people were reluctant to surrender their power. (Manager)

Changes in Company Structure

In order to transform the company into a service provider, Julio Boechat championed major changes in the structure of the company. Instead of being oriented towards the dictums of engineering, the company's structure now had to become sensitive to market requirements. This involved the creation of units focusing on distinct types of clients, namely large mobile clients, metropolitan regions and the interior of Minas Gerais. His plans included the separation of the operational and maintenance processes from the business plant. Two new departments were created, the Department of Services and the Department of Engineering. The former was primarily dedicated to identifying clients' needs and fostering the development of new services. The latter had the task of coping with the engineering requirements of the different business units. *Building Telemig's Transformation 1994* also mentioned the creation of business units for large clients, mobile clients and market development.

Some of the changes envisaged in *Building Telemig's Transformation* were only implemented from 1995 onwards, following the government's official announcement that the telecommunications sector was to be privatized. Comparison of Telemig's organizational charts in 1993 and 1994 shows little change in the company's structure. By the end of 1995, however, the chart shows that the newly created departments, Engineering and Services, still maintained the constituent units as well as much of the functional duplication that had characterized their predecessors, the Technical and Operations Departments. For example, each region in the Engineering Department had a subunit dedicated to marketing.

The organization charts from end-1995 to end-1998 reflect Telebrás's intentions to concentrate power in the hands of the vice-presidents of the companies in the system. Until then the VP position had been mostly absent from Telemig's organization charts. Now, the VP gathered a substantial amount of power, taking responsibility for corporate development, strategic planning and implementation, and the management of technological innovation.

Comparison of the charts through the 1990s suggests that the company's structure reflected the intentions put forward in *Building Telemig's Transformation*. Maintenance functions previously under the responsibility of the Services Department went to Engineering. The company created a Support Department, which now took over the functions of three previous departments: Administration, Human Resources and Finance.

From 1995, Telemig employed an outsourcing strategy. A former manager mentioned that:

> Within limits imposed by legislation, Telemig tried to outsource everything that it could, with the exception of services to customers. Ranging from legal to human resources tasks, training, contracting courses, in the administrative area, telephone cleaning, underground path cleaning – a number of things were outsourced.

Company Performance

Before 1994 the company's performance had failed to meet expectations. The 1997 document *Histórico da Telemig* (*History of Telemig*) indicates that investment in management and employee education was helping the company to recover its credibility. In the pre-privatization period, Telemig's performance improved substantially. As table 6.2 indicates, net profit increased from US$104 million in 1994 to US$445 million in 1997. There was a reduction in both profit and investment with privatization, when Telemig lost the status of an independent company in the acquiring group.

Just before privatization Telemig was viewed by the market as a promising company. A historical analysis of Telemig's performance since the foundation of CTMG in 1954 points out that in 1996 the company was viewed by financial analysts as one of the most profitable in Latin America: 'Profit margin increased from 11.9 per cent in 1995 to 24 per cent in 1996. Its shares increased by 150 per cent in the stock market. Financial analysts indicate that Telemig's shares are being sold at 4 per cent above their market value' (*Histórico da Telemig*, 1997). *DDdicas*, the management newspaper, also pointed out that for the first time in its 44 years of existence the company was able to distribute dividends to its employees amounting to nearly R$12 million (*DDdicas*, June 1997).

Privatization

Privatization completely changed the company's ownership configuration, with fundamental and fatal consequences for its corporate identity and employment. Restructuring was part of the package of changes brought by the new owners, most of whom were financial and institutional investors. The culture and system of state ownership was replaced by a shareholder value style of management and governance. This was experienced by Telemig's employees as a breach in their psychological contract with the company. This section discusses these issues and their association with the weakening of the trade union as a significant evolutionary force.

As indicated in chapter 2, telecommunications is a sector that has adjusted very quickly to a business environment driven by innovation and competitive pressures. Organizational forms in the sector became more flexible but also leaner. Privatization has encouraged telecommunications companies to revise their psychological contracts and the nature of their obligations towards employees. The outsourcing that generally accompanies privatization and restructuring has been used to justify revisions in the terms of the psychological contract, while at the same time it weakened the power of trade unions (Keefe and Batt, 1997). Recently privatized organizations are therefore likely to replace the employment relationships of state enterprises, based on secure, tenured contracts, with temporary contracts based on self-reliance, and no expectations of mutual loyalty (Robinson and Rousseau, 1994). The following sections describe how these changes were introduced into Telemig.

Strategy

At the time of its privatization and incorporation into the Telemar group, Telemig was split into two different companies, Telemig Cellular and Telemar. Telemig Cellular was formed from a small group from Telemar and young people from the principal local university. During its first two years of existence, Telemar pursued a strategy of integration and unification of the geographically disperse companies inherited from the previous state companies. In 2002 Telemar created 'OI', a mobile company. However, its ambition to secure a dominant position in the long-distance market, through a bid to acquire Embratel, encouraged Telemar to maintain two separate and independent structures for the mobile and fixed-line businesses. These were kept apart until 2004 when it became clear that the plan to acquire Embratel could not be realized.

1 The emerging shareholder value model of governance

Interviews with former Telemig employees suggest that the company's structure and culture changed fundamentally after it became Telemar. Our interviews indicate that decisions became more centralized, the company became more focused on its core business, there was a greater emphasis on adding value to the business and on costs, and restructuring was used as a tool to create value for shareholders. According to an engineer:

> The owners have just one main objective which is to add value for the shareholders. However, I feel that people are not comfortable. There is a regression in the processes and everything is becoming more centralized. I have the impression that we are going back to the military period, but without the advantage of the 'big family'.

A former manager of Telemar explained that:

> The new holding has progressively shrunk into two units, corporate clients and retail business. The shareholders do not influence matters of daily life, only strategic matters. However, they are the main decision makers when it comes to restructuring. The impetus for this comes directly from head office. It is now very different from old Telemig. There is no movement up from the bottom. The owners' view was that the current structure was not adding value and the solution was to go for optimization. Nowadays, they are contracting an external consultancy company to do the job.

2 Restructuring

An organizational chart published by the company at the beginning of 2002 indicates a major change in the company's structure after privatization. It points to a refocusing on to the core business and it reflects the segmentation of the market. The chart shows a simplification of the structure, with four units responding to the Chief Executive, the highest post for each regional subsidiary. This structure comprised departments for corporate clients and for the retail business, a network department and a finance department. The new structure was very indicative of the new priorities. The Finance Department became one of the largest units, while other departments such as the Information Technology (IT) and the Human Resources (HR) departments lost their centrality. IT became a unit of the Finance Department, and though HR still reported to the Chief Executive, it lost its status as a function headed by a director.

The company suffered from successive downsizing after privatization. A manager commented on the downsizing of managers that accompanied this reorganization: 'When deciding on downsizing, the CEO invites some executives to stay. He selects the ones to survive the "tsunami". He has created a sub-group and asked a consulting firm to advise on the best structure and how to proceed with downsizing.' This structure then changed again when Telemar merged with the mobile company of the group called OI and it was slimmed down when the plan to acquire Embratel failed. The rate of headcount reduction intensified from 2000. Interviews with former Telemig and Telemar managers, as well as with the Telecommunications Union, suggest that downsizing occurred in several stages. A former manager mentioned that, in comparison with other companies, Telemar's approach to downsizing was 'light', as the following suggests:

> The Spanish did worst with Telesp [another telecommunications company]. In their first day in office they kicked everybody out, including the district heads. However, some guys in the city held on to strategic information so as to retain their position. Everyone knows that for each telephone apparatus there are two pairs of wire, one red and one green. These wires go into cables that contain around 10,000 pairs of wires. This information is organized into a file of cable registering. The guys in Telesp disappeared with the books in order to keep their positions. They knew that if there was a telephone defect and the company did not address it, it would have to pay huge fines. So, in São Paulo there was chaos for eight months following the acquisition. The company was able to control the situation only after paying huge fines. (Retired engineer)

However, in 2004 the company went for a huge downsizing in which it reduced its seven units down to two. According to an interview with a former manager of Telemar, the company laid off five vice-presidents, 40 directors, 100 managers and 200 coordinators (project managers). A trade union official reported that in 2005 the company sent an e-mail around warning of its intention to make 5,000 employees redundant.

The Breach of the Psychological Contract

Studies of the state sector in Brazil have argued that 'corporativism' was a main characteristic of the state sector (Murillo, 2000).[2] Its *reason d'être* was to protect the advantageous relational contract that characterized employment in state companies. There was a public understanding that state enterprises suffered from two types of malaise, one of them being their captivity by politicians and the second being the corporativism of employees and the union. Privatization enjoyed the support of the Brazilian public at the time, since it was assumed that it was the best cure for both malaises. Privatization was viewed as a tool to break down the hardened corporativism that stood in the way of change (Kaufman, 1977; Schneider, 2004). State enterprises in Brazil were well known for offering an employment contract that was superior to those of private companies. Not only did their employees have the right to a 13-month additional salary that was guaranteed for all salaried employees in the country, but sometimes they were entitled to a 14- or even 15-month bonus depending on their rank. They also had the right to full pension and other security benefits. In the pre-privatization period, a scheme for employee participation in profits had been widely applied in state-owned companies. The state also guaranteed security of employment. Privatization has changed various aspects of the previous employment relationship and taken away some advantageous features of the employment contract. Some of the lost features comprised a psychological contract in the sense that they were subjective and implicit.

As noted in chapter 5, the concept of psychological contract refers to organizational members' perceptions of mutual obligations in an employment relationship. Newer thinking recognizes that individuals have a mental perception of their relationship with the organization, and that this may not reflect the formal specifications of the contract. Expressions of a breach in the psychological contract may be subjective and they do not necessarily correspond to managers' views or to the formal terms of employment. Our analysis of Telemig's evolution suggest that employees' perception of breaches in the psychological contract may be expressed indirectly, through rejecting and contesting organizational changes that are disadvantageous not only to their salaries but also to their employment security, benefits, privileges and status. The Telemig union newspaper also contained many expressions of employee unease concerning their psychological contract with Telemig, even to the extent of perceiving that a breach of trust had taken place (see chapter 10).

The most intensive perception of threats to the employment contract came shortly before and after privatization. They were expressed in several ways: in terms of losses of taken for granted benefits and lifestyle, the intensification of work pressures, a feeling of exploitation by management, employment insecurity and the way that the company carried out downsizing.

The profit-sharing scheme in Telemig had provided benefits that employees came to take for granted. For example, prior to privatization, if the company made profits, they were distributed to all employees in proportion to their salaries. After privatization, this distribution not only became unequally differentiated into hierarchical categories; it was also linked to the company's performance and creation of added-value. The union reacted to this change in a combative manner. From 1998 to 2000 the trade union newspaper carried various pieces denouncing the company's failure to meet its obligations concerning the payment of profit shares. Many

Figure 6.1 The beggar.
Source: Bodim Semanal, n°60. 30/Apr/1998.

of the trade union claims about the scheme were presented in an ironic figurative
way. Figure 6.1 is an example where employees are presented as beggars pleading
for their shares in the profit.

The change of location of the headquarters was also perceived as a threat to the
stability of their employees' families. For the employee, his or her assignment to
Belo Horizonte was part of the implicit terms of the contract. The scaling down
of activities in Belo Horizonte resulted in some personal costs for employees. Many
were transferred to other states and this had negative personal consequences such
as having to live away from their families. A manager mentioned: 'We think that
transfer to Rio was a threat to the family since we would have to move and be
away from our friends and family. So there is a real dilemma' (Manager). Another
issue was the perception of unfairness in the balance between inducements and
contributions. According to an engineer, 'everybody is feeling smashed and mas-
sacred. We spend at least ten hours a day in the company. Some people stay put
for twelve hours and some spend the night here. Other people have to travel and
have to stay away from their families for fifteen days.' Another engineer echoed
this perception of being exploited:

> We spend more than the contracted eight hours a day here. We give our blood to
> this company. Many people stay here twelve hours. You just have to look in our
> car park to see that. At eight in the evening it is as full as at three in the afternoon.
> Managers go home at ten in the evening and we have to stay over too.

The perception among former members of Telemig was that the new owners
were not keeping promises made before privatization. For example:

At first, Telemig was like a Diaspora. They took our best professionals to the North-east. What we know is that they used us. After a given time, top management began to replace the people that helped them to restructure the company. They replaced them with less expensive young people. (Retired Manager)

Telemig has now become a 'milch cow'. We now have to pass on material to every-one else so that they can solve the problems of Rio and other regions. (Manager)

The breach of the psychological contract was also expressed in terms of a manage-ment failure to maintain procedural justice: there was a lack of proper voice and information in the decision-making process (Brockner and Siegel, 1996). The restruc-turing that took place on various occasions at Telemar was described as ruthless:

Making people redundant was a terrible process, but it did lead to a change in atti-tude. In this company it was done in an American way, with people being dismissed over the telephone. People changed because they were afraid of losing their jobs. After privatization, entire sections were closed down with an e-mail. It was a ruth-less process. Telemig was like a conquered land. That's how they changed the men-tality, by replacing people. There are only two ways you can change mentalities: either by promoting people or by firing them. (Human Resources Manager)

The Breach of the Psychological Contract and Employability

Current studies suggest that restructuring is a characteristic of a shareholder-value style of governance, associated with an emphasis on employability and with breaches of the psychological contract (Börsch, 2004). The Telemig case illustrates how an emphasis on employability helped to prepare for a shareholder-value type of governance and for a change in the psychological contract from a relational basis to a transactional form. Companies that adopt relational contracts tend to make a long-term investment in employees' education and to offer benefits that encourage their permanence in the organization. Such contracts also provide employ-ment security in exchange for loyalty. A transactional contract, on the other hand, is based on economic exchange and stresses short-term commitment by both par-ties (Lee, 2001).

Interviews with senior managers indicate that they expected that, with privatiza-tion, the employment contract would soon change from a relational to a transac-tional form. Their discourse on employability was intended to prepare the employees for further extension of restructuring in the years following privatization. For example, a director said: 'Employability is a discourse that began in the pre-privatization period. The discourse was that a society cannot guarantee employment for every-body. People should be responsible for their own employability' (Director).

One way to try to reduce resistance to change was to argue that the existing organizational culture, which supported the psychological contract based on long-term employment and loyalty, was no longer appropriate. Top management's discourse argued that the previous organizational culture was outdated in the new business environment. Following privatization, the new top management attempted to convince employees that practices such as job security and employee profit-sharing were paternalistic, and that they led to rigidity and passivity. In their view, the only way to secure change was to get rid of the old paternalism and reject the notion that Telemig was like a family that had an obligation to preserve jobs. Directors expounded this view at length. For example:

> People in this company have to understand that paternalism is a practice that is not acceptable any more. People have to achieve for themselves, not live on what others achieve for them. . . . Once privatization could be considered a certainty, we adopted the discourse of employability. There is way that societies can guarantee employment. This is through individuals taking responsibility. It is the responsibility of the employee and not of the company to improve his education and skills. (Director)

> Today we need a multifaceted professional who is able to adapt to new situations. . . . The change is intended to allow us to offer better quality services by having better quality employees. The professionals whose skills do not help to develop what the company wants are going to be replaced. If one does not think like that, the company cannot survive. We want a company with a long life and to be the best in the country. At first, employees may become depressed about this and feel rejected. They may say 'I worked here my whole life and what do I get?' This is just nonsense. They should shake themselves up and say that they are going to undertake a programme of personal improvement. However, they should not expect any financial support for this. They have to arrange it for themselves. (Director)

Management was looking for a different kind of employee with a different mind set; one who was prepared to go and find employment elsewhere when the need came and one who was able to accept an extension and diversification of his or her responsibilities if need be. We frequently found an internalization of such top management discourses in employees' own narratives. What the engineers said illustrates this:

> People need nowadays to be eclectic and able to do different kinds of things. Every professional has to be able to adapt to different circumstances and be able to change. If one does not adapt he or she cannot survive. (Engineer)

> The world has changed. You cannot assume that it is still normal for you to keep your job. The employee must be responsible for keeping his job. Nobody is going to do it for us. (Engineer)

Employee Identification

The transformation that took place in the periods before and after privatization changed the nature of relationships inside the company. It affected people's trust in management and colleagues as well their affections towards the company. Their attachment to the company had been linked to the perception that Telemig had a particular identity. It was seen to be like a family and a mother, with all the emotional and financial security associated with this identity. So when managers came to profess a market-oriented identity for the company and to engage in an employability discourse that emphasized independence in the sense of standing on one's own feet, employees mourned what they thought they had lost. For example: 'Telemig was like a mother. It was like heaven's blessing is for the Catholics who believe in God' (Engineer).

Studies of identity and identification suggest that when changes are forced on people who suffer from their effects, they tend to take refuge in the past and embellish it (Brown, 2006). Some reflection back to a rosier past was evident in the discourse of employees following privatization. For example:

> Top management says we are going to be alright. But we know this is just talk. In the corridors you know that this is not the case. I think that we are returning to centralization and control, but it is worse because now relations within the company are no longer characterized by much friendship to compensate for this and to support the love for the company which existed before. There is no identification with this new company. We do not know what it is anyway. (Engineer)

Declining Union Power

Management's ability to introduce radical changes disadvantageous to employees was enhanced by declining union power. With the introduction of neoliberal reforms in the mid-1990s, it was very difficult for the Confederation of Brazilian Unions (CUT) and its member unions to maintain the confrontational strategy that had been successful in the 1980s. A strategy of mass mobilization could not be sustained in an economy in which unemployment was rising and inflation falling. Whereas much of the drive behind the union movement at the end of the 1980s had arisen from the inability of successive governments to control rampant inflation, in the 1990s industrial restructuring forced unions to concentrate on defending jobs (Sandoval, 2001).

The union was by this time too weak to mobilize any effective opposition to privatization. Some managers suggested that the union failed to gain support because its approach to mobilization did not work as well as it had done in the past. Trade union strategies in Brazil relied excessively on verbal protest rather than action. Activism became an end in itself (Boito, 1994). The union was more concerned with engaging in opposition *per se* – in a general political struggle – than with formulating relevant and specific policies. According to a former human resources manager in the company:

> In my view the union movement grew weaker because of the kind of negotiating strategy it was using. The movement's problem is that it values politics as an end

itself. It does not matter if they win causes. What is important is mobilization itself, not achieving goals. The character of their motivation is political only. When top management discovered that, it became easier to deal with the union. The union believes that what unifies workers is the political fight itself. But nothing is gained from that.

He continued:

In Brazil, union officials have been trained by the Catholic Church. There was an institute in São Paulo named Casa Mar where this training took place. They were educated to articulate discourses and engage in political fighting, but they did not have a Plan B if their fight failed. They did not prepare for the possibility of a failure to prevent privatization. It is just like when a dog runs barking after a car. What can the dog do, if the car stops?

Another interpretation is that in Brazil, union goals became confused with those of the Workers Party (PT). Like the PT, their focus was on exerting influence in the capital, Brasília, rather than at ground level:

The goal of these guys was to get to the government. The unions were the instrument of the PT's political fight. When privatization arrived they felt lost. They fought and fought against it, but were unprepared for a situation in which it went ahead despite their opposition. Their main target was to prevent privatization. When it actually happened, they did not know what to do. (Manager)

Other factors behind the decline in union power during the 1990s include the rise in unemployment and, taking the longer view, the loss of the political and social cause to be fought against the military regime for the restoration of democracy and its attendant rights.

Conclusion

During the period 1993–8, Telemig redefined its core business. In order to achieve its purpose senior management constructed a platform to support its goals by changing mentalities and building new competencies. The perception of the government's intention to deregulate the sector in the near future encouraged senior managers to develop strategies to obtain resources externally, through forming strategic alliances with the private sector, rather than internally within the state.

Examination of Telemig's strategic change and reconstruction highlights two relevant issues. The first is the notion of strategy as movement mentioned by one of the managers. This simile seems to combine the elements of an emerging strategy as defining by Whittington's (2003) idea of strategy as practice and Mintzberg's (1994) earlier work on emerging strategies. In his work, Whittington (2003) discusses how strategy emerges informally from managerial activities, such as through team projects, through learning and through daily experience such as writing reports and giving *Powerpoint* presentations. This closely describes what took place in Telemig. However, the idea of movement seems to incorporate another very important element of strategy making, namely the notion of negotiated strategy. The ways in which managers in this chapter describe strategy suggest that a negotiated strategy is one in which mobilization and legitimation play an important role in its evolution.

Mintzberg suggests that the results achieved by an emerging strategy can be totally distinct from what had been planned. Within the overall plan laid down by the government, preparation for privatization emerged within Telemig from the grass roots as the outcome of a political process of negotiation, mobilization and building legitimation. A group of senior managers had to mobilize to re-invent Telemig. This involved various actions, including building legitimation through benchmarking, by showing to Telemig what kind of processes successful organizations were using. The issuing of the document *Building Telemig's Transformation* represented a further attempt to legitimate the proposed changes. Senior management also took action to obtain resources externally through strategic alliances with the private sector and through negotiation within the state telecommunications hierarchy to get their projects approved.

Mobilization was an important engine in the process of privatization. Through their place within the government's network, Telemig's senior managers were co-participants in the design of privatization and in the redefinition of the future institutional environment. Telemig's CEOs and VP, and some of its engineers and managers, belonged to inter-organizational networks in favour of change and privatization. Its managers made connections with MNCs and took them as the model. Some were involved in the government's designs for privatization. These ideas were then fed back and disseminated within the company through educational programmes and training.

The recognition that privatization was the best alternative to political influence in the company's policies and strategies gained it substantial support among senior managers. Two main factors lent legitimacy to privatization as an adaptive option. Managers' conceptions of privatization were anchored in neoliberal discourse, which defended the advantages of the free market as a driver of economic development and performance improvement at the company level. There was an understanding among senior career managers that privatization would enhance managerial choice and, like in the old days, would put the company back on the track of economic rationality. Second, there was an internal consensus on the importance of eliminating direct interference by populist politicians in the company's policy-making. Privatization was viewed as the most feasible path to that end. In short, privatization was a movement that co-evolved within both government and the company, a co-evolution that progressed through networking between the both levels.

This chapter also describes the new factors in Telemig's co-evolution that occurred following privatization. It draws attention to the relevance of the corporate governance changes that took place during 1998–2000 and their consequences for employees and the union. It indicates how the change of ownership brought about company restructuring and a revision of employment contracts. It indicates how the discourse on employability was important in preparing the ground for downsizing and the breach of trust that followed privatization. The revision of the employee contract that followed privatization was important in 'breaking the union's bones' and, according to one director, it neutered its capacity to act against subsequent restructuring initiatives by management. It laid the ground for a less obtrusive implementation of the shareholder-value culture and structure. In short, the contribution of this chapter is to show how a company's evolution is driven by a simultaneous combination of issues that interact and mutually reinforce each other, such as redefinition of the core business, downsizing and the breach of the psychological contract.

An important development was the weakening of the trade union's capacity for counter-mobilization. Senior management mobilization to get privatization under way generated a counter-mobilization movement by the union. However, as privatization came to affect core elements of the employment contract, such as employment security and remuneration, this weakened the union's capacity to mobilize against these changes. By this time, the trade union movement in Brazil had substantially lost its mobilization capacity, and one of the reasons for this was growing unemployment. The perception of a weakening trade union movement left management relatively free to break with the past and to introduce radical changes. Breaking with the past had a particular meaning for senior managers. In their mind, it represented the move towards an ideal organization, regulated by the economic rationalities of the financial markets, free from state ties and union pressures.

Notes

1 Earnings Before Interest, Depreciation Taxes, and Amortization. This is an approximate measure of a company's operating cash flow.
2 Corporativism, in Latin American political science, refers to the organization of interest groups to promote their vested interests though close links with the state.

References

Boito, A. (1994) The state and trade unionism in Brazil. *Latin American Perspectives*, 21, 7–23.

Börsch, A. (2004) Globalization, shareholder value, restructuring: the non-transformation of Siemens. *New Political Economy*, 9, 365–87.

Brockner, J. and Siegel, P. (1996) Understanding the interaction between procedural and distributive justice: the role of trust. In R. M. Kramer and T. R. Tyler (eds), *Trust in Organizations. Frontiers of Theory and Research*. Thousand Oaks, CA: Sage, pp. 390–413.

Brown, A. D. (2006) A narrative approach to collective identities. *Journal of Management Studies*, 43, 731–53.

Carrieri, A. P. (2001) O fim do mundo Telemig: A transformação das significações culturais em uma empresa de telecomunicações. Doctoral thesis, UFMG-CEPEAD.

CEPAL (1998) *La inversión extranjera en América Latina y el Caribe*. Santiago de Chile: CEPAL.

Fransman, M. (2001) The evolution of the telecommunication industry into the internet age. *Communication and Strategies*, 43, 57–113.

Gonçalves, R. (2000) Centralização do capital em escala global e desnacionalização da economia brasiliera. In P. da M. Veiga (ed.), *O Brasil e os desafios da globalização*. Rio de Janeiro: Relume-Dumara, pp. 79–95.

Histórico da Telemig [History of Telemig] (1997) Belo Horizonte: Telemig.

Kaufman, R. R. (1977) Corporatism, clientelism, and partisan conflict: a study of seven Latin American countries. In J. M. Malloy (ed.), *Authoritarism and Corporatism in Latin America*. Pittsburgh: University of Pittsburgh Press, pp. 109–48.

Keefe, J. H. and Batt, R. (1997) Restructuring of telecommunications in the United States. In H. Katz (ed.), *Telecommunications: Restructuring Work and Employment Relations Worldwide*. Ithaca, NY: ILR Press, pp. 31–88.

Lee, G. (2001) Towards a contingent model of key staff retention: the new psychological contract reconsidered. *South African Journal of Business Management*, 32, 1–9.

Luz, T. R. da (2001) *Telemar-Minas: competências que marcam a diferença*. Thesis submitted for the title of Doctor in Administration at Universidade Federal de Minas Gerais, Belo Horizonte.

Mintzberg, H. (1994) *The Rise and Fall of Strategic Planning*. New York: The Free Press.

Murillo, V. (2000) From populism to neoliberalism. Labor unions and market reforms in Latin America. *World Politics*, 52, 135–74.

Pinheiro, A. C., Giambiagi, F. and Gostkorzewicz, J. (1999) O desempenho macroeconômico do Brasil nos anos 90. In F. Giambiagi and M. M. Mesquita (eds), *A economia Brasileira nos anos 90*. Rio de Janeiro: BNDES.

Pires, J. C. L. (1999) Políticas regulatórias no setor de telecomunicações: a experiência internacional e o caso brasileiro. Textos para Discussão no. 71. Rio de Janeiro: BNDES.

Robinson, S. L. and Rousseau, D. M. (1994). Violating the psychological contract: not the exception but the norm. *Journal of Organizational Behavior*, 15, 245–59.

Sandoval, S. A. M. (2001) The crisis of the Brazilian labor movement and the emergence of alternative forms of working-class contention in the 1990s. *Revista Psicologia Politica*, 20, 173–95.

Schneider, B. R. (2004) Organizing interests and coalitions in the politics of market reform in Latin America. *World Politics*, 56, 456–79.

Shima, W. T. (2004) The implications for innovation in Brazilian telecommunications. *International Journal of Technology Management and Sustainable Development*, 3(1), 3–16.

Whittington, R. (2003) The work of strategizing and organizing: for a practice perspective. *Strategic Organization*, 1, 117–25.

Wohlers de Almeida, M. and Crossetti, P. (1997) *Infra-estrutura, perspectivas de reorganização: telecomunicações*. Brasilia: IPEA.

PART III

Multidimensional Co-evolution

CHAPTER SEVEN

Organizational Culture

Introduction

As pointed out in the previous chapters, the evolution of Telemig is marked by various dimensions of change, one of them being organizational culture. This chapter discusses the emergence of organizational subcultures at different periods of the organization's life. It describes Telemig's root metaphor as the common element between different periods of the organization's history and across different groups and levels. The company's root metaphor – the idea of the organization as a family – was simultaneously an element of common organizational identification across groups, and a managerial tool to control opposition and discourage the formation of countercultures.

A root metaphor conveys basic assumptions (Smircich, 1983; Schein, 1992) about the organization that are meaningful to employees. It carries meanings that are cognitive and emotional in nature, but it can also represent material conditions of significance for employees. Root metaphors usually symbolize values or organizational features that members cherish and wish to maintain despite their different interests. Unifying meanings are embedded in tradition and they can survive for a long period of time, as organizational members protect these meanings under threatening situations. Root metaphors have an important role in organizations, as they are embedded in meanings that tie different groups together, preventing the organization from falling apart in periods of crisis and radical change.

Several studies view organization culture as holistically comprising shared values (Kotter and Heskett, 1992; Schein, 1992). This is a problematic view, however, as research indicates that organizations are pluralistic in nature, and that conflict is endemic within them (Hinings et al., 1973; Pfeffer, 1981; Greenwood and Hinings, 1996). Individuals see themselves only to a partial extent as members of an organizational culture. It may therefore be difficult to attain a cultural consensus beyond the scope of particular groups or specific issues (Martin, 1992, 2002), but as this chapter shows, there are some cultural values that the whole membership of an organization may fight to preserve.

This chapter contributes to our knowledge on organizational evolution by discussing how the root metaphor can be a tool for political infighting and resistance to change. In times of crisis, the root metaphor helps to maintain the organization's equilibrium, preventing it from falling apart. Telemig's root metaphor – the 'Telemig family' – was the guiding ideal that supported employee's mobilization against changes that could threaten their interests, such as in the employment contract. A root metaphor is a symbolic representation of what members define as being the organization's most precious characteristic, but this symbolic representation also stands for material conditions.

Symbols emerge from history and are rooted in practice (Anthony, 1994). Symbols have a strategic importance to organizations in the sense that they connect imagination and idealization with the material features of the organization. A symbol may become an object of contest if its material representation is the focus of dispute between groups. Because of that symbolic characteristic, root metaphors can promote conflicting situations as they may endow legitimacy to political infighting. They can offer a frontier of resistance to change and in so doing keep the interests of groups hidden. It is more reasonable and unobtrusive to fight for an organizational symbol that represents given conditions then to expose group self-interests.

Under conditions of intense external and internal pressure, the organization's root metaphor may be the only thread that binds the organization together. Root metaphors may emerge strongly in periods of organizational transformation, not only as a defence mechanism to provide some stability in periods of greater uncertainty and ambiguity (Brown, 1995), but also as a reminder to organizational members of their past. Root metaphors embellish the past in order to protect the organization from the future.

When managers introduce radical changes that affect the power basis of groups – their material and symbolic representations – cultural differentiation and fragmentation are likely to become more evident. The concepts of cultural integration, differentiation and fragmentation have been employed by Martin (1992, 2002) to understand conditions of consensus, division, contradiction and ambiguity in organizations. Martin identifies three *cultural conditions* that are useful to our analysis. An organizational culture is 'integrated' when it reflects a wide consensus, 'differentiated' when it is confined to certain subcultures in opposition to others and 'fragmented' when there is little consensus at all and a root metaphor is absent.[1]

Key Concepts

Organizational culture consists of ideas, values and activities that are specific to a given organization and have special relevance to its members (Brown, 1995). Collective

manifestations, such as beliefs, rituals and other activities, establish meaningful connections between the past, present and future (Pettigrew, 1979). These meanings
constitute the social and emotional 'thread' that holds people together in the
organization. This emotional thread may encompass various levels and units in the
organization and be stronger at particular points of its trajectory. Root metaphors
convey meanings that can be shared widely throughout an organization, such as
those associated with its survival. Other meanings are nurtured in specific groups
or collective categories, such those that mediate issues relating to members' identity (Alvesson and Willmott, 2002) or represent claims to resources and power (Pfeffer
and Salancik, 1978). Though it is often assumed that an organizational culture is
widely shared, closer analysis reveals that organizations can be differentiated into
various subcultures, sometimes appearing so fragmented that even a minimal level
of consensus is hard to establish (Van Maanen and Barley, 1985). Organizational
culture is therefore composed of a mosaic of meanings that are shared to various
degrees and in small as well as large compartments.

Subcultures can develop both around common bases for identification and through
the activity of groups, which mediate and protect the interests of their members.
They may remain acquiescent for a time, but their adherents can form alliances
to advance their interests (Pfeffer and Salancik, 1978; Pfeffer, 1981). The groups
bearing different subcultures vary in their capacity to mobilize material and
symbolic resources. A subculture can become a dominant culture if the groups
concerned unify adherents around ideas that incorporate wider interests (Clarke
et al., 1987). These adherents can include various stakeholders, such as government agencies in the case of organizations subject to institutional ownership and/or
regulation. If a subculture reflects a cohesive group and defends 'plausible' ideas,
or there is a recognition that it can address specific situations better than other
subcultures (Abravanel, 1983), it may become a credible alternative for the entire
organization (Gagliardi, 1986).

A subculture that attains a dominant position can then be advanced as the
organization's *corporate culture*. A corporate culture can be both integrative and
dominant if it is able to incorporate disagreements and contradictions and finds
modes of expression that highlight mainly the points of unification (Anthony, 1994).
Usually these points of unification conciliate differences among groups and encourage the sense of belonging. If the corporate culture loses legitimacy through being
unable to provide positive meanings for organizational members, they may turn
to their group membership for identification, forming subcultures around different
occupations, organizational levels or associations (Gagliardi, 1986). In this situation, members tend to identify more with peers and occupational values than with
the organization as a whole (Van Maanen and Barley, 1985).

A subculture may be defined as a *counterculture* when one or more significant
occupational groups consider a corporate culture to be illegitimate, because it
challenges core values – the root metaphor – and, therefore, basic assumptions are
not being put into practice (Gagliardi, 1986). In order to protect root metaphors,

adherents of countercultures can increase their power by making key alliances externally. Trade unions, for example, can increase their bargaining power if they establish
cross-industry links and if they are associated with political parties. Political actions
such as these can evidence the oppositional nature of countercultures (Scott, 1990).
Another way in which countercultures manifest themselves is by using metaphors
and subversive humour, which articulate opposition in subtle ways. These manifestations permit a negotiation of meanings and disguise the identity of contenders.
They may appear frequently in organizations where consensus is fragile and obtained
through ongoing negotiation, and where oppositional cultures are ineffective in
leading radical change (Rodrigues and Collinson, 1995).

Method

Telemig's organizational culture was accessed through interviews with managers
and employees and by examining company documents. Documents such as the
autobiographies of the founders of the sector were essential to understanding their
role in the creation of Telemig's culture. Company reports and the trade union
newspaper provided key insights in the understanding of the different cultures present within the company. Questions 1.5, 1.7 and 3.6 in the interview checklist
shown in table 3.2 were relevant to organizational culture. Narratives on the issues
arising in the company's history and concerning its corporate identity were also
used to inform our analysis. Organizational culture was captured by content analysing
all interviewees' narratives about the company's history in terms of anecdotes,
rituals, myths, heroes and leaders. We also analysed materials from the trade union
newspaper, in particular metaphors, stories and cartoons.

Integration around a Founding Culture: 1973–1985

The period 1973–85 set the conditions for the installation of a normative isomorphism that extended across the whole telecommunications sector and for the
creation of a root metaphor that encouraged employees to continue to identify
with the company. The normative isomorphism and the root metaphor provided
the basis for cultural integration during the foundation period.

Integration was enforced by a dominant military/engineering coalition united
by a military ideology and structure that was isomorphic throughout the sector.
As the agents of professionalization in telecomunications, the dominant coalition
created the conditions for a normative isomorphism that tended to reproduce
rules and discourses that mirrored those of educational institutions (DiMaggio and
Powell, 1991). They held that the best way to organize was through technocracy,
bureaucracy and rigid discipline. This led to a favourable context for the institutionalization of technocracy as a powerful organizational ideology.

Technocracy was pervasive throughout the whole sector and was viewed as one of the most important features of Telemig's culture in this period. One of the basic assumptions in the organization was that technical considerations should override political criteria. Politics were considered to be illegitimate: 'parochial, divisive and, above all, not based on expertise' (O'Donnell, 1979, p. 81). These beliefs boosted the image and influence of the engineers in technical departments. Engineers were considered to be the heroes of the organization, because of their innovative capacity and, even more, because they were responsible for implementing the company's mission – contributing to the social and economic development of the country.

Technocracy was 'the way we did things in the company', one manager mentioned. The importance of engineering and innovation was made evident in ceremonies for the distribution of awards for technical invention and innovation. In these ceremonies the company also recalled its founders and the values they enforced: hard work, honesty and achievement. General Alencastro, Telemig's first CEO, was remembered as a hero of the telecoms sector, and for his moral qualities and charisma.

Nationalism was an important component of the technocratic mentality that was reflected in the company's policies. It emphasized the protection of national boundaries and the prevention of predatory multinational activities (Evans, 1979). Being associated with the protection of national interests meant that the company was growing on the basis of its own independent efforts; it also meant 'sweating blood' for the benefit of the country. It reflected an enthusiasm in contributing to the 'economic miracle'. Pioneering represented the 'superhuman' efforts to expand the system under unfavourable conditions. Nationalism also maintained the importance of insulating the company from global competitive pressures.

There are some conditions that define military governance, including the suppression of voice, control of information through a rigid hierarchy and centralized command and communications (Winsor, 1996). All these features define an authoritarian rule. They were evident in the way things used to be done in Telemig. For example, relationships between the union and employees were primarily bureaucratic, with a focus on legal and social benefits. The union had to conceal any opposition to the military and it was, in general, perceived to be aligned with management interests. Communications were linear. A manager could not directly communicate with a superior of his superior. Circulation of information was also restricted. 'Even irrelevant information was controlled', said one interviewee. Employees complained that managers were 'those guys in suits and locked in their rooms'.

The root metaphor – the shared notion that Telemig was a 'big family' – mitigated authoritarianism. Telemig 'family' represented the ethos of collaboration and friendship created at the time. The principal functions of the 'family' were to bridge hierarchical and occupational differences and solve practical problems.

The family metaphor was rooted in the way Telemig was first constituted. Most people had relatives in the company. One manager mentioned the following about the military period:

Telemig has an interesting characteristic. It is a family organization. I am a product of this. I am a son of an ex-employee, my sister works in the company, I met my wife in the company, and my sister met her husband here. Thus it is a family environment. I do not know whether this is bad or not. I think it is good because everybody loves this company and cares for it.

The Telemig family represented an entrenched paternalism. As one engineer commented, 'If an employee had a personal problem, the company provided assistance to the whole family.' The paternalist system ingrained in Telemig could also be noted through related metaphors mentioned by employees in their interviews. Telemig was also termed 'a widow' to indicate benevolence and compassion towards employees. Other equivalent metaphors were those of 'a father and a mother'.

The family metaphor also has a material expression and this was represented by an advantageous and protective employment contract. State enterprises were recognized as good employers, and Telemig provided benefits generally unavailable in the private sector. Employees had a generous salary and pension fund, and the company provided 13 'monthly' salaries a year and other benefits. Most important was security of employment. As one employee put it, 'The problem with this company is that we cannot lay off the bad employee. Reasons for layoffs could be very serious, such as stealing or when the government decides to do this. I do not think it should be like this.' The following extracts suggests how the family metaphor was linked to the prevailing employment contract:

In the 1970s there was a policy of employment stability, which reinforced the idea of a big family. The majority of employees have 17 years of service. The staff grew old and as a result there was a stable and permanent relationship between the employees. This created a type of togetherness that you can only find in a family relationship. (Manager)

This company is a family. Being a family it cannot dismiss people. It is inconceivable to sack a member of your family. (Manager)

Security of employment was reinforced in organization rituals and ceremonies where employees received awards for long service to the company. The terms of employment could be defined as a psychological contract where employee protection was paid back with loyalty and hard work. According to two engineers:

People were very loyal to the company. There was comradeship. If one needed blood many people offered their help. There was commitment with the organization and with what we do. Work in Telemig was like working for a community.

During the military time, the employees were more attached to the company. We loved it. We looked after the company as it looked after us. It was like that despite their authoritarianism.

Disintegration of the Founding Culture and Growing Differentiation: 1985–1993

The military regime began to be challenged as early as 1978, when the government announced a political amnesty and its intention gradually to restore civil liberties. One of the most important factors contributing to the decline of military legitimacy was the growing popular demand for democracy (Dreifuss, 1981; Rodrigues and Child, 2003). Democracy brought social pressures for the institutional reinstatement of political rights, and this led to the re-emergence of trade unions as key political actors.

The weakening of the military regime encouraged the creation of the PT and the Central Labour Union. The national telecommunications union strengthened itself through building a political alliance with the PT. This enabled the union to become more active within the companies. Institutional change granted more latitude to organized labour, which soon learned to make demands on management. The union played a leading role in the social movement opposing the military regime. By the end of the 1970s, the regime had lost political support among the population and in 1985 Brazil returned to democracy. Knowing of the importance of the family for the employee, the union resorted to the family metaphor in its attempts to mobilize against management policies and practices, but so did management, as we describe next.

1 The corporate culture

From 1985 onward, appointments to Telemig's board and management were governed by party political affiliations. Managers were viewed as part of a political rather than technical coalition, with consequences for their capacity to create an integrated culture. To secure legitimacy as power holders, managers tried to differentiate themselves from the Telemig techno-bureaucracy by introducing a new corporate culture that was less militaristic and more democratic. Accordingly, they decentralized the organization and encouraged middle and lower management involvement in decision-making. They did, however, retain those organizational values and ceremonies from the military period that they thought would be useful to their purposes, trying to revive the family metaphor by inviting employees' families to visit the organization. This was to make public the presumed unity between the 'Telemig family' and that of the employee.

2 Subcultures and the emergence of a counterculture

Senior and middle managers viewed themselves as agents for the new corporate culture, though this failed to gain widespread acceptance. The interviews portray an increasingly divided Telemig during this period. The engineers and the union saw themselves as having identities of their own. Both groups detached themselves from the corporate culture, but in different ways. Engineers did not share corporate views on how the organization should be managed, but they did not engage in public opposition. The union developed and expounded a counterculture. With strong and articulate union opposition during this period, Telemig's organizational culture became differentiated.

Under military management, technocracy had been considered superior to other forms of rationality. This was reinforced by the founders' culture at the top and reiterated at the operational level by engineers and technicians. Their 'rare competence' granted engineers status and power. Their position was reaffirmed in the organization's public rituals, such as award ceremonies, and in assumptions that engineers were competent to hold positions of power in the organization and in the telecommunications system in general. When the new management took control, it put an end to these rituals and proved generally insensitive to the assumed superiority of technical rationality.

In the 1980s, government money for state companies began to dry up, forcing telecommunications companies to redefine their mission as solely service-providing organizations. The power of the planning and development department declined, bringing further serious consequences for the engineers who were already seeing their prestige wane. A conflict arose as to whether engineers or career managers were better equipped to occupy management positions, with the union taking the side of the engineers. Managerial discourse revealed an attempt to delegitimize the position of engineers as the core professional group and at the same time created justification for the corporate culture. Comments that managers made during the 1986–90 interviews illustrate this view. For example:

> There are cases when the person is a qualified engineer, but not a good manager.

> Because Telemig is a state company we need to have an interface with public powers and politicians.

The following are taken from interviews with engineers at the same time:

> Politicians can now place all kinds of demands on the organization.

> It used to be necessary to have an engineering qualification to get a position in this organization. Now top management bring in their political allies.

The fact that management now gave precedence to political criteria over technical concerns created a credibility gap, because the founding culture had institutionalized technocracy. In the engineers' views, top managers contributed to an erosion of the sense of community identification and loyalty to the organization. As one engineer stated: 'Today loyalty is not linked to institutions, but to those who have power.' One of the company's founders said:

In 1985 the opening up of politics permitted interference in telecommunications, which I think is bad. In the 1970s the military had control over decision-making and finances, which is why it worked. When the system had to coexist with politics, it went backwards. (Ex-president)

Political interference was a main reason for lack of motivation:

The level of motivation is completely different. During the company's foundation the employee used to 'dress in the company's shirt' for 24 hours a day. Everyone stood up for the company when needed. Nowadays it is completely different as people have their own vested interests in the company. (Manager)

During the period 1985–93, the trade union newspaper, *The Goat*, employed various metaphors to criticize management for pursuing an even worse version of the militaristic culture and for allowing political interference in the company. Managers were portrayed as pigs and animals in a circus. They were castigated for being 'nepotistic', 'patrimonial' and 'corrupt', while management practices were classified as 'insulting' and 'revolting' (Rodrigues and Collinson, 1995). Managers were also criticized for bringing relatives and friends to work in the company without going through a proper recruitment and selection process. 'This was a disaster for the Telemig family, because others refused to integrate with them', a manager said.

At that time the company union in association with the national telecommunications union and the PT achieved an impressive degree of mobilization. It pushed aggressively for changes in the corporate culture, and pressed for a more democratic and open organization; one that would also preserve the company's technocratic values. This union activism caught managers, who were short of political skills, by surprise. As the Human Resources Manager admitted, managers were not able to argue and negotiate effectively. One way to deal with union activism was to appeal to the metaphor of the Telemig family. Recollecting this period, a manager said:

Union activism at that time caught management wearing 'their shorts, rather than their trousers'. The union got employees' families on their side. What we did was to appeal to people's families as well to try to get their support. We visited them; we sent messages explaining why employee involvement in activism could jeopardize their jobs and their positions in the company.

He continued:

We created a programme of organized visits by employees' families to Telemig to neutralize the union's influence. In this programme we brought the family for a tour of the company in which we presented our main goals and showed the relevance of the employee's work. On that occasion the worker's family received a small token, a T-shirt stating: 'The Telemig family. You are part of it.'

Table 7.1 Frequency and meanings of the family metaphor in the union newspaper

Period	Meanings	Frequency of mention
1980–5	Friendly cooperative environment. Communitarian organization. Organization that values employment security and years of service. Paternalist organization: helps employees to solve family and personal problems.	84
1986–93	Telemig family and employment security as propaganda, manipulation and myth.	204
1994–2000	Telemig family defunct. Present in the collective memory. Reminder of the good old times.	68

However, the union claimed that the founding culture had actually been subverted in order to manipulate and control the employees: 'When the union showed its opposition to restructuring, managers contacted the employees' families to get their support against the union. This is manipulation' (Union official).

Investigations by the first author of the family metaphor in the union newspaper indicate that the meanings associated with the 'family' changed from denoting a 'cooperative and friendly environment' during the foundation period to a parody during 1985–93. The 'family' and the 'mother' metaphors appeared together and in periods of crisis.

As indicated in table 7.1, the family image appeared more frequently from 1986 to 1993, appearing 204 times in the newspaper (57 per cent of all appearances), during which time employees felt threatened by the implementation of redundancies. As the table indicates, the family metaphor appeared many times in the union newspaper with different meanings. During this period, the union portrayed the open door policy as a poor joke and a myth, signifying management's attempts at propaganda and manipulation:

> Top management talks a lot about defending the Telemig family, but this does not exist any more. It is mere propaganda. (Manager)

> In the past there was a culture of a big family. Nobody sent anyone away. Now the big family is a myth. (Manager)

> The open door is a joke. In reality it means that it is the door to the street that has been opened to the employees. (Union official)

A comparison of the newspaper information with interview data leads to the conclusion that management's introduction of a redundancy scheme and discontinuation of the long-service policy lay behind the sense that Telemig family had been lost, and behind calls for its restoration.

At the end of the 1980s the federal government demanded a reduction in the size of state enterprises. Telemig's management made the decision to lay off 300 employees. A director explained that:

> The government had demanded that telecoms companies cut costs. We then called all the managers on a Sunday and asked them for a list of employees to be dismissed. . . . This was kept most secret inside the organization. Each manager had a number of people to reduce. On Monday afternoon we provided the employees in the list with a dismissal letter. The union tried to shout, but they did not have prior information about this.

The way employees felt about this had been captured in the interviews:

> Today there is terrorism in the organization. Management has dismissed people, but they did not convince us about the reason why they did that. (Engineer)

> There is no loyalty in this organization. What management has done was a betrayal of our notion of a big family in Telemig. (Engineer)

From Differentiation to Increasing Fragmentation: 1993–2000

During this period, institutional pressures became relevant in changing the relationships between Telemig and the market, with significant implications for the organization's culture. By the early 1990s it was apparent that the development model based on state intervention was not meeting economic and social expectations. The government that took office in 1993 expressed its preference for a neoliberal framework by putting forth a message that idealized market virtues. Ministers, officials and politicians in the government parties were the main conveyors of neoliberalism (Boschi et al., 2000). The role of CEOs was to turn state companies around, change values and make practices more compatible with neoliberal ideals (Pires, 1999), including privatization.

In 1993, the government started to deregulate the telecoms sector. It allowed competition in equipment manufacturing and announced its intention to open the market to foreign investors. The Ministry of Telecommunications injected resources for improving the financial and managerial aspects of companies in order to proceed with further deregulation that culminated in the privatization of the sector in 1998. Deregulation and an injection of funding sought to make companies more responsive to market pressures.

1 The corporate culture

During 1993–2000 Telemig went through radical changes. It is reasonable to separate this period into two periods because this division represents the sharp changes that took place in the company and its environment. The period of pre-privatization, 1993–8, was marked by significant competitive and institutional pressures to develop into a market-oriented organization. The new corporate culture incorporated ideas not only about what the organization should be but also about the ideal employee. It began by insisting on market virtues. An important concept behind the new corporate culture was that of 'organizing for the clients', stressing the need to become sensitive to market changes and pressures from different types of customers. As one manager put it, 'The company has to be more aggressive now. It cannot wait for the clients to come to it. Now it has to go after them.' Another said: 'Managers used to spend 90 per cent of their time managing technical staff. Today we spend 90 per cent of our time looking for clients' (Manager).

There was no mention by management of the family ideal as in the earlier periods. The values of the corporate culture were now those of the market-oriented organization. 'Speed and flexibility' was another message of the corporate culture. One of the directors proudly compared Telemig's pace of change to a 'jet engine replacing a turbo-prop during flight'. Another referred to the pachyderm structure of the former system, saying that Telemig was 'an elephant that mutated into a bird . . . it can now fly wherever there is a more favourable environment'. This idealized image of a market-oriented organization was understood by management as being linked to a learning process involving 'oxygenating, erasing or cleansing the organization of antiquated ideas and practices' (Manager). A process of resocialization was initiated through an early retirement programme and intensive training in market skills. Preparation for privatization was also seen to require extensive renewal through re-engineering, delayering and downsizing. There was a reduction in the number of managerial and engineering positions.

The market-oriented organization idea involved concepts of the role of employees in the organization. An important idea was the 'employable employee', involving the need for continuous improvement. Employees should find ways of upgrading skills. The more these competencies were valued in the labour market, the greater the possibility of keeping their current job at Telemig or finding a job elsewhere. Linked to this idea was that of the 'renewable employee'. This implied that employees should be prepared to change their opinions of the world. There was no place for employees that were stuck in old ways of doing things. Another metaphor was 'multifunctionality', by which employees were expected to change jobs and locations. This set of expectations involved preparing employees for downsizing after privatization. A complementary idea was that of 'the competitive employee'.

2 Subcultures and the counterculture

Culture fragmentation has been described by Martin (1992, 2002) as being marked by contradiction and ambiguity. Root metaphors do not serve as points of unification. One of the reasons is that they lose the material basis that sustains their symbolic value. In other words, resource allocation and practices do not confirm their centrality in life in organizations.

In Telemig, the union became progressively weaker in the 1990s. The union movement in Brazil was losing power significantly (Donadone and Grun, 2002), while engineers had lost much of their glamour and centrality due to changes in technology and the strategy of turning Telemig into a service-provider company.

Job insecurity became an important issue for the subgroups within Telemig. It contributed to the rejection of the new corporate culture, but at the same time its threat maintained opposition within limits. It was an important management strategy to secure acquiescence from different categories of staff. Employees did not accept competition, the motto of the new corporate culture, as readily as the company's leaders envisaged. Engineers offered comments such as the following:

> Nowadays it is like we were all at war, with each one of us wanting to hold on to our jobs tightly as possible. The idea of 'wearing the company uniform' has gone.

> They say that we are in a battle for clients, but inside there is a war of nerves. They are afraid of competition that does not exist; it is a phantom. Instead, they should be afraid of failing to create an environment that encourages what they say they want: quality and efficiency.

Managers and engineers both resented the collapse of Telemig's earlier identity as a family. As a source of meaning for employee identity, the market-orientated corporate culture failed to achieve the same level of integration as that of the founding period. In many people's perceptions, the bonds that had kept the company together had now gone. The following interview extracts illustrate this point:

> The organization is now worse than it was during the time of the military in terms of control over what we do. It is in fact even worse because the environment of the 'big family' has been taken away from us. (Engineer)

> There are no friends or family any more; everyone has to see the other as a competitor. (Manager)

In the period between 1993 and 2000, the company was often referred to by the union newspaper as a 'stepmother'. This new image, of Telemig as a stepmother who now 'worked against the family instead of being pro-family', was mentioned in the newspaper 80 times, generally to represent top management betrayal of the family ideal. Another, even more dramatic, portrayal was that of the company as a 'vampire', exploiting its employees. This representation appeared 50 times in the union newspaper during the same period. The interviews conducted during the period 1998–9 point to the meanings now attributed to the mother and the family metaphors:

> Telemar is more a stepmother than the mother that Telemig was. (Engineer)

> I do not like this situation. Do you know the feeling of losing a mother? (Engineer)

> Telemar is more a stepmother than anything else. You can call it Telemá.[2]

After privatization, Telemig started to build a shareholder culture. The new owners were business investors and bankers with little knowledge of the business. Their immediate concern was to restructure the company and thus integrate the various companies that were part of the group but spread in different geographic areas. This resulted in Telemig being completely decharacterized and being transformed into a sales office. It was obliged to change its name to Telemar Minas. The company went from being an elite unit in the telecommunications sector to a mere sales office that had no influence on conglomerate decisions or even decisions that concerned it individually. After privatization, several of Telemig's best executives were transferred to the central office and other companies in the group. Managers and technicians felt that their self-esteem had been undermined by the destruction of the organization they once fought to build. Several of Telemig's previous departments disappeared and the first one to go was the Human Resources Department:

> Looking to what happened to the third floor [where the Human Resources Department had been located] you understand that Telemig is not the same any more. When they say that the company needs to be shaken up that means pressure upon us.

> Have you seen what happened to the HR Department? What is the kind of feeling that it gives you? It has been completely dismantled. It is really awful to look at the place. At old Telemig HR had a whole floor in the head office and each regional office had its own HR Department. Today they have just a tiny bit of the floor and there is just one person doing the old operational stuff.

The shareholder value culture involved an emphasis on costs, extracting higher productivity from employees, greater accountability, employability and refocusing of tasks, downsizing and a change of location. Some of these policies clearly represented a move away from the former psychological contract that defined Telemig as a family. Previously, training and education was part of the implicit contract with the company. Now, Telemar's employees were expected to look after their own education and development:

> Telemar is another world. The employee has to compete and has to look after his or her own employability. I do not think that this is happening only in this company. Everywhere is like that. (Engineer)

> In the mid-1990s the company warned everyone that we had to pay for our own training. (Engineer)

A former engineer said the following:

> In my memory there is just old Telemig. I do not wish to remember my time in Telemar. Although they increased productivity substantially and improved the effectiveness of meetings they did awful things. Everybody was scared stiff that they would be next in the line to be sacked.

Downsizing was seen by employees as breaching the contract that was taken for granted in old Telemig:

> The company wanted to multiply the valued added and did things that would have be seen as inconceivable. For example, in the old Telemig we used to make 20 links a month. In Telemar with the same people we did 180 links per month. What people resented was that productivity was going well, the company was going well and yet they found that they still had to downsize further. (Engineer)

> Telemig as a family is dead.

A heightened emphasis on saving and making money out of transferring wealth from the employees to shareholders, a common phenomenon in companies that stress shareholder value (Blair, 1995), has been detected in Telemar:

> Telemar is very different from Telemig. Telemig used to value its engineers. In Telemar it was all focused on numbers. They lay off our best engineer, a genius, without any further thought. It is just very silly. How is the company going to retain its knowledge? Everything goes, including what they need. (Engineer)

> They were completely ruthless and intended to save money on layoffs by sacking people before they could exercise the right to compensations and bonuses. They played with redundancies to avoid paying the employees their share of the profits. (Engineer)

During the period 1998–2004, the company undertook various restructurings. The first involved unification of various companies in various regions of the country in order to form a distinctive holding. The second consisted of the creation of a separate company, the mobile business, called OI, and the third major change involved the merger between Telemar and OI. The restructuring that occurred after 1998 involved fundamental changes in the psychological contract. According to more recent interviews with former managers, the employees have been continuously suffering from the 'survivor syndrome', a phenomenon described by Cascio (2002) as involving fear of imminent redundancy, low morale and trust. For example, two engineers said:

> There was a feeling of injustice around. People knew that the company was doing well, but that it would still lay off people. Many people became ill. The company did not care about the social aspects of its work. People did not trust each other and least of all management.

> It was all very unstable. People could make money and have better salaries compared with the old system. However, they knew they could be out at any moment.

Table 7.1 indicates that during the period 1994–2000, the family metaphor was mentioned in the newspaper as something present in the collective memory, as a reminder of good old times. As in the earlier period, managers tended to embellish the positive characteristics of the old technocracy. Residuals of the founders' culture were often evident in the discourse of managers, technicians and engineers. The virtues of the founders' culture came to be appreciated. For example, 'Telemig was a very good organization while it lasted. It is like a picture on the wall; it is a reference that we cannot lose' (Manager).

The union was the only group that displayed its antagonism to the corporate culture openly and publicly. This antagonism nevertheless was expressed more in terms of suffering than the open opposition that had been prevalent in the previous period. While managers who benefited from privatization argued that it was necessary for the company's survival, a metaphor representing the organization as a dark 'cave' was now introduced, appearing 57 times in the union newspaper between 1993 and 2000 and accompanied by cartoons and captions indicating anomie, such as 'Who am I?' This portrayed an insecurity concerning the future of the organization and its employees. The metaphor revealed a de-identification from top managers and the company. A manager commented that 'Telemig is now Telemar. This is like leaving one organization and entering another' (Manager).

Political and Institutional Dynamics of Organizational Culture Change

The development of Telemig's culture can be divided into three phases. The first represents a period of integration and dominance of the founding culture, which served as a basis for constructing the unifying ideal of the Telemig family. Although some characteristics associated with military management, such as authoritarianism, were openly rejected as the country adopted democracy, the family metaphor remained the essential source of cultural integration and indeed served to mitigate the authoritarianism. It was associated with various practices that contributed to integration, such as ceremonies recognizing long service and social events that involved employees' families with the company. Analogous to the distinctions made by Argyris and Schon (1978) with reference to organizational learning, one might say that an integrated organizational culture is likely when the 'espoused culture' is the same as 'the culture-in-use'. This consistency in putting into practice an organizational culture that was legitimate in the eyes of employees provided the foundation for its integration.

Military officers together with engineers were the main mediators of knowledge, managerial expertise and financial resources for the organization. The dominance of this group can be attributed in particular to its institutional embeddedness, reflecting the simultaneous existence of coercive, normative and professional isomorphism (DiMaggio and Powell, 1991), backed by the guarantee of resource supply (Oliver, 1992; Simons and Ingram, 1997). Cultural homogeneity within Telemig was justified by strong values and isomorphism, both reinforced by the state through its application of universal rules to all companies in the sector.

The second period is characterized by differentiation (Martin, 2002), evident with the formation of two subcultures: engineers/technicians, and the counterculture that developed with union support. The founding culture became deinstitutionalized and the 'culture-in-use' was no longer seen to reflect the espoused culture. Employees considered the discrepancy between the new managers' discourses and their practices to be illegitimate. Contributors to the union newspaper clearly suggested that managers were breaching trust in the Telemig family by dismissing career employees and instead employing their own friends and relatives. In their view, when Telemig's family ideal became divorced from practice, it became a myth manipulated by managers. This included using it as a tool to demobilize the trade union.

The third period is appropriately characterized as one of cultural fragmentation, when the root metaphor lost its power to unify the organization through either the corporate culture or the counterculture. Subcultures were visible and allied with a counterculture expressed by the union, but with a progressively weaker voice. The union was handicapped in advancing its interests because of the threat of unemployment through privatization. There was a feeling that the family metaphor was being undermined in favour of free market ideals but, because their jobs were threatened, no one risked open opposition. The union continued to express its views, but did not attack managers publicly as it had in the previous period. Further detachment from the public sector created a sense of anomie and a feeling of bereavement comparable to the loss of a family member. In this period, the family metaphor served as a reference point to remind the employees of the prospect of losing the core values of Telemig through privatization. It also reminded the employees of good times bygone. This appears to have been a case of what Emirbayer and Mische

(1998, p. 984) called 'creative reconstruction', namely reinterpreting the past in a positive light.

In Telemig, the family metaphor was the main touchstone for the legitimacy of its organizational culture through all three periods of integration, differentiation and fragmentation. As indicated in table 7.1, the meanings attached to the family metaphor changed over time. Initially, top managers were regarded as faithful to the family ideal because they followed practices that supported it. The family metaphor may be regarded as a 'super-rational truth' (Bate, 1994, p. 2) that served as a palliative to undesirable management strategies such as authoritarianism. In the second period, senior managers continued to proclaim their adherence to the family ideal but contrary practices served to undermine the legitimacy of their professed support. This was seen to make a myth of core values. Managers therefore lost legitimacy and employees transferred their loyalty to the union when it publicly condemned the managerial attack on Telemig's family ethos. In the third period, management no longer proclaimed its adherence to this ethos and the union therefore lost its legitimate focus for opposing management's implementation of privatization. This case therefore points to the presence or absence of a central unifying ideal as an important distinction between conditions of differentiation and fragmentation.

Based on the preceding analysis, table 7.2 summarizes the factors that the Telemig case suggests support different cultural conditions. Changes in these factors are therefore operative in promoting organizational culture change. An integrated culture

Table 7.2   Factors supporting different organizational cultural conditions

Organizational cultural condition	Root metaphor of the family as a unifying ideal	Legitimacy of the leading group in the eyes of employees	Relative power of leading group
Integration	Meaningful and universal	High	High. Backed by government and facing no significant opposition
Differentiation	Unifying ideal becomes a myth as practice diverges from it	Decreasing	Weakening. Reduced governmental support and opposition by key groups
Fragmentation	Present only in the collective memory	Low	Strengthening primarily due to support of government with privatization programme

is supported by the legitimacy of the leading group in the eyes of employees. It derives this legitimacy from its capacity to sustain a unifying ideal that organizational members accept as meaningful and that is applied consistently throughout the organization. Sustaining the ideal requires an ability to mobilize necessary political and material support. In the case of an organization like Telemig, which operated within a highly institutionalized environment, this support had to come from policy-makers, regulators and providers of finance.

Differentiation happens when the power or motivation of a leading group is unable to sustain a unifying ideal so that it comes to be regarded as a myth. When a leading group depends on institutional support for organizational resources, as was the case with Telemig, a withdrawal of that support weakens its ability to satisfy various interests within the organization. The constraint on resources obliges the leading group to adopt practices that diverge from the organization's unifying ideal, such as declaring redundancies. This further reduces the leadership's credibility and at the same time encourages the emergence of one or more oppositional groups who in turn solidify opposition to management's culture-in-use.

Fragmentation is associated with anomie, when a unifying ideal has lost its original meaning and now resides mostly in the collective memory (Halbwachs, 1992). It is likely to occur when oppositional groups are weak relative to the leading group. This situation creates a propitious terrain for the introduction of radical changes, such as in ownership and corporate culture. Fragmentation is encouraged when the power of oppositional groups is further weakened by the fact that the introduction of a new corporate culture – in this case one emphasizing a shift from a public service to a market orientation – deprives them of a traditional rallying point from which to contest change. A counterculture may lose its power of mobilization to defend a root metaphor when breaches in the psychological contract undermine the basis for attracting affiliates to the cause. A continuous pressure of imminent dismissal discourages opposition to management policies.

The Telemig case suggests a broader framework for understanding organizational culture change in companies that operate in an institutionalized environment. In these organizations, political changes are likely to occur as the result of ideologically inspired institutional changes in policies and rules. The latter can give rise to transitions in organizational ownership and leadership. These transitions have consequences for internal organizational politics that in turn modify the fragile equilibrium between the espoused culture and culture-in-use. Oppositional groups are likely to exert more pressure when inconsistencies between the two is deeper. If cultural differentiation evolves into fragmentation, however, the state of anomie together with a weak voice creates room for the introduction of radical change. Thus, while differentiation is likely to maintain continuity, fragmentation paradoxically may pave the way for the introduction of major changes in corporate culture. A fragmented culture could therefore be a relatively transitory phenomenon.

Anthony (1994) argues that corporate cultures asserting market values are likely to become powerful when supported by institutions that consider such values to be legitimate. The introduction of neoliberal ideology was the first point of support for the changes that took place in the period pre-privatization. The shareholder value model of management introduced by the new owners was a further point of support for the succeeding breaches of trust that happened after privatization. Eventually, employees may accept market and shareholder values as pragmatic reality. In this way, an ideology can obscure conflicts of interest in the eyes of organizational members, even when some alienation persists. The Telemig case adds to this argument by indicating that shareholder cultures also gain sway because their exponents control a key factor in the eyes of employees, namely the rules of employment. Thus, organizations based on shareholder values enforced by private owners may be able to enforce adherence to the corporate culture just as effectively as organizations subject to high institutional dependence.

Conclusion

Despite the considerable attention that organizational culture has received in recent years (Brown, 1995), there remains a need to understand how organizational culture changes over time and what drives the process. The longitudinal study that we develop here brings some insights into the nature and the origin of these changes. Central to the discussion is the notion of root metaphor as a unifying element among groups that stand for different values and beliefs. This chapter shows how the root metaphor facilitated mobilization of subcultures and countercultures by lending legitimacy to their causes.

This chapter suggests that cultural change is a multifaceted and multilevel process. It contributes to theory in two main ways. First, it highlights the political nature of the process, showing that deep cultural change can be attributed not to a single agent but to the mobilization of different groups within and across organizational levels. Second, it suggests that change towards either cultural integration or differentiation depends on the legitimacy of internal coalitions and their capacity to sustain integrative ideals.

This chapter has presented a historical and contextual account of organizational culture. Its aim was to shed light on the factors giving rise to different conditions of organizational culture and how such culture changes over time. It contributes to our knowledge of organizational cultures in several ways. First, it extends our understanding of 'root metaphors' (Smircich, 1983) and Martin's (2002) idea of 'home perspectives'. These authors employ these concepts with reference to the ontology of organizational culture, whereas the present study suggests that they can also usefully refer to the substance of culture in terms of what an organization's members perceive to be its central values. The ability of an organizational culture to represent a collective enterprise through use of a root metaphor or home perspective depends on the capacity of the symbolism to maintain unifying ideals, supported by practices that are meaningful to employees (Gagliardi, 1986).

Unifying ideals have different functions in times of integration, differentiation and fragmentation. Differentiation and fragmentation may ensue when managers are perceived as challenging the moral ground upon which a unifying ideal is based, such as perceived relations of reciprocity between managers and employees. For example, perceptions of secure employment are regulated by norms of reciprocity and the symbolic and material outcomes associated with it (Anthony, 1994). If the moral bases of cultural values weaken, organizational members may engage in a revisionist strategy (Gioia et al., 2000). The tendency is to reconstruct past metaphors as a basis for group identification, while the organization is viewed more in terms of self-interest. In conditions of cultural differentiation, the root metaphor maintains its unifying power by exposing the inconsistency of management practices with its main principles. With cultural fragmentation, it is reconstructed such that future images of the organization contain some elements of the past. Here, the root metaphor has a function in retaining a common identity among organizational members in situations of discontinuity, even when members' trust in management fails or they cannot identify with the corporate culture. Thus, the meaningfulness of root metaphors can be reconstructed and persist over time, even when the conditions that supported their origin no longer apply. In this respect, our analysis contributes to the construction of a meta-theory on organizational culture, with parallels to the work of Pettigrew (1979), Child and Smith (1987) and Greenwood and Hinings (1996), recognizing that continuities of organizational culture can be maintained alongside significant changes.

A further contribution is the extension of the three perspectives put forward by Martin (1992, 2002). She indicates that an organizational culture simultaneously exhibits elements of integration, differentiation and fragmentation at any given time. This chapter goes a step forward by clarifying how and why such conditions prevail in organizations. Most studies of organizational culture, including those that focus on the three perspectives, are cross-sectional and therefore unable to explore in any depth the questions of how and why culture changes in the direction of differentiation or otherwise over time. What we can learn from this case study is that, when organizational culture is examined over time, one of these conditions may be found to predominate as a result of political and institutional pressures.

We have also sought to clarify the relevance of institutions and the role of political actors in culture formation and change, thereby filling a gap in the literature, which has traditionally viewed organizational culture through a cognitive lens. Because of methodological limitations, most studies are limited in their understanding of environmental influences on culture change (Martin, 2002). The present study goes beyond mere recognition of external forces. It indicates how institutional forces interact with internal political actors in organizational culture change. Institutions can create conditions that impact on the activity of subcultures by empowering or disempowering social actors and creating or deactivating the rules that foster alliances and different social formations. An organizational culture tends to be integrated when a powerful group or leading coalition supports it. By contrast, fragmentation reflects not only anomie but also the incapacity of the leading group to satisfy the interests of other groups. The more institutionalized an organization's environment, the more likely that institutional agencies will influence its prevailing culture. In such environments, power and legitimacy do not necessarily cohere. An organization's leadership can survive without legitimacy, because its mandate is controlled from above and voice alone cannot overturn it. In other types of organization, such as the privately owned company, leadership can more readily be changed through stakeholder pressures.

Notes

This chapter derives from Rodrigues (2006) and is also informed by Carrieri (2001).

1   Though Martin's intention was to address the ontology of organizational culture, her framework is applied here to advance the understanding of change in cultural conditions and the role of subcultures in this process.
2   By employing the term 'Telema', the employee was making a word play in which he joined the word 'tele' with the word 'má' which in Portuguese means 'bad'.

References

Abravanel, H. (1983) Mediatory myths in the service of organizational ideology. In L. Pondy, P. Frost and T. Dandridge (eds), *Organizational Symbolism*. London: JAI Press, pp. 273–93.

Alvesson, M. and Willmott, H. (2002) Identity regulation as organizational control: producing the appropriate individual. *Journal of Management Studies*, 39(5), 619–44.

Anthony, P. (1994) *Managing Culture*. Buckingham: Open University Press.

Argyris, C. and Schon, D. (1978) *Organizational Learning: A Theory of Action Perspective*. Reading, MA: Addison-Wesley.

Bate, P. (1994) *Strategies of Cultural Change*. Oxford: Butterworth-Heinemann.

Blair, M. (1995) *Ownership and Control: Rethinking Corporate Governance for the Twenty-first Century*. Washington, DC: The Brookings Institution.

Boschi, R., Diniz, E. and Santos, F. (2000) *Elites Politicas e Economicas no Brasil Contemporaneo*. São Paulo: Fundação Konrad Adeneur.

Brown, A. D. (1995) *Organizational Culture*. London: Pitman Publishing.

Carrieri, A. (2001) O fim do 'mundo Telemig': a transformação das significações culturais em uma empresa de telecomunicações. Thesis submitted for the title of Doctor in Administration at Universidade Federal de Minas Gerais-Brazil.

Cascio, W. F. (2002) *Responsible Restructuring*. San Francisco: Berrett-Koehler.

Child, J. and Smith, C. (1987) The context and process of transformation – Cadbury Limited in its sector. *Journal of Management Studies*, 24(6), 565–93.

Clarke, J., Hall, S., Jefferson, T. and Roberts, B. (1987) Subcultures, cultures and class. In T. Bennett, G. Martin, C. Mercer and J. Woollacott (eds), *Culture, Ideology and Social Process*. London: Open University Press, pp. 53–79.

DiMaggio, P. J. and Powell, W. W. (1991) The iron cage revisited: institutional isomorphism and collective rationality. In W. W. Powell and P. J. DiMaggio (eds), *The New Institutionalism in Organizational Analysis*. Chicago: University of Chicago Press, pp. 63–82.

Donadone, J. C. and Grun, R. (2002) Participation, participations: semantic inflections and social transformations in Brazil in the last three decades. Society for Advancement of Economics Conference, Minneapolis.

Dreifuss, R. A. (1981) *A Conquista do Estado: Ação Política, Poder e Golpe de Classe*. Petrópolis: Vozes.

Emirbayer, M. and Mische, A. (1998) What is agency? *American Journal of Sociology*, 103, 962–1023.

Evans, P. (1979) *Dependent Development: The Alliance of Multinational, State, and Local Capital in Brazil*. Princeton, NJ: Princeton University Press.

Gagliardi, P. (1986) The creation and change of organizational cultures: a conceptual framework. *Organization Studies*, 7, 117–34.

Gioia, D. A., Schultz, M. and Corley K. G. (2000) Organizational identity, image and adaptive instability. *Academy of Management Review*, 25, 63–81.

Greenwood, R. and Hinings, C. R. (1996) Understanding radical organizational change: bringing together the old and the new institutionalism. *Academy of Management Review*, 21, 1022–54.

Halbwachs, M. (1992) *On Collective Memory*. Chicago: University of Chicago Press.

Hinings, C. R., Hickson, D. H., Schneck, R. H. and Pennings, J. (1973) Structural conditions of organizational power. *Administrative Science Quarterly*, 23, 454–65.

Kotter, J. P. and Heskett, J. L. (1992) *Corporate Culture and Performance*. New York: The Free Press.

Martin, J. (1992) *Culture in Organizations*. New York: Oxford University Press.

Martin, J. (2002) *Organizational Culture: Mapping the Terrain*. London: Sage.

O'Donnell, G. (1979) *Modernization and Bureaucratic Authoritarianism*. Berkeley: Institute of International Studies.

Oliver, C. (1992) The antecedents of deinstitutionalization. *Organization Studies*, 13, 563–88.

Pettigrew, A. M. (1979) On studying organizational cultures. *Administrative Science Quarterly*, 24, 570–81.

Pfeffer, J. (1981) *Power in Organizations*. London: Pitman.

Pfeffer, J. and Salancik, G. R. (1978) *The External Control of Organizations: A Resource Dependence Perspective*. New York: Harper & Row.

Pires, J. C. L. (1999) *Políticas regulatórias no setor de telecomunicações: a experiência internacional e o caso brasileiro*. Textos para Discussão no. 71. Rio de Janeiro: BNDES.

Rodrigues, S. B. (2006) The political dynamics of organizational culture in an institutionalized environment. *Organization Studies*, 27, 537–57.

Rodrigues, S. B. and Child, J. (2003) Co-evolution and transformation in times of deconstruction: a dynamic multi-level process. *Journal of Management Studies*, 40, 2137–62.

Rodrigues, S. B. and Collinson, D. (1995) 'Having fun?' Humour as resistance in Brazil. *Organization Studies*, 16, 739–68.

Schein, E. H. (1992) *Organizational Culture and Leadership*, 2nd edn. San Francisco: Jossey-Bass.

Scott, J. C. (1990). *Domination and the Arts of Resistance. Hidden Transcripts.* New Haven, CT: Yale University Press.

Simons, T. and Ingram, P. (1997) Organization and ideology: kibbutzim and hired labor, 1951–1965. *Administrative Science Quarterly*, 42, 784–814.

Smircich, L. (1983) Concepts of culture and organizational analysis. *Administrative Science Quarterly*, 28, 339–49.

Van Maanen, J. and Barley, S. R. (1985) Cultural organization: fragments of a theory. In P. J. Frost, F. Louis, C. C. Lundberg and J. Martin (eds), *Organizational Culture.* Beverley Hills, CA: Sage, pp. 31–53.

Winsor, R. D. (1996) Military perspectives of organizations. *Journal of Organizational Change Management*, 9, 34–42.

CHAPTER EIGHT

Corporate Identity

A corporate identity denotes a set of attributes that senior managers ascribe to their organization. It is therefore an organizational identity articulated by a powerful interest group. It can constitute a claim that serves *inter alia* to justify the authority vested in top managers and to further their interests. The academic literature on organizational identity, and on corporate identity in particular, pays little attention to these political considerations. It focuses in an apolitical manner on shared meanings when corporate identity works, or on cognitive dissonance when it breaks down. In response to this analytical void, in the present chapter we elaborate a political analysis of corporate identity and its development, using the Telemig case as an informative illustration. Our analysis suggests a cyclical model in which corporate identity definition and redefinition involve power relations, resource mobilization and struggles for legitimacy.

The study of organizational identity has attracted a large literature (e.g. Whetten and Godfrey, 1998; Albert et al., 2000; Hatch and Schultz, 2004). This interest reflects Gioia et al.'s (2000, p. 78) claim that 'the concept of identity is key to understanding modern organizations'. Yet there is little agreement on what the concept of organizational identity denotes, on a relevant theory or on an appropriate methodology for studying it (Hatch and Yanow, 2006). Instead, as one authority has commented, 'anarchy reigns . . . even after more than 15 years of active conversation about organizational identity' (Harquail, 2004, pp. 141–2).

A major problem resides in the tacit insistence found within much recent analysis on an apolitical treatment of what is a politically charged topic. We argue that the study of organizational identity needs to come to terms with the fact that organizations are arenas within which conflicting as well as joint interests are pursued. A political perspective extends our appreciation of organizational identity from being a set of meanings to constituting a political claim and, in so doing, moves away from the quiescent logic of identity construction found in much purely constructionist scholarship. An identity claim is informed by collective views as to what the organization's priorities should be. Such a claim requires the mobilization of political support and the garnering of legitimacy. That claim can subsequently be mobilized as an ideational resource in the contexts of further political processes and power relations. In developing this argument, we recognize the asymmetric distribution of power that characterizes most organizations, and we therefore focus on 'corporate identity', which refers to the identity attributed to an organization by what is normally its most powerful group – senior (corporate) management. The distinction we are making here between corporate identity and organizational identity is comparable to that between corporate and organizational culture made by Linstead and Grafton-Small (1992).

The following section presents the essence of a political perspective on corporate identity. It also clarifies the concept of corporate identity, arguing that it is a particular, but important, form of organizational identity. We then highlight relevant findings from the Telemig case. The case study illustrates the application of a political perspective to corporate identity and advances the argument insofar as it suggests a cyclical model of corporate identity development that is driven by political factors.

A Political Perspective on Corporate Identity

1 The political view of organizations

The political view of organizations regards them as internally differentiated by interests and asymmetric power (Pfeffer, 1981; Clegg et al., 2006). Just as governments are the subject of special attention within political science because of the differential power they normally wield in society, those in leading organizational positions are similarly deemed worthy of particular attention. The political perspective is deeply rooted within political and social science, and is far from novel within organization theory. Thus the study of pressure group politics (e.g. Bentley, 1908; Berry, 1997) draws attention to how organizations can be used by those controlling them to articulate their interests to government officials and politicians. The 'resource dependence perspective' (Pfeffer and Salancik, 1978) adds the observation that in order to survive an organization needs to secure the support of external resource providers. In some cases, an organization requires institutional approval or support in order to continue. Such dependence does not rule out the possibilities of exerting influence on external parties through cooptation, persuasive lobbying and the other proactive measures that 'old institutionalists' like Selznick (1949) and political analysts such as Berger (1981) have identified.

The role of internal coalitions and shifting forces of power has been central to the political perspective on organizations. For example, studies of strategic decision-making point to the role of leading groups or internal coalitions with sufficient initiative and power to define an organization's mission and develop the competencies appropriate to that mission (e.g. Hickson et al., 1986; Hitt and Tyler, 1991). Organizational decision-making has been studied explicitly as a political process (e.g. Pettigrew, 1973), while the dialectical view of organizations as comprising different conflicting interest groups traces its origins to a Marxist conception (Benson, 1977). The 'strategic choice' perspective argues that the leading coalition or group in an organization attempts to implement policies that it values, and by implication to maintain a preferred organizational identity, through a political process of negotiation both within and outside the organization (Child, 1997). There is, then, a political tradition within organizational analysis that regards organizational attributes as reflective of the ability of powerful groups to negotiate with, persuade or impose upon others to accept their preferred policies. Insofar as this ability varies over time in changing circumstances, a political perspective should help to account for variation in an organization's attributes, including the identity that is publicly claimed for it.

2 Limitations of an apolitical organizational identity discourse

Our opening assumption in this chapter is that one of the limitations of much current discourse on organizational identity lies in its tacit insistence on an apolitical treatment of what is a politically charged topic. Albert and Whetten's (1985) seminal definition of organizational identity as that which is central, distinctive and enduring about an organization served to launch the identity literature off on this apolitical track. Their definition is holistic and contains an implicit assumption of consensus. Both centrality and endurance become questionable attributes if the possibility is acknowledged that an organizational identity could be simply the expression of a particular interest group and thus open to contest by other parties. Some have argued against this holistic notion of organizational identity from an interpretive perspective. They maintain that the identity of an organization is an essentially inter-subjective phenomenon residing in the perceptions and understandings of its various membership and stakeholder groups (Hatch and Schultz, 2002). According to Ravasi and Schultz (2006, p. 435), 'organizational identities reside in shared interpretive schemes that members collectively construct in order to provide meaning to their experience'.

The interpretive perspective thus acknowledges that different categories of social actor, such as owners, managers, engineers, workers, trade union officers and customers, may well have their own shared understandings of what an organization's identity is (Scott and Lane, 2000). These different interpretations can conflict (Pratt and Foreman, 2000; Brown and Humphreys, 2006). This, in turn, raises the question of how potentially divergent meanings are negotiated between organizational actors, and whether such negotiations are an impetus for organizational identities to change over time (Gioia et al., 2000). The interpretive perspective can in this way draw attention to essentially political issues concerning conflict over the identity ascribed to an organization by different social actors and the potential exercise of power in resolving such conflict. In practice, however, it has usually treated conflict in terms of cognitive dissonance.

The notion of 'social actor' has also been employed in the analysis of organizational identity at two different levels (Whetten and Mackey, 2002). At one level, insofar as an organization is a player within its industry, community and other segments of society, it can be considered as a social actor in its own right (Meyer et al., 2006). An affirmation of what an organization's role in society is and should be constitutes a political statement about its identity since it denotes concern with 'a cause' that is likely to reflect the interests of a particular stakeholder group. This identity can be expressed by 'strategizing and organizing' (Whittington, 2003) as well as by defining the organization's obligations to principals or stakeholders. At another level of analysis, however, an organization includes various categories of social actor among its stakeholders and employees. As the interpretive perspective has recognized, each of these actor groups may well attach a somewhat different, and possibly more specific, identity to the organization.

This dual level analysis presents a disjuncture between the notion that an organization's identity can be defined in terms of its having a clear role in society and the probability that its members and stakeholders may not agree upon what this identity is. Whetten and Mackey (2002) try to resolve the disjuncture by emphasizing areas of agreement over organizational identity, in terms of what they call 'shared identity claims' (p. 399) and 'identity congruence' (p. 400). This, however, is to ignore the possibility of contest between social actors in their definitions of an organization's identity. It is, in effect, to adopt what Martin (2002) terms an integration perspective, which depicts only one of several possible situations and which draws attention away from the tensions that are likely to lead to the development of organizational identities over time.

A political perspective, which recognizes the role of interest and power, can help to resolve the apparent disjuncture in social actor analysis. With regard to *interest*, the political perspective would see organizational identity as a set of attributes that social actors ascribe to an organization, but it would also enquire whether those collectively held identities constitute claims that can further their interests. In other words, the political view can accept, along with most identity theorists, that definitions of an organization's identity derive from subjective interpretations, but it would expect such interpretations to be informed by a sense of how that organization can serve the interests of the people concerned. Insofar as these interests vary for different categories of stakeholder, each group is likely to attach its own preferred identity claim to an organization.

With regard to *power*, a political analysis would recognize that in hierarchically constituted organizations such as most business firms, power and authority are unevenly distributed. One particular interest group – senior management – normally has privileged control over an organization's material and informational resources, which implies that it is likely to enjoy greater power than other groups to articulate its identity claim for the firm and to project this both internally and externally (Anthony, 1994; Soenen and Moingeon, 2002; Currie and Brown, 2003). So, in effect, the representation of the organization as a social actor is likely to be heavily conditioned by the identity that its leading group articulates for it. This leading group is in an advantageous position to project its identity claim for the organization on to the identity of the organization per se as a 'social actor'. It is *this* identity claim on which we focus in this chapter, and to which we give the term 'corporate identity' in order to *distinguish* it from the organizational identities held by other groups. Our focus on corporate identity is consistent with the approach adopted by Clegg et al. (2007), except that it does not assume, as these authors appear to do, that the identity expressions of the principals of firms can be equated to a more general organizational identity.

3 A political view of corporate identity

We use the term 'corporate identity' to refer to senior managers' definitions of their organization through characterizations of its central and distinctive features (van Riel and Balmer, 1997; Melewar and Jenkins, 2002; Moingeon and Soenen, 2002). Although these characterizations may not be entirely consistent among themselves or between different senior managers, their common and salient components together provide the elements of an 'identity claim'. An identity claim is a statement about the organization's political stance and its role in society. It normally includes declarations about the main interest groups the organization serves, and about who has the right to determine the use of organizational resources. In the case study to be reported, the question of 'for what and for whom the company stands' served as our main criterion of relevance to capture the leading group's definition of the organization's corporate identity. This is compatible with Cornelissen et al.'s (2007, p. S3) view that a corporate identity is 'the distinctive public image that a corporate entity communicates' about itself. Conceptions of corporate identity are also evident in categorization schemas, in prototypical characteristics and abstractions of corporate leaders (Ashforth and Mael, 1989). In the minds of managers, characterizations may reflect organizing for a given constituency, such as customers, employees or shareholders. As a political statement, an identity claim is a persuasive representation of an organization's accountability in society, be it to private or public interests. Such claims may be publicly expressed, through documents, such as company reports and publications, as well as through branding, communications, graphic design and other aspects of image creation (Olins, 1995; Dowling, 2001).

Corporate identity claims can have a political purpose. By framing an organization in terms of a particular logic and order, they can inform and justify the managerial use of power to maintain that order (see Foucault, 1982; Knights and Morgan, 1991). They may also serve to justify the authority of the leading corporate group insofar as it is expected to take the lead in articulating an organization's identity and is remunerated highly for so doing. Moreover, in conveying a view of an organization's accountability, identity claims locate that organization in relation to interest groups within the wider society.

Conceptions of corporate identity derive from a process of interaction and sense-making between different corporate actors and the principals to whom they as agents are beholden. Despite the often hidden nature of this process, corporate identity is nevertheless expressed in more public forms accessible to the researcher. These forms include written corporate statements as well as narrative descriptions offered by corporate managers. Thus while a corporate identity is an expression of the distinctive set of meanings that is attached to an organization by its corporate leaders, this subjectively held meaning-set can be expressed or be projected into public statements that have a more objective ontological status. Moreover, there may be mutuality between senior managers' characterizations of their organization and its objectified routines. Their characterizations may be sedimented into routines that in turn become tangible points of reference for an articulation of their characterizations of the organization. The researcher's challenge is to understand these diverse expressions of corporate identity and make sense of them with the help of the extant literature. This corresponds to recognizing the value of a 'constructivist-interpretivist' position concerning the process whereby the identity is formed and the meanings that inform it, while at the same time adopting a 'naturalist-realist' position concerning the manifestations of a corporate identity (Hatch and Yanow, 2006).

It is also necessary to differentiate a corporate identity from an organizational or corporate culture. While an organization's culture can help to support the identity that its top management seeks to articulate, the two are not conceptually the same. Corporate identity is a characterization of the organization as a whole by top management, including the organization's role as a social actor. By contrast, an organizational culture is concerned with acceptable and habitual conduct *within* an organization. It denotes the beliefs, norms and collective rituals common among organizational members, or significant sub-groups (Brown, 1995; Martin, 2002). Top managers may try to foster an organizational culture that lends credibility to their desired corporate identity. However, that identity can be recognized by the organization's internal and external publics without their necessarily being aware of its internal culture. Moreover, an organizational culture is likely to be embedded in its customs and rituals and hence endure for longer than the corporate identity articulated by top managers. If the two are inconsistent, this could reduce the legitimacy of the corporate identity. We have maintained this distinction in the previous chapter, which treats the development of Telemig's internal culture with reference to its degree of integration, differentiation and fragmentation. In addition to this substantive distinction, our assessment of Telemig's organizational culture relied upon the responses of all employees interviewed, in contrast to the assessment of its corporate identity, which derives from interviews with executive directors and the documents they produced.

There are several considerations that lead us to focus on corporate identity rather than on other organizational identities, and these derive directly from a political perspective. First, as already argued, the hierarchical nature of most organizations lends particular significance to the corporate definition of what an organization is. This informs actions taken by management on behalf of the organization, which impinge upon the interests of its members and external constituencies. Employees are encouraged to take corporate identity as a significant point of reference, and indeed some of its components may be directed specifically at them in an attempt to enforce their compliance (Alvesson and Wilmott, 2002).

Second, the dynamics of proposition and opposition around corporate identity claims are likely to play a particularly active and salient role in the process of organizational development and they may shape internal features such as strategy, organizational design and training. Corporate identity definitions established for an organization at its foundation and during its formative years may have an enduring impact, at least as a point of reference against which the legitimacy of subsequent changes is evaluated (see Stinchcombe, 1965). On the other hand, if a corporate identity and supporting policies negatively affect the self-esteem and interests of others, they are likely to oppose it (Brown and Starkey, 2000). This loss of legitimacy could lead to alienation and the mobilization of protest, thus jeopardizing the claims of the corporate identity. Non-managerial parties to an organization are not necessarily powerless. The discursive struggle around identities highlighted by Phillips and Hardy (1997) showed that power can be exercised by groups lacking formal power or control over resources through their creation of meaning in terms of offering an interpretation of what is going on in their organization. Their collective mobilization around the articulation of a distinctive interpretation consistent with their interests secured for them a legitimate voice and hence influence. In other words, actors can put effort into ensuring that their interests have a voice within organizational discourse and, in so doing, challenge the dominance of a corporate identity and the managerial ideology that informs it (Brown and Humphreys, 2006; Poggi, 2006). Corporate identity is therefore liable to be contested, in some circumstances effectively.

A third consideration is that it is part of top managers' justification of their leading role to give a corporate identity greater salience than other organizational identities. They do this through the documents and reports they issue and through the public statements they make. This accessibility aids an investigation that is concerned to explore the processes that lead to identity articulation and development.

4 Corporate identity development

Although attention has been paid to the issue of continuity and change with regard to organizational identity, we still have only a limited understanding of its development over an extended period of time (Gioia et al., 2000; Peverelli, 2004). Some studies have indicated the presence of systemic identity conflicts (e.g. Humphreys and Brown, 2002) and these offer useful leads. Changes in the definition of corporate identity can be stimulated by external pressures as interpreted by corporate managers (Chreim, 2005). Divergence between the corporate identity of an organization articulated by its leaders and the identity conceived as legitimate by significant external parties such as government agencies or consumers has been said to give rise to an 'identity dissonance' (Chreim, 2002) or 'perceived discrepancy' (Gioia et al., 2000). If this is experienced as an 'identity threat' by those leaders, it will encourage them to revise the organizational identity they hold and articulate (Elsbach and Kramer, 1996). When such dissonance or discrepancy arises, there are likely to be managerial responses aimed at restoring consistency between projected and attributed identity (Gioia et al., 2000). Nevertheless, should management seek to redefine a corporate identity, employees may organize resistance in order to preserve what these elements they value in that identity (Ravasi and Schultz, 2006). Equally, a negative reaction by the members of an organization against the prevailing corporate identity could generate pressures for it to change if their stance is supported by strong collective action mobilized by a labour union or occupational association.

Notions of 'identity dissonance' or 'perceived discrepancy' contribute useful insights into the process of corporate identity formation. These insights can be strengthened if their analytical grounding on cognition and interpretation is extended to include the political considerations of interest and power. With regard to interest, a dissonance or perceived discrepancy between a corporate identity and other organizational identities, or between a corporate identity and managerial behaviour, may affect the legitimacy of the practices it is intended to reinforce, and generate mistrust in management's capacity or willingness to satisfy the interest of other parties. That could encourage mobilization by groups and individuals who feel their interests are threatened.

Identity dissonance may also stimulate the exercise of power. Insofar as managers take active measures to reduce dissonance between their definition of an organization's identity and that held by others, they require resources to research the nature of the dissonance, activities to create and project a new or reinforced identity message and, not least, efforts to formulate organizational policies and practices that support the identity. These measures depend on their power to command and coordinate organized activities and appropriate resources. The persons at the top of organizational hierarchies have the internal authority to initiate these measures, but unless an organization is autonomous and self-financing, they may also require the approval of owners and other resource providers. The more that organizational leadership depends on external approval, the more such approval is likely to be necessary for the viability of a corporate identity that the leadership is seeking to project (Pfeffer and Salancik, 1978). Similarly, in circumstances when the reaction of internal stakeholders to an identity claim is unfavourable, the power they may have to oppose this claim has implications for its sustainability and perhaps the continuance in office of the incumbent top management team. A combination of high dependence on external support and collective employee power is often found in organizations, such as the one reported in this chapter, that are located within the public sector or subject to public regulation. As LaPalombara (2001, p. 565) comments, 'politics in both the organizational environment and political organizations actually infuses every aspect of what public-sector organizations are and what they do'. These considerations indicate that it is simplistic to regard the construction and maintenance of an identity claim just as a process of arriving at a collective agreement on shared meanings. For, if a corporate identity is the product of political manoeuvring, its social construction has to be understood as involving power relations, resource mobilization and conditional legitimacy.

5 Mobilization and legitimacy

These considerations call for an analysis in which top managers' ability to construct and sustain a definition of corporate identity is not taken for granted. Political analysis suggests that this ability may depend importantly on two factors: mobilization and legitimacy. *Mobilization* is a concept often applied to the development of a collective consciousness and the energizing of action in social and political movements (e.g. McCarthy and Wolfson, 1996; Newton, 1999). Rowley and Moldoveanu (2003) propose that stakeholder group mobilization will be enhanced by both a sense of common interest and common identity. This suggests that acceptance of a collective identity and group mobilization may be mutually reinforcing factors.

Two kinds of mobilization are potentially relevant to understanding corporate identity development. The first concerns the activation of conditions that sustain a particular corporate identity discourse, including its modification in order to reduce identity dissonance and threat. These conditions are likely to include both material and ideational supports. External material supports could include the provision of financial resources and institutional support in the form of mandatory freedom to pursue policies and practices consistent with a given identity claim. Internal material support could include the allocation of investment to socialize employees to accept a corporate identity claim through propaganda and training. The political ideology dominant in a society, such as neoliberalism, could provide an important ideational support for a corporate identity claim, feeding into its content and rationale. Mobilization often involves the formation of coalitions and/or the co-optation of support from outside the organization, and these are likely to have particular relevance for an organization providing a public service. The classic case in the literature is the Tennessee Valley Authority (Selznick, 1949). Greenwood and Hinings (1996, p. 1040) refer to mobilization as 'the act of leadership', and this reinforces the argument that an understanding of the process by which a given articulation of corporate identity is constructed and reconstructed requires a primary focus on an organization's corporate management.

The other kind of mobilization might more precisely be termed 'counter-mobilization' (see Burnham, 1970; Green, 1984). It is the mobilization of forces opposed to a prevailing corporate identity by, for instance, NGOs or organized labour. While these forces may be purely oppositional rather than offering a well worked-out alternative identity for the organization in question, they could hasten the redefinition of an existing corporate identity if they were motivated by a denial of that identity's legitimacy and supported by effective collective action. Counter-mobilization may also depend on material resources such as NGO and union funds and ideational ones that speak for the reform of corporate identities such as 'the unacceptable face of capitalism'. Examples include Greenpeace's campaign against Shell concerning the disposal of the Brent Spar oil rig and the British GMB union's campaign against the employment-reducing effects of acquisitions by private equity firms.

Legitimacy is the second relevant concept. Within the sociological tradition, legitimacy denotes a condition of positive valuation and acceptance enjoyed by persons in positions of power, and by the organizations through which that power is exercised, with particular reference to the policies and actions they undertake (Bierstedt, 1964). Habermas (1975) maintains that 'legitimacy crises' arise when those in power are unable to meet social expectations. Suchman (1995, p. 574) argues that applied to organizations, 'legitimacy is a perception or assumption in that it represents the reaction of observers to the organization as they see it'. It reflects the extent to which an organization's goals and actions are congruent with wider social values, norms and beliefs (Parsons, 1956; Pfeffer and Salancik, 1978). The degree of legitimacy accorded to a corporate identity may be taken to refer to how far it is positively accepted by other groups or stakeholders within the organization or outside it. The legitimacy of an organization's corporate identity claim may also depend importantly upon institutional approval in sectors such as telecommunications, in which the state has a stake in the ownership of member organizations, or acts as their regulator in the public interest (Powell and DiMaggio, 1991). Thus 'conscious and explicit attempts on the behalf of the organization to justify what it is and what it stands for' (Christensen and Cheney, 2000, p. 248) are aimed at securing legitimacy for the ideas behind a corporate identity and the actions associated with it.

The evaluation by stakeholders of a corporate identity claim will inevitably be associated with the legitimacy that they accord to the authority of an incumbent corporate management. A withdrawal of this legitimacy could arise from various developments, ranging from broad changes in wider socio-political sentiment to a specific failure by top management to deliver good organizational performance. The severe criticisms that firms like Gap and Nike faced concerning employment conditions in their developing country subcontractors' factories illustrate the impact of changes in public sentiment in their domestic economies. A lack of legitimacy, especially when combined with counter-mobilization against a prevailing corporate identity claim, is likely to generate pressures for that identity to be changed. Insofar as legitimacy is a cognitive process through which an organization or its actions are regarded as consistent with taken-for-granted assumptions (Zucker, 1977), the extent to which continuity is preserved within a changing corporate identity may help to preserve its legitimacy (see Child and Smith, 1987).

A political perspective thus draws attention to the conditions under which support may be mobilized for a given articulation of corporate identity, while at the same time allowing for opposition should that identity fail to gain legitimacy among non-corporate groups. It suggests a number of factors that may be relevant for an understanding of changes in the articulation of corporate identity. They include the circumstances under which a collective identity first emerged, including the interpretations of an organization's founders, and the support they mobilized. Other factors include subsequent events leading to identity crises, including a loss of legitimacy among stakeholder groups, the ability of organizational leaders to adapt to such crises and the power of corporate leadership to prevail with their preferred claim relative to the power of other groups to oppose it. The political perspective is a dynamic one that points to a developmental process in the articulation of corporate identity. This process is now illustrated through reference to the case of Telemig during the period from its foundation in 1973 to its demise as a legal entity in 2000.

Telemig's Corporate Identity

1 The ontology of corporate identity in its political context

As indicated earlier, we adopted the middle ground suggested by Hatch and Yanow (2006) with respect to the ontological status of corporate identity. This middle ground envisages 'a social reality [that] is socially constructed *and* that the world, both social and natural, exists independently of any of us, even though we only know it through interpretation' (p. 42). While a corporate identity is a socially constructed reality (Berger and Luckmann, 1966), it has an existence and, more importantly, consequences that become to some degree independent of the process by which it was generated. Managerial reports, such as mission statements and managerial philosophy, are the most tangible manifestations of the reality of a corporate identity. This social construction of a corporate identity is, however, limited in that it is the expression of a certain group that does not capture or even recognize the potentially conflicting and contested nature of the identity claims being made. Documents issued by particular groups need to be interpreted in the context of other organizational members' accounts of corporate identity. The extent to which other parties to an organization contest a corporate identity can only be revealed by reference to accounts emanating from outside corporate management. Therefore while documentary evidence could reveal differences in the characterization of corporate identity over time, sole reliance on such sources could be misleading, giving a false impression of artificial consensus and unity. Reference to narratives and discourses, on the other hand, allow us to understand corporate identity as a contested creation of meanings that are far from neutral within the ambit of organizational politics. Meanings are embedded in groups and individuals frameworks of self-interest and, therefore, are subject to forces of mobilization and counter-mobilization. Moreover, an understanding of identity in its context and its transformation through time necessarily demands interpretation by the researchers. It involves the co-production of meanings between the researchers and its subjects whereby knowledge emerges from a continuous dialogue between data and scholarship. In short, understanding identity from a middle ground approach requires the use of multiple sources.

2 Sources and method

We therefore proceeded on the basis that the descriptions of, and claims about, an organization's central characteristics that constitute a corporate identity are present in senior managers' spoken narratives as well as in documents they issue (Humphreys and Brown, 2002; Hardy et al., 2005). During the interviews with Telemig's executive directors, we asked them to define the main characteristics of the company, and to describe for what and for whom the company stood both at the time of interview and in its previous history (see questions 1.6, 1.8, 3.4 and 3.8 in table 3.2). They were encouraged to elaborate on their answers, which were tape-recorded. In order to capture the shared views that the directors held on Telemig's identity, two researchers (the first author and one other Brazilian researcher) independently analysed the content of the answers to discern categories underlying their statements about the company's distinctive features at different times in its history. The first analysis of interview data gave rise to broad constructs that represented categorizations of the organization. These emerged from discussion between the researchers. We then examined the directors' interviews again and identified the category into which each extracted sentence or passage could be placed. This yielded a 93 per cent agreement between the researchers. The extracts over which there was some ambiguity were discussed between the researchers until agreement was reached about which category to place them in. The main categories and the percentage of total interview extracts falling into them are presented in table 8.1 for each period of the company history.

We complemented this assessment of Telemig's corporate identity by reference to the documentary sources noted in chapter 3. The autobiographical interviews with 25 telecommunications sector leaders who were associated with Telemig's foundation and development under Brazil's military regime until 1985 were content analysed against the categories arising from the analysis of the directors' interviews. Other documentary sources used were Telemig's annual reports and key internal documents. These documents provided overall information on identity claims. Here the two researchers analysed the organizational priorities and preferences expressed towards particular stakeholders and expressions about accountability (for what and for whom the company stood). A content analysis of these documents, and the interviews, according to the themes they expressed indicated that corporate claims about Telemig's social role changed over time.

The study was not originally designed to assess the legitimacy of Telemig's corporate identity or the kinds of mobilization that affected it. An awareness of these factors emerged in a grounded manner from the case itself. Insights into legitimacy were gained from two available sources, both reflecting opinions expressed by employees or their representatives in the context of changes in the wider political environment. The first source was 145 interviews that had been conducted with Telemig's middle managers and engineers, also during the periods 1986–90 and 1997–2000.[1] In the course of each interview, respondents were invited to describe what they saw as the company's main characteristics, both at the time and in its previous history, and to comment on these. Analysis of these interviews focused on the views expressed about top managers' discourses on for what and for whom the company stood. In particular, we took account of how the interviewees perceived the compatibility of top managers' claims with employee interests, and the consistency of managerial discourses with corporate actions and resource provision. The interviews normally lasted for around 90 minutes and were transcribed verbatim.

Because it was not possible to interview lower-level employees, analysis of the Telemig union newspaper was used as a second source of insight into legitimacy. The newspaper was established in 1980. It was considered an appropriate source of opinion because it circulated widely within the company, and because until 1990 over 90 per cent of Telemig's employees outside corporate management belonged to the union. Every copy of the newspaper produced by Telemig's labour union was analysed, in order to assess its characterization and evaluation of management's identity claims and behavior. The newspaper mentioned 9,408 different topics over the period 1980–2000. The researchers selected 2,288 subject matters that contained narratives about the stance of the company and its management towards its employees. The criticism of management contained in this discussion provided an indication of the approval or otherwise granted by the union towards Telemig's corporate identity.

We sought insights into the mobilization behind the formation of Telemig's corporate identity through evidence about internal coalitions and their links with external networks that enabled its top management to secure resources and to gain external support. Particularly significant insights were offered for the early part of Telemig's life by the autobiographies of Brazil's telecommunications sector founders. The interviews offered further insight into the processes of mobilization and counter-mobilization, and the parties involved, during the whole of the company's life. Information on the activity and power of Telemig's labour union, including its alliances with national unions and political parties, was also taken into account as an indication of attempts at counter-mobilization. Finally, further follow-up interviews with nine union officers, 14 retired employees and two former CEOs provided additional information and perspective on events relevant to mobilization.

3 The development of Telemig's corporate identity over time

The analysis of interview and other material confirmed that the three distinct periods we have already discerned in Telemig's history were also a valid basis for according periods to the development of its corporate identity. Examination of its directors' discourse suggests that in each of these three periods they conceived of Telemig performing a different role as a social actor. In the first period, 1973–85, this was an agency for economic and social development. In the second period, 1985–93, it was an agency for multiple interests. In the third and last period, it was an agency for shareholder value.

Table 8.1 presents our classification of the characterizations and claims relevant to Telemig's corporate identity for each of these three periods that were most frequently mentioned by its directors and, for the first period, in the founders' autobiographies. Short quotations from their narratives are shown in order to illustrate the meaning attached to each category. Table 8.1 also summarizes the main features of mobilization and legitimacy in each period. The case offers a basis for elaborating the political perspective through a discussion of the roles played by mobilization and legitimacy in the process of Telemig's corporate identity development.

4 Mobilization

The Telemig case offers several insights into how mobilization can be used by top managers and other interest groups to support or oppose corporate identity claims. During the foundation period a professional network comprising engineers and military telecommunication engineers, linked to power circuits in government, served as transmission belts for the government's plans to design a telecommunications sector that could contribute to the country's social and economic development. In addition to facilitating the sharing of ideas, this network was also an instrument for mobilizing the regulative changes and investment necessary for such ideas to have salience (Granovetter, 1992). In the period between 1973 and 1985 managers characterized the company as being missionary, technocratic and military (table 8.1).

With the end of the military regime, the incoming civilian top managers mobilized to change Telemig from a technocratic military to a pluralist organization. This was evident in the managerial philosophy document issued in 1987. This document affirmed managers' intention to make the organization responsive to demands of diverse interests, including shareholders, the community, customers and politicians. This new claim encountered resistance from engineers and managers below director level, as well as from the trade union. Engineers opposed this claim as they saw it as a corporate justification for binding the organization to external political interests. The trade union saw the inclusion of politicians as the main stakeholder group as a threat to the employees' employment security and control over recruitment process. A common thread in the discourse of this alliance was the inconsistency between top managers' claims to be constructing a more pluralist organization and the persistence of a military culture and practices. Though they did not advance an alternative claim, their activities of counter-mobilization

Table 8.1 Central characteristics of Telemig's corporate identity, mobilization and legitimacy in different periods

Corporate identity definition in each period of time[a]	Percentage of total identity characterizations falling into each category	Mobilization[b]	Legitimacy[c]
1973–85			
Identity claim: *Agency for economic and social development* Technocratic agency of the military government to help promote national development and integration		Close network of military officers and engineers, many sharing a common educational background. This network linked military officers to federal governmental bureaucrats and, via the holding company, to top managers and engineers in Telemig. This network channelled strong financial and ideological support from the government. It publicly articulated the role of telecoms companies in fostering the development of Brazilian society through seminars, meetings and publications. Opposition by organized labour was proscribed by law until 1979. As the military regime lost support after 1978	Telemig's contribution to economic and social development helped to secure a high level of legitimacy for its founding corporate identity. Legitimacy was sustained by the esteem that the company enjoyed within the state of Minas Gerais due to its combination of economic success and social delivery. An internal culture of benevolent paternalism encouraged an acceptance of the corporate identity. The legitimacy of the founding corporate identity started to decline
Identity characterization			
Missionary 'Our job was to integrate Brazilians into the world and the community.' 'We were entrepreneurs, we had to innovate and do everything from the smallest task to the bigger.' 'We considered the interests of the country as being those of the company.'	30.8		
Technocratic 'Telemig was an engineering company. Decision-making was guided by technical criteria'. 'We were proud that technical criteria prevailed in our decisions.' 'We were known for our innovativeness in technology. Our systems were transferred to other companies.'	23.6		

Table 8.1 (cont'd)

Corporate identity definition in each period of time[a]	Percentage of total identity characterizations falling into each category	Mobilization[b]	Legitimacy[c]
Military 'Telemig was a professional organization. We learned this from the military.' 'Telemig was like an army where "the good soldier is the one who obeys".' 'Telemig was a military company, obedient to rules and hierarchy.'	13.2	and the opposition workers' movement gained strength, mobilization behind the founding corporate identity progressively weakened and counter-mobilization strengthened.	after the late 1970s as the military regime with which it was associated was progressively rejected by a growing proportion of the Brazilian public.
Cumulative percentage of total identity characterizations	67.6		

1986–93

Identity claim: *Agency for Multiple Interests*
A state enterprise accountable to elected politicians in Brazil's new democracy and operating in ways responsive to the needs of employees and the community. Former characterization as a technocratic company now played down. Company reports in the six years between 1986 and 1993 contained 44 per cent more mentions of Telemig's democratic and pluralist aspirations than in the previous twelve years. However, the new corporate identity claim was not clearly articulated.

In this period, there were strands of mobilization and counter-mobilization. The formation of a new democratically elected government based on a coalition of political interests was the primary driver of mobilization towards modifications in Telemig's corporate identity. Company

Telemig's modified corporate identity gained only partial legitimacy within the company. The claims of increased openness were welcomed but this was tempered by criticism that the openness was very limited and by regret that political interference was

Identity characterization

Political	35.0	directors were now political appointees. However, mobilization behind the revised corporate identity was weakened by the lack of a clear post-military political ideology in Brazil as well as by reduced government funding for the company.
'This company now has to listen to the demands of politicians; we depend on their goodwill.' 'Today the board concerns itself whether a political demand will result in some votes.' 'In 1985 we had a political opening in Brazil which gave scope for political interference.'		
Democratic and community oriented	33.5	Pressures for change were also exerted by the emergence of labour unions, which, allied to the Workers Party, were active and powerful at both macro and micro levels. The union demanded a more pluralistic organization and open management but it did not accept that this reformed corporate identity was actually implemented. Telemig's founding technocratic and apolitical identity was defended, and the new identity resisted, by the company's Managerial Council, consisting of managers below corporate level.
'This company had previously never looked to the community as an intelligent voice. Now it does.' 'Telemig is now an open company, it listens to its employees.' 'We are much more inclusive than in the past. We now listen to our managers through proper channels.'		
Corporativist	9.9	
'Telemig is an organization that is centred on employees. It is the interests of employees that guide decision-making.' 'This company exists for its employees.' 'It is obvious that as a state company, Telemig is corporativistic. The employees think that the company is theirs and exists for their own benefit.'		
Cumulative percentage of total identity characterizations	78.4	

Table 8.1 (*cont'd*)

Corporate identity definition in each period of time[a]	Percentage of total identity characterizations falling into each category	Mobilization[b]	Legitimacy[c]
1994–2000 **Identity claim**: *Agency for shareholder value* An enterprise being prepared for privatization in a market opening to competition. Corporate identity characterized by a growing accountability for shareholder value, market orientation, self-reliance and cost-effectiveness. **Identity characterization** *Shareholder value* 'Telemig was previously constructed around the goal of bringing benefit to society; today the main concern is with profit.' 'We have now to do everything for the owners. If we don't, we are out.' 'As a state enterprise there was no visible owner. Now everything has to be for the owner.' *Market orientation* 'The company is now solid and firm . . . an organization that is ready to impose itself in a	 31.7 24.4	The emergence of global players in telecommunications encouraged Brazil to open its telecommunications market and to privatize its state companies. The reforming government that took office in 1993 put out a clear message that idealized the virtues of 'the market' in contrast to the deficiencies of 'the state'. In 1993, it announced its intention to privatize telecommunications companies. It encouraged experienced executives in Telemig to substantiate the new corporate identity through a programme of major restructuring (including	While the changes post-1993 helped the company to recover the financial deficit it had incurred in the early 1990s, they were perceived by many employees and their union as threatening their interests. There was a widespread feeling among employees that the company's new identity and actions breached the trust they had vested in it, and that the company's founding identity was now dead. Most employees did not regard Telemig's new corporate identity as legitimate,

although privatization was favoured by many senior and middle managers as well as by the government.

competitive market' (*DDdicas*, Telemig's corporate magazine, March/April 1999).

'Telemig has changed from an introverted identity oriented towards itself to an extroverted identity where leadership is oriented to the outside world, to the clients.'

'Under the new incoming president the company is redefining its priorities. The president is a leader. He has put pressure for the company to prepare for competition; we have to be a company that is oriented towards the market, not only at the level of discourse, but primarily in practice.'

layoffs) and training. However, the affinity of those managers with the government was now based on a shared ideology rather than being activated through a tight social and administrative network as had been the case in the 1973–85 period. The union movement was considerably weakened by growing unemployment and despite taking industrial action could not effectively counter-mobilize against the new corporate identity and its implementation.

Self-reliance and cost-effectiveness

'We have to live on what we can get. The state doesn't support us any more.'

'Competition is now a reality and we have to prepare for this new world.'

'Costs come first, then the rest.'

20.2

Cumulative percentage of total identity characterizations

76.3

Source: [a]interviews with directors and (for the period 1973–85) analysis of founders' autobiographies; [b]founders' autobiographies, interviews, background information on union power and action; [c]145 interviews with employees and analysis of the trade union newspaper.

lent cohesion and forcefulness to the critical ideas that contributed to a redefinition of Telemig as a company more sensitive to and in tune with the community's interests.

The third period of the company's history witnessed senior managerial efforts to mobilize for privatization and a redefinition of Telemig's stance towards customer service and subsequently towards being an agency for shareholder value. In 1995, top management issued a document, *Building Telemig's Transformation*, in which it defined Telemig as a service organization, responsive primarily to the demands of customers. This was accompanied by re-engineering and restructuring, which culminated in the separation of the mobile and the fixed business and the recognition of Telemig as one of the best service providers in the country. Managerial mobilization involved training and education for the provision of superior services and the formation of alliances with multinational companies and the neoliberal government of Cardoso to prepare for privatization.

These new identity claims were again opposed by engineers and the trade union, because they devalued engineering in favour of marketing and also undermined Telemig's identity as a state company, which during its lifetime had defined employees' interests as an essential component of its ethos. The prospect of privatization particularly enflamed union activism. The number of strikes in the telecommunications sector rose to ten in 1995 when the legislation for privatization was introduced, compared with an average of two strikes a year during the previous two years. However, by contrast with the 1980s, little was gained from this attempt to counter-mobilize because by this time the threat of unemployment was undermining the union's capacity to sustain industrial action.

5 Legitimacy

We have defined an identity claim as top management's definition of the organization's stance towards different constituencies, internal and external, through formal representation and public diffusion. The acceptability of this claim by these constituencies confers legitimacy to it. An identity claim gains legitimacy when it is embedded in discourse that relates sympathetically to the wider context (Suddaby and Greenwood, 2005). This discourse can be informed by an ideology and/or articulated by a social movement. Legitimacy has also been associated with successful recipes (Gagliardi, 1986) and can be enhanced by evidence of consistency between claims and stakeholder expectations (Gioia et al., 2000).

The Telemig case suggests that all these factors are relevant to the sustainability of corporate identity claims, and that their intensity may vary over the course of a company's development. As mentioned, interest groups can increase their legitimacy by mobilizing resources for articulating a discourse that finds resonance in changes that are socially supported. In the mid-1980s, corporate managers' claims were largely informed by the political changes that affected the country during this period, such as the move to a democratic regime. A change of political regime fostered an emphasis on decentralization of decision-making and on participation across Brazilian society. Later in the mid-1990s, Telemig's corporate identity claims were significantly informed by an ideology when they accorded with neoliberalist policies in their emphasis on competition and employability.

The legitimacy of a claim is closely related to the authority of those who make it. However, this conferred authority is unstable. It depends on the acceptance of others, who may decide to withdraw this 'right'. Thus the end of the 1970s witnessed a delegitimation of the military regime due to a withdrawal of Brazilian public support and the incapacity of the system to deliver economic growth. This led to a breakdown of the political forces that supported the regime, including the alliance between the military and engineers in state enterprises. The civilian government that replaced the military regime failed to assure adequate resources for the company and its declining performance contributed to a delegitimization of top management. A discrepancy developed between the normative expectations attached to the company and its institutional resource provision. This handicapped the company's ability to respond to global market pressures. While global telecommunications were moving towards service provision and market segmentation, Telemig was still stuck in the old model in which engineering continued to be viewed as a distinctive competence of the company. Telemig was prevented by the lack of funds from carrying out technological innovation. The inability to sustain its distinctive competence led to a failure of clear vision and of credible plans for the future, which resulted in a sense of confusion and crisis. This further reduced the legitimacy of Telemig's definition as a technocratic engineering company.

The instances in which there was a withdrawal of the legitimacy granted to Telemig's corporate identity suggest that such legitimacy can take two forms. The first reflects a *cognitive consonance* in the minds of stakeholders between a corporate identity claim and the actions of corporate management (Suddaby and Greenwood, 2005). Thus in the 1985–93 period, a cognitive dissonance arose when managerial proposals to transform Telemig into a pluralist organization and claims to stand for participation and openness lost credibility because of the perceived failure to put these claims into practice. The trade union newspaper exposed these inconsistencies between top management's discourses and practices. It did this primarily through creating metaphors, often depicted as cartoons and elaborated in stories, which criticized management as being authoritarian and operating behind closed doors. For example, the 'open door' metaphor was used to claim that these were doors that showed employees out to the street rather than ones offering access to a participative process. This cognitive dissonance undermined the legitimacy of the corporate identity. Chapter 10 offers a detailed analysis of the metaphors advanced by the union newspaper.

The second form of legitimacy is *interest-based*. It relies upon compatibility between the corporate identity, and associated managerial policies, and the interest of other parties. In the last period of Telemig's life, 1994–2000, there was a clear conflict of interest between the implications of the newly reconstructed corporate identity and the interests of employees, even though there was little cognitive dissonance between what corporate management claimed and the actions it was seen to be taking. The conflict of interest was manifested through metaphors, such as that portraying the company as a stepmother, which implied a lack of caring for the welfare of employees. Statements made in interviews and the content of the union newspaper indicate that during this period employees considered that the positive aspects of Telemig's previous corporate identity, particularly its corporativist strand, were now being undermined.

Discussion: Cycles of Corporate Identity Definition and Redefinition

The Telemig case suggests a model of corporate identity definition that could be further investigated and extended by further research. It indicates that the definition of a corporate identity evolves over time as a result of dynamic tensions associated with different conditions of mobilization and legitimacy. When viewed from a long-term perspective, Telemig's experience suggests a cyclical process whereby in some periods new claims and definitions of corporate identity are advanced and gain acceptance, whereas at other times these lose support. This postulated cycle is portrayed schematically in figure 8.1. It is framed in terms of the two key dimensions that have emerged from the case study and that are also suggested by existing theorizing, namely mobilization and legitimacy.

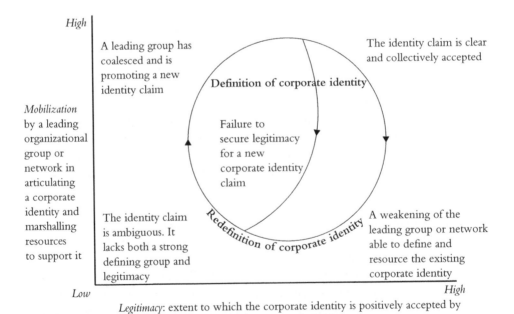

Figure 8.1   The cycle of corporate identity definition and redefinition.

The upper left-hand part of the cycle in figure 8.1 represents a situation in which an effective leading group has coalesced, probably with the support of significant external groups. This leading group has a shared sense of what the organization's role in society should be, its priorities and its preferred stakeholder group. These ideas become an identity claim when this leading group is sufficiently powerful to exert influence across different organizational levels and to mobilize the conditions that will give life to this claim. The first is a cognitive mobilization in the sense of bringing together the ideas, knowledge and expertise necessary to articulate the organization's role and its distinctive competence. The second is a political mobilization in the sense of reaching accommodations with the interests of external and internal groups that provide the organization with the autonomy to pursue that role, and permit it to secure and allocate necessary resources (Aldrich, 1999). The foundation of Telemig's corporate identity illustrates this situation.

Movement towards the upper right-hand part of the cycle represents the results of the efforts put into identity definition. At this point of the cycle, top managers have a clear and distinctive identity claim that is reiterated in its discourses and reaffirmed in structure and routines. The identity claim's cognitive and interest-based consonance also secures legitimacy from both within and outside the organization. The identity claim articulated by top management comes closest to being accepted as legitimate by the organization as a whole, as was the case for Telemig up to the end of the 1970s.

A move towards the lower right-hand part of the cycle in figure 8.1 takes place when there are changes in the environment that begin to undermine the resourcing and effectiveness of the leading group projecting an identity claim. These may create a gap between the identity and perceived reality, which will set in train the process leading to identity redefinition. For the social actors involved, this period represents a withdrawal of support for the prevailing identity claim. This situation developed in Telemig during the last years of the military regime.

As conditions shift towards the lower left-hand part of the cycle, corporate managers experience an increasing loss of legitimacy for their identity claim. The corporate identity becomes confused, discredited and challenged – in other words, delegitimated. The corporate group is weak and the corporate identity has lost centrality for both organizational members and external groups. In this situation a corporate identity crisis arises, which for Telemig in the late-1980s was exacerbated by a crisis of performance. Taking refuge in an idealized past or seeking a new identity, such as privatization, may be seen as a way out of the current uncertainties.

Identity cycles can be more or less complete. An identity cycle can be interrupted if there is a clear inconsistency between the identity claim and managerial practices. If this inconsistency represents a threat to employees' interest, or affects deeply rooted values, this situation can give rise to counter-mobilization for identity redefinition. The 'agency for multiple interests' identity characterizing Telemig from the mid-1980s did not gain full support from the bulk of the company's managers and employees, because its leadership was not rooted in the tradition of the company or the sector and was seen to be a tool of external political interests.

Progression from the top left-hand to the top right-hand segments of the cycle was cut short and the process returned to a sense of crisis and confusion before a new corporate management advanced a new identity claim in the early 1990s. The 1990s also witnessed a thorough attempt to construct a new identity for the company. Top management's mobilization involved a considerable investment in strengthening the organization's capabilities to sustain its core theme of market-ization and also to resocialize its personnel accordingly. Nevertheless, the new identity retained elements of contradiction as long as the company remained state-owned, and only achieved a high level of consistency upon privatization in 1998. Two factors contributed to identity redefinition in the period leading up to privatization. Senior managers tackled the opposition by initiating an attractive early retirement programme. They also obtained the support of middle managers for privatization because the latter believed that this was a better solution then having an organization captive to politicians or corporativism.

Conclusion

We have advanced a political perspective that calls for a revised conception of corporate identity. If corporate identity is a set of statements made by its leader-ship on the political stance of an organization – what it is and what it stands for – these statements are highly consequential for organizational members because they imply differential access to resources by groups and disparity in the demands placed upon individuals. One of the latent functions of corporate identity is to justify and secure legitimacy for the incumbent top management. But a corporate claim may also have the dual function of justifying the right of the corporate group to govern and, at the same time, of creating and constraining opportunities for different groups to pursue their interests. Because organizational members' con-ceptions of what the organization is and should be are embedded in vested inter-ests, corporate identity transformation is essentially political and contentious in nature. The fragmentation and fragility that many have described as characteristic of organizational identity may have its origin in the complexities of reconciling different interests even inside the same group. Given its political nature, identity transformation is sensitive to mobilization and counter-mobilization by diverse forces, both inside and outside the organization. Its transient and fragile nature captures not only cognitive dissonance and variance in meanings, but also the political insta-bility of power in organizations. Identity claims are at the heart of the politics of co-evolution.

Some two decades ago, Pettigrew (1985) decried the apolitical nature of studies of organizational change. A major contribution of this chapter is to reinforce his point with reference to studies of organizational identities. The mainstream of such work has substantially advanced the understanding of the cognitive complexities of the phenomena of identity definition and change, especially among individuals and groups. However, the nature of an organizational identity, such as corporate identity, is very different from that of an individual identity. Organizations are engines of power that move through resource mobilization and counter-mobilization. One interesting point that Hatch and Yanow (2006) raise in their discussion of research on identity concerns the underlying dominance of western aesthetic in our interpretations of organization identity. Taking their point further, one may ask whether the notion of managerial stewardship, and the consensus-building and rationality claims associated with management processes, have encouraged a neglect of the political nature of corporate identity definition. The analysis offered in this chapter serves to reframe the debate in these terms. It endorses and amplifies the warning some have made recently (e.g. Alvesson and Willmott, 2002; Brown, 2006; Clegg et al., 2007) that we need to move beyond the simplistic notion of shared meanings that have dominated much of the discussion on organizational identity to date. Indeed, one aspect of this notion that deserves further investigation is the extent to which top executives themselves may not always act as a homogeneous political unit when formulating corporate identities. Studies have indicated the presence of political rivalry and conflict within top management (e.g. Morrill, 1995; Ravasi and Zattoni, 2006). While our evidence suggested nuances rather than serious conflict within Telemig's top management, the narratives and documents we used as sources could have obscured its presence. The company's heavy dependence on the state for much of its life may also have reduced the scope for conflict within its top management.

Before leaving the subject of corporate identity, we should note that the Telemig case has some unusual features that speak for further work to examine how far our conclusions have wider application. First, the organization was heavily embedded in an institutional context due both to its long period of state ownership and to its public standing as the provider of an infrastructural service. While organizations in regulated environments may experience similar dynamics around the definition and redefinition of their identities, such as those associated with privatization, other companies may not be embedded to the same degree as the present case. Second, the study spanned a long period of time, 27 years. The time period adopted will inevitably bear upon an investigator's judgement as to the stability or otherwise of an organization's identity. Over a long period, there is more chance of changes taking place and for the dynamic properties of those changes to become apparent.

Notes

This chapter is drawn from Rodrigues and Child (2008).

1   As explained in chapter 3, engineers fell into two categories: those with university degrees and those with technical qualifications. It was not feasible to interview unqualified employees.

References

Albert, S., Ashforth, B. E. and Dutton, J. E. (eds) (2000) Special topic forum on organizational identity and identification, *Academy of Management Review*, 25, 13–152.

Albert, S. and Whetten, D. A. (1985) Organizational identity. In L. L. Cummings and B. M. Staw (eds), *Research in Organizational Behavior*, volume 7. Greenwich, CT: JAI Press, pp. 263–95.

Aldrich, H. (1999) *Organizations Evolving*. London: Sage.

Alvesson, M. and Willmott, H. (2002) Identity regulation as organizational control: producing the appropriate individual. *Journal of Management Studies*, 39, 619–44.

Anthony, P. (1994) *Managing Culture*. Buckingham: Open University Press.

Ashforth, B. E. and Mael, F. (1989) Social identity theory and the organization. *Academy of Management Review*, 14, 20–39.

Benson, J. K. (1977) Organizations: a dialectical view. *Administrative Science Quarterly*, 22, 1–21.

Bentley, A. F. (1908) *The Process of Government*. Chicago: University of Chicago Press.

Berger, P. and Luckmann, T. (1966) *The Social Construction of Reality*. New York: Anchor.

Berger, S. D. (ed.) (1981) *Organized Interests in Western Europe*. Cambridge: Cambridge University Press.

Berry, J. M. (1997) *The Interest Group Society*, 3rd edn. London: Longman.

Bierstedt, R. (1964) Legitimacy. In J. Gould and W. L. Kolb (eds), *A Dictionary of the Social Sciences*. Glencoe, IL: Free Press, pp. 386–7.

Brown, A. D. (1995) *Organizational Culture*. London: Pitman.

Brown, A. D. (2006) A narrative approach to collective identities. *Journal of Management Studies*, 43, 731–53.

Brown, A. D. and Humphreys, M. (2006) Organizational identity and place: a discursive exploration of hegemony and resistance. *Journal of Management Studies*, 43, 231–57.

Brown, A. D. and Starkey, K. (2000) Organizational identity and learning: a psychodynamic perspective. *Academy of Management Review*, 25, 102–21.

Burnham, W. D. (1970) *Critical Elections and the Mainsprings of American Politics*. New York: Norton.

Child, J. (1997) Strategic choice in the analysis of action, structure, organizations and environment: retrospect and prospect. *Organization Studies*, 18, 43–76.

Child, J. and Smith, C. (1987) The context and process of organizational transformation. *Journal of Management Studies*, 24, 565–93.

Chreim, S. (2002) Reducing dissonance: closing the gap between projected and attributed identity. In B. Moingeon and G. Soenen (eds), *Corporate and Organizational Identity*. London: Routledge, pp. 75–90.

Chreim, S. (2005) The continuity–change duality in narrative texts of organizational identity. *Journal of Management Studies*, 42, 567–93.

Christensen, L. T. and Cheney, G. (2000) Self-absorption and self-seduction in the corporate identity game. In M. Schultz, M. J. Hatch and M. H. Larsen (eds), *The Expressive Organization: Linking Identity, Reputation and the Corporate Brand*. Oxford: Oxford University Press, pp. 246–70.

Clegg, S. R., Courpasson, D. and Phillips, N. (2006) *Power and Organizations*. London: Sage.

Clegg, S. R., Rhodes, C. and Kornberger, M. (2007) Desperately seeking legitimacy: organizational identity and emerging industries. *Organization Studies*, 28, 495–513.

Cornelissen, J. P., Haslam, S. A. and Balmer, J. M. T. (2007) Social identity, organizational identity and corporate identity: Toward an integrated understanding of processes, patternings and products. *British Journal of Management*, 18, S1–S16.

Currie, G. and Brown, A. D. (2003) A narratological approach to understanding processes of organizing in a UK hospital. *Human Relations*, 56, 563–86.

Dowling, G. R. (2001) *Creating Corporate Reputations: Identity, Image, and Performance*. Oxford: Oxford University Press.

Elsbach, K. D. and Kramer, R. M. (1996) Members' responses to organizational identity threats: encountering and countering the *Business Week* rankings. *Administrative Science Quarterly*, 41, 442–76.

Foucault, M. (1982) The subject and power. *Critical Inquiry*, 8, 777–95.

Gagliardi, P. (1986) The creation and change of organizational cultures: a conceptual framework. *Organization Studies*, 7, 117–34.

Gioia, D. A., Schultz, M. and Corley, K. G. (2000) Organizational identity, image and adaptive instability. *Academy of Management Review*, 25, 63–81.

Granovetter, M. (1992) Economic action and social structure. In M. Granovetter and R. Swedberg (eds), *The Sociology of Economic Life*. Boulder, CO: Westview Press, pp. 53–84.

Green, D. J. (1984) Countermobilization as a revolutionary form. *Comparative Politics*, 16, 153–69.

Greenwood, R. and Hinings, C. R. (1996) Understanding radical change: bringing together the old and the new institutionalism. *Academy of Management Review*, 21, 1022–54.

Habermas, J. (1975) *Legitimation Crisis*. Boston: Beacon Press.

Hardy, C., Lawrence, T. B. and Grant, D. (2005) Discourse and collaboration: the role of conversations and collective identity. *Academy of Management Review*, 30, 58–77.

Harquail, C. V. (2004) Review of Moingeon, B. and Soenen, G. (eds) (2002). *Corporate and Organizational Identity*. London: Routledge. *Administrative Science Quarterly*, 49, 141–4.

Hatch, M. J. and Schultz, M. (2002) The dynamics of organizational identity. *Human Relations*, 55, 989–1018.

Hatch, M. J. and Schultz, M. (eds) (2004) *Organizational Identity: A Reader*. Oxford: Oxford University Press.

Hatch, M. J. and Yanow, D. (2006) Methodology by metaphor: painting and the study of organizational identity. Paper presented to the 22nd EGOS Colloqium, Bergen, July.

Hickson, D. J., Butler, R. J, Cray, D., Mallory, G. R. and Wilson, D. C. (1986) *Top Decisions: Strategic Decision-making in Organizations*. Oxford: Blackwell.

Hitt, M. A. and Tyler, B. B. (1991) Strategic decision models: integrating different perspectives. *Strategic Management Journal*, 12, 327–52.

Humphreys, M. and Brown, A. D. (2002) Narratives of organizational identity and identification: a case study of hegemony and resistance. *Organization Studies*, 23, 421–47.

Knights, D. and Morgan, G. (1991) Corporate strategy, organizations and subjectivity: a critique. *Organization Studies*, 12, 251–73.

LaPalombara, J. (2001) Power and politics in organizations: public and private sector comparisons. In M. Dierkes, A. Berthoin Antal, J. Child and I. Nonaka (eds), *Handbook of Organizational Learning and Knowledge*. Oxford: Oxford University Press, pp. 557–81.

Linstead, S. and Grafton-Small, R. (1992) On reading organizational culture. *Organization Studies*, 13, 331–55.

McCarthy, J. D. and Wolfson, M. (1996) Resource mobilization by local social movement organizations: agency, strategy and organization. *American Sociological Review*, 61, 1070–88.

Martin, J. (2002) *Organizational Culture*. London: Sage.

Melewar, T. C. and Jenkins, W. (2002) Defining the corporate identity construct. *Corporate Reputation Review*, 5, 76–90.

Meyer, J. W., Drori, G. S. and Hwang, H. (2006) World society and the proliferation of formal organization. In G. S. Drori, J. W. Meyer and H. Hwang (eds), *Globalization and Organization: World Society and Organizational Change*. Oxford: Oxford University Press, pp. 25–49.

Moingeon, B. and Soenen, G. (eds) (2002) *Corporate and Organizational Identity*. London: Routledge.

Morrill, C. (1995) *The Executive Way: Conflict Management in Corporations*. Chicago: University of Chicago Press.

Newton, K. (1999) Mass media effects: mobilization or media malaise? *British Journal of Political Science*, 29, 577–99.

Olins, W. (1995) *The New Guide to Identity*. Aldershot: Gower.

Parsons, T. (1956) Suggestions for a sociological approach to the theory of organizations – I. *Administrative Science Quarterly*, 1, 63–85.

Pettigrew, A. M. (1973) *The Politics of Organizational Decision Making*. London: Tavistock.

Pettigrew, A. M. (1985) *The Awakening Giant: Continuity and Change in Imperial Chemical Industries*. Oxford: Blackwell.

Peverelli, P. J. (2004) Creating corporate space in search of Chinese corporate identity. Unpublished paper, Faculty of Economics and Business Administration, Vrije Universiteit Amsterdam, August.

Pfeffer, J. (1981) *Power in Organizations*. New York: Pitman.

Pfeffer, J. and Salancik, G. R. (1978) *The External Control of Organizations: A Resource Dependence Perspective*. New York: Harper & Row.

Phillips, N. and Hardy, C. (1997) Managing multiple identities: discourse, legitimacy and resources in the UK refugee system. *Organization*, 4, 159–86.

Poggi, G. (2006) Power. In B. S. Turner (ed.), *The Cambridge Dictionary of Sociology*. Cambridge: Cambridge University Press, pp. 464–9.

Powell, W. W. and DiMaggio, P. J. (1991) *The New Institutionalism in Organizational Analysis*. Chicago: University of Chicago Press.

Pratt, M. and Foreman, P. (2000) Classifying managerial responses to multiple organizational identities. *Academy of Management Review*, 25, 18–42.

Ravasi, D. and Schultz, M. (2006) Responding to organizational identity threats: exploring the role of organizational culture. *Academy of Management Journal*, 49, 433–58.

Ravasi, D. and Zattoni, A. (2006) Exploring the political side of board involvement in strategy: a study of mixed-ownership institutions. *Journal of Management Studies*, 43, 1671–702.

Rodrigues, S. B. and Child, J. (2008) The development of corporate identity: a political perspective. *Journal of Management Studies* (forthcoming).

Rowley, T. I. and Moldoveanu, M. (2003) When will stakeholder groups act? An interest- and identity-based model of stakeholder group mobilization. *Academy of Management Review*, 28, 204–19.

Scott, S. G. and Lane, V. R. (2000) A stakeholder approach to organizational identity. *Academy of Management Review*, 25, 43–62.

Selznick, P. (1949) *TVA and the Grass Roots*. Berkeley: University of California Press.

Soenen, G. and Moingeon, B. (2002) The five faces of collective identities. In B. Moingeon and G. Soenen (eds), *Corporate and Organizational Identity*. London: Routledge, pp. 13–34.

Stinchcombe, A. L. (1965) Social structure and organizations. In J. G. March (ed.), *Handbook of Organizations*. Chicago: Rand McNally, pp. 142–93.

Suchman, M. C. (1995) Managing legitimacy: strategic and institutional approaches. *Academy of Management Review*, 20, 571–611.

Suddaby, R. and Greenwood, R. (2005) Rhetorical strategies of legitimacy. *Administrative Science Quarterly*, 50, 35–67.

van Riel, C. B. M. and Balmer, J. M. T. (1997) Corporate identity: the concept, its measurement and management. *European Journal of Marketing*, 31, 340–55.

Whetten, D. A. and Godfrey, P. C. (eds) (1998) *Identity in Organizations: Building Theory through Conversations*. Thousand Oaks, CA: Sage.

Whetten, D. A. and Mackey, A. (2002) A social actor conception of organizational identity and its implications for the study of organizational reputation. *Business and Society*, 41, 393–414.

Whittington, R. (2003) The work of strategizing and organizing: for a practice perspective. *Strategic Organization*, 1, 117–25.

Zucker, L. G. (1977) The role of institutionalization in cultural persistence. *American Sociological Review*, 42, 726–43.

CHAPTER NINE

Metaphors and Reflective Imaging

Introduction

This chapter examines changes in the use of metaphors applied to Telemig's management and organization by its employees and their trade union during the period from 1980 to 2000. It deepens our co-evolutionary analysis through the concept of 'reflective imaging'. This concept provides a link between changes in the inner and outer contexts of the company and the use of metaphors by employees. Attention to reflective imaging is instructive in revealing the meaning and status of metaphors in an evolving organizational context that presented employees with conditions which were at variance with their expectations and even threatening to their economic livelihood. Like the other chapters in part III of the book, this chapter also addresses a specific literature that had developed on its particular theme, namely organizational imaging through metaphors. It contributes to the development of that literature in three main ways. First, by placing the subject of organizational metaphors within a co-evolutionary framework, the chapter demonstrates ways in which we can better understand the role they play in organizational life. Second, it draws attention to the political role of metaphor as a weapon of protest against managerial actions that threaten the interests of other groups. This in turn contributes to the political perspective on organizational co-evolution that this book is developing and which will be presented more formally in chapters 10 and 11. Third, the chapter also contributes a methodology that permits the multidimensional aspects of metaphors to be demonstrated, and the incidence of different metaphors to be assessed both in a given period and over time.

The Study of Organizational Metaphors

Students of organization have shown an increasing interest in metaphors (Morgan, 1986, 1993; Oswick and Grant, 1996; Cazal and Inns, 1998; Vaara et al., 2003). The appeal of metaphors in empirical studies derives from the way they can provide insights into the hidden perceptions and feelings that individuals and groups have about organizations, and from the way metaphors are able to convey complex meanings in a concise manner (Koller, 2003). Metaphors have the power to break free from previous conceptions of organizational phenomena, as in the analysis of different types of organizational change (e.g. Marshak, 1993; Weick and Quinn, 1999). They also have the potential to generate and crystallize new insights among organizational members that may help to mobilize support for such change (Sackman, 1989; Gibson and Zellmer-Bruhn, 2001).

In view of the attention given to metaphors in connection with organizational transformation (Tsoukas, 1991), it is paradoxical that the extent to which organizational metaphors themselves change over time, and the circumstances under which this may take place, have not attracted much research. Insofar as metaphors are vehicles for conveying shared understandings that groups of people have about the characteristics of organizations, they do not stand alone from actions and events that shape those characteristics. Metaphors are likely to reflect and convey an interpretation of the context in which those articulating the metaphors find themselves. This implies that the ability of scholars to make sense of metaphors will be enhanced by taking their context into account. If that context changes over time, one might expect the metaphors in use to change correspondingly or at least for there to be a modification in the meanings attaching to existing metaphors.

The study of changes in organizational metaphors could provide a test of the thesis that they play a significant role in organizational life. Metaphors have been studied within organizational discourse with respect to their role in conveying social interpretations of phenomena such as change and conflict, and in differentiating categories of organizational members (Wilson, 1992). However, progression beyond a relatively time-limited analysis offers an opportunity to examine whether the use and meaning of metaphors changed through time in a way that followed or paralleled developments in the organizational context. This can contextualize metaphors and provide insights into the factors that encourage and inform their use. Evidence on the process of reflection on new developments that accompanies metaphorical change would add yet further insight into the construction or amendment of organizational metaphors.

This chapter therefore examines changes in the use of metaphors applied to management and organization by the employees of Telemig and their trade union during the 20-year period following 1980 in which the union was free to act independently of company and government. The concept of 'reflective imaging' provides a link between changes in the inner and outer contexts of the company and the use of metaphor. Attention to reflective imaging will be seen as instructive in revealing the meaning and status of metaphors in an evolving organizational context that presented employees with conditions which were at variance with their expectations and even threatening to their economic livelihood. In this way, the chapter contributes to a theory of metaphor within an evolving organizational and environmental context. A second contribution lies in its use of a methodology that permits the multidimensional aspects of metaphors to be demonstrated, and the incidence of different metaphors to be assessed both in a given period and over time. The chapter proceeds within the simple analytical framework shown in the next section, and its purpose is to elaborate this framework and assess its validity in order to develop theoretical insight rather than to test specific hypotheses.

The chapter is organized as follows. It begins by discussing its analytical framework and the concepts employed within that framework. It then describes the specific methodologies employed to examine context, reflective imaging and metaphors. The next section presents relevant material from the Telemig case. The chapter closes with a discussion of theoretical implications and main contributions.

Analytical Framework and Conceptual Foundations

The framework guiding our study of metaphors and reflective imaging in an evolving corporate context is shown in figure 9.1. This envisages changes in the organization's context, including the intra-organizational context of employment, to be the main trigger of a reflective process on the part of employees and their representatives. This process in turn is seen to give rise to a choice of apt metaphors and to shape the meanings attached to them. We use the term 'reflective imaging' to refer to the combination of reflection and imaging through metaphors.

The distinction made in figure 9.1 between the outer and inner context of an organization parallels that between inter- and intra-organizational fields (Pettigrew, 1985; Scott, 1995). The *outer context* consists of the national and international material and ideational systems in the environments within which the organization operates. Material systems primarily comprise features of economic consequence, such as markets and technologies. Ideational systems primarily comprise cultural values and political ideologies, which are likely to bear upon the institutional conditions that constrain organizations (Child, 2000). New circumstances in the outer context can change ownership and corporate management through entire reconfigurations of businesses, as with privatization of the telecommunications

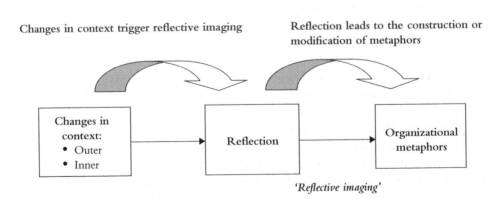

Figure 9.1 Metaphors and reflective imaging in an evolving corporate context.

sector, with profound implications for work organization and the employment relationship (Keefe and Batt, 1997).

The *inner context* consists of organizational properties that affect members and
are wholly or in large measure subject to the discretion of its top management.
Normally they derive from the overall strategy that management is pursuing and
include structuring, employment conditions and management practices. Senior
managers are normally the initiators of changes in the inner contexts of organizations. In so doing, they are not only influenced by material conditions in the
outer context, such as market forces, but may also draw upon external ideational
discourses to justify attempts to change the inner context (Alvesson and Willmott,
2002; Chreim, 2005).

In recent decades, neoliberal ideas have been of particular relevance to changes
in telecommunications companies in many countries (Hemming and Unnithan,
1996). They have encouraged and justified the restructuring of such companies so
as to become leaner and more attractive for eventual privatization. Studies of organizational change in emerging economies indicate how the managerial elites in
these countries have frequently drawn on neoliberalism to encourage privatization
(Schneider, 2004). Neoliberalism is founded on a discourse that sings the praises
of the market and of enhanced competitiveness (Sirico, 2001). This kind of
discourse legitimizes corporate restructuring and changes in the conditions of employment (Katz, 1997). The literature on discourse in organizations suggests that the
active propagation of ideas such as neoliberalism is applied to management practice through processes of institutionalization and normalization (Chreim, 2005; Hardy
et al., 2005).

Thus, privatization often brings in new managers who may have no inclination
or legal obligation to abide by the terms of longstanding relationships with their
employees (Blair, 1995; Child and Rodrigues, 2004). The introduction of new
owners and corporate managers who restructure and downsize organizations, and
hence revise the nature of commitments to employees, exemplifies how policy changes
in the outer context can initiate radical changes in the inner context (Lee, 2001).
The latter have often involved sudden and ill-considered mass dismissals that are
perceived as a breach of trust both by those made redundant and by survivors (Littler,
2000; Cascio, 2002). A change of business ownership can therefore alter the fundamental basis of the inducements–contributions exchange with consequences
for the employment relationship (Sims, 1994). This bears upon the well-being of
employees through changes in job security, levels of participation and information
sharing, and the criteria for appointments and personal advancement. When
changes of ownership or corporate management affect an organization's core
values and/or the interests of employees, the latter can call the managerial discourse into question, based on a process of reflecting on the new situation.

Referring again to figure 9.1, *reflective imaging* is a term used in neuropsycho-
logy that refers to a process in which the receiver redefines or reinvents an object
or item of information (Lieberman, 2003). It was originally understood as a search
for an alternative through reinvention when there is frustration of expectations. In

this chapter we understand the concept in a broader sense, as referring to a process whereby people reflect upon characteristics of the organizational context in which they are located and express their interpretations by constructing images of those characteristics (Rodrigues, Child and Carrieri, 2006).

Hatch and Schultz (2002) apply the term 'construed image' with reference to employees' perceptions of how *external* stakeholders perceive the organization. We shall employ the concept of reflective imaging with an *internal* orientation to employees' perceptions about their organization. Reflective imaging has three main properties. First, it can be understood as a narrative (Sødeberg, 2006) or a discursive form (Hardy et al., 2005; Suddaby and Greenwood, 2005) that has a strong emotional content. Second, it is a collective activity that is both sensitive to an organization's history and tempered by a political awareness of group interests. Third, reflective imaging is also sensitive to the more immediate context in which organizational actors find themselves. In other words, reflective imaging consists of descriptions of past and current events that situate actors and their reactions in particular contexts. This is done by constructing narratives that reinforce collective identity, by making clear the differences between groups and by constructing symbolic barriers between 'us and them' (Sødeberg, 2006).

Reflective imaging is therefore more than simply a reflection upon perceived reality; it can have political consequences. It may be defined as a collective sense-making activity (Weick, 1995) in which reflection simultaneously conveys beliefs and constructs collective mental models of social and political relations. By using different resources such as stories, cartoons or metaphors, reflective imaging is aiming to reconstitute reality, not only at a symbolic level, but also in practice. This reflection may be embedded in a discursive form such as in humour, and expose contradictions and inconsistencies in managers' discourses (Collinson, 1992).

The *Concise Oxford Dictionary* defines a *metaphor* as 'the application of a name or descriptive term or phrase to an object or action to which it is imaginatively but not literally applicable'. Linguists have defined metaphorical processes as 'experiencing one kind of thing in terms of another' (Lakoff and Johnson, 1980; Fairclough, 1995). Morgan (1986) has used the term to denote the different images by which scholars have interpreted organizations. Similarly, we shall focus on how employees represent the organization in terms of a set of images. In this sense we are interested in metaphors as comprising systems of ideas that can carry multiple, often contradictory, meanings that are nonetheless complementary.

Method

1 *Operationalization of concepts*

The methodology employed reflects a grounded iterative approach (Glazer and Strauss, 1965). The relevance of the metaphors became evident during our analysis of the trade union newspaper and also from the interviews with employees (Carrieri, 2001).

These raised the question of how metaphors could arise from reflections about changes in the evolution of the company and the changing context this presented to employees. Iteration between the data and our emerging conceptions of reflection and organizational metaphor occurred in two stages. We started by examining all the cartoons that the trade union newspaper contained up to 1990. These 304 cartoons conveyed meanings about the relationship between the organization, management and employees. Most criticized the organization or managers' handling of matters that concerned employees. The cartoons were then classified according to the content of the message and the target at which the message was addressed; for example, managers, the government or the employees. The cartoons expressed ideas through images and metaphors, and some were accompanied by stories. Both cartoons and stories often conveyed a political message.

We subsequently analysed a random selection of 104 additional cartoons published from 1991 to 2000, and compared their content with those published in the previous decade in an attempt to understand whether the images and metaphors persisted through time. Our findings in this second phase suggested that some of these metaphors that appeared in the newspaper in the first period of investigation had waned or now presented different meanings, while others disappeared from the newspaper and new ones emerged. It became clear that in order to understand the logic of these metaphors and images, we needed to relate them to the historical context in which they emerged. This then led us to analyse all the metaphors appearing between 1980 and 2000 through a longitudinal perspective with reference to the evolving situation of the company.

During the third phase of research we therefore read through every issue of the trade union newspaper from 1980 to 2000 and examined not only cartoons, but also figures and text that contained a metaphorical expression involving the organization, managers or employees in their title. As noted in chapter 8, during this period the newspaper mentioned 9,408 different topics. We identified 7,056 items that involved a discussion of the stance of the company and its management towards its employees. From these items, we selected 2,288 representations that conveyed images, gestalts and stories of managers, management and the organization. These were grouped according to the common themes they conveyed, in terms of the 'ways of thinking about the organization' and its managers (Morgan, 1986). Metaphors of organization were empirically defined in two ways: (a) when pictures, cartoons, figures and stories compared the organization and its management with other forms of organizing, by means of imagery such as of machines, a circus or animals; and (b) when these portrayed relationships between managers and employees by comparing them with other forms of relationships, such as with mothering, fathering, stepmothering or dictatorship. We then further grouped these images according to the common themes they conveyed.

These grouped images formed the metaphor systems that we present later in this chapter. Kovecses (2002) defined metaphor systems as those where various metaphors fit together in a coherent fashion to articulate abstract interrelated themes. The images appearing in the union newspaper related to one another in various

Figure 9.2 The military metaphor.
Sourece: O Bode Berra! First Year. n°06. December/1980 and January/1981.

ways: they could extend meanings, and mutually intensify, attenuate or even con-
tradict each other. In our analysis, single metaphors that confirmed and supported
a particular overarching theme were deemed to belong to a particular family of
metaphors. For example, cartoons about the 'Powerful Little Chief' were deemed
to belong to the category of military metaphors because they conveyed images of
an authoritarian hierarchical and rigid organization (see example in figure 9.2). Another
recurring set of metaphors was that of the 'Open Door' (figure 9.3), the 'Flying
Train', the 'Circus' and the 'Pig', which were grouped together because they focused
on the dubious ethics of managers and power abuse (see example in figure 9.4). Other
metaphors conveyed stories about how Telemig was a bad mother through cartoons
and figures, and these were grouped as the 'Stepmother' (see figure 9.5). The frequency with which each individual metaphor appeared in the newspaper, and the
date, were noted. We considered each different mode of metaphorical expression
that appeared in the newspaper as a separate self-contained matter, constituting
one occurrence. Thus, if an issue of the newspaper contained a story, a cartoon
and a picture of the 'Powerful Little Chief', this would be taken as representing three
instances of the military metaphor. Independent classification by two researchers
led to eight distinct primary metaphor systems, with a 96 per cent agreement between
the coders.

The analysis of reflective imaging required a contextualization of the metaphors
with reference to particular events or organizational characteristics. Information
on *outer* and *inner contexts* as previously defined has been provided in part II of this
book. We therefore only summarize key points in this chapter. The periodization
we apply is that used throughout this book. It is informed by key events in Telemig's

Figure 9.3 Open doors metaphor.
Sourece: O Bode Berra! Sep/1986.

context: the nationalization and reorganization of the sector in 1973, the fall of the military government in 1985 and the advent of Brazil's economic reform with the *Plano Real* in 1994.

2 Summary of the outer and inner contexts

Particularly relevant aspects of Telemig's outer and inner contexts included the regulatory framework for telecommunications, prevailing political ideologies and governmental policies, trade union organization and power, and the character-istics, values and practices of corporate management. The Telemig case indicates how changes in these contextual features affected employment relationships. A sum-mary of these changes is presented in table 9.1.

Reflective Imaging

The union newspaper reflected different images of Telemig over time, expressed by the changing use of metaphors. The images were often expanded by a text that accompanied the metaphorical expressions, and through pictures, cartoons and photos that conveyed implicit categorizations about the organization and/or its management. Some metaphors were mentioned more frequently in particular periods of the organization's history, and the same metaphor could carry different meanings over time. Table 9.2 presents the frequency with which the metaphors occurred and the meanings associated with each of them.

Figure 9.4 The circus and the flying train.
Sourece: O Bode Berra! n°107. Jul/1987. This figure was originally published in *Organization Studies*, Vol. 16, No. 5, page 762, published by SAGE Publications, 1995.

Figure 9.5 The mother and the step–mother.
Sourece: Bodim Semanal, n°03. 23/Jan/1997.

Table 9.1 Outer and inner context and associated metaphors

Date	Outer context	Inner context	Dominant metaphors
Telemig as an agency for economic and social development 1973–85	1 Military government 2 Nationalism: emphasis on national integration and development; closed market and import substitution 3 Economic growth 4 Nationalization of telecommunications companies 5 Unification of telecommunications through Telebrás 6 Improving performance and growing legitimacy of state enterprises (in the 1970s)	1 Military on the board and management of telecommunications companies 2 Military and engineers as the most powerful groups within such companies 3 Repression of union activities 4 Authoritarian labour relations	The military The family
Telemig as an agency for multiple interests 1986–93	1 Civilian and populist government 2 Pressures for participation in civil life 3 Continuing nationalism 4 Economic decline 5 Foundation of the Workers' Party (PT) 6 Increasing integration of the labour movement and trade union activism	1 Political interference in company affairs 2 Increasing attention of the company to societal demands 3 Increasing pressure of the trade union for more participation in the company's affairs 4 The company creates the opportunity for managerial participation in decision making 5 The company begins to recognize the trade union for purposes of discussion 6 High union membership and increasing activism	The military The open door The circus, flying train and pig The family The mother
Telemig as an agency for shareholder value 1994–2000	1 Development of new technologies and services in the telecommunications sector 2 Neoliberalism as the espoused doctrine of the government 3 Opening the market to foreign and private investors 4 Reduction of the state's role in the economy	1 Re-engineering and restructuring in preparation for privatization 2 Privatization of telecoms 3 Financial investors and bank become owners of the company 4 Telemig loses its separate identity 5 Significant downsizing and outsourcing 6 Declining union membership	The cave The stepmother The vampire

Table 9.2 Frequency of reflective imaging through metaphors at different phases of Telemig's corporate identity development

Metaphor systems and meanings	1980–5	1986–93	1994–2000	Total
Military				
Rigid, inflexible, authoritarian and bureaucratic organization	120	93	7	220
Exploitative organization: workers as objects, work intensification	210	253	14	477
Insensitive and dictatorial management	98	128	1	227
Total	428	474	22	924
Flying Train, Circus and Pig				
Organization is a floating machine adrift from its technical foundations	2	10	2	14
A shelter for corrupt, nepotistic and illegitimate managers	13	56	9	78
Chaotic, absurd and anarchical organization	4	6	7	17
Total	19	72	18	109
Open Door				
A deceptively pluralist, participative organization	12	242	73	327
Family				
Friendly environment, non-demanding and cooperative organization	84	0	0	84
The Telemig family as propaganda and myth	0	188	0	188
The family lodged in the collective memory	0	16	68	84
Total	84	204	68	356
Mother				
Caring and protective organization	3	31	15	49
Fatherly and providing organization	1	28	5	34
Generous organization	2	24	6	32
Total	6	83	26	115
Stepmother				
An organization that punishes its employees, uncaring and harsh	0	0	37	37
An organization that takes from employees, rather than gives	0	0	43	43
Total	0	0	80	80
Cave				
Confused organization at the mercy of events	0	0	17	17
An organization that has lost its identity	0	0	26	26
Employees have lost their identity	0	0	14	14
Total	0	0	57	57
Vampire				
An exploitative organization that takes money and jobs from its employees	0	0	50	50
Overall total	549	1,075	394	2,018[1]

Note: [1]270 images out of the total of 2,288 did not fit the classification of eight primary metaphors shown here.
Source: Text, cartoons, figures and pictures from Telemig's trade union newspaper.

The image of the 'Military Organization' began to appear very frequently in the union newspaper right from its inception in 1980. It was usually presented in the form of cartoons criticizing managers and the punishment-centred character of the company. Thus, the military metaphor included cartoons depicting the 'Powerful Little Chief' and other images of exploitation. The stories in these cartoons conveyed ideas about an authoritarian and rigid organization. It is the ideas implicit in these cartoons that constituted the metaphorical system of a military organization. An example is given in figure 9.2.

These cartoons challenged top managers' discourses about the positive aspects of Telemig as a military organization. Military metaphors have been frequently used by managers to emphasize efficiency and loyalty in business (Winsor, 1996). The union metaphors challenged the legitimacy of this image by emphasizing its inherent injustices and rigid rules. By comparing disciplinary procedures with forms of slavery, their messages both reflected and reinforced employee antagonism towards excessive and unacceptable levels of control and surveillance. They compared Telemig to the army, portraying the organization as a bureaucratic machine, controlled by dictatorial managers. One of the most frequent images of a victim of this approach was 'Zizi the Telephonist', which was used to highlight exploitation and excessive managerial demands placed upon staff. The 'Powerful Little Chief' was the second most frequently used cartoon image. It described an obsessive and autocratic manager whose little black moustache in a Nazi uniform was a clear reference to Hitler. These two metaphors are illustrated in Rodrigues and Collinson (1995). The appearance of military imagery reached its peak in 1986 and 1987, the first two years of democracy, at a time when the growing power of unions in Brazil was juxtaposed with the legacy of a military managerial style. The military metaphor continued to be heavily used until the early 1990s, but with different meanings attached to it. Thus the depiction of the company as rigid and inflexible appeared less frequently in the years following the end of the military government, whereas its use to depict exploitation and insensitivity increased.

Other images that also contested management's discourse and the legitimacy of its practices appeared more frequently between the mid-1980s and the early 1990s. The 'Flying Train', 'Circus' and 'Pig' images contested the claims that Telemig was an honest and rational organization, an essential part of the military culture. These images together with that of the 'Open Door' peaked after management's announcement in 1990 of the first redundancy scheme in the history of the company. At that same time, management suspended internal promotion and selection on the basis of qualification and began to employ friends and relatives instead. The 'Flying Train' portrayed a Telemig out of control and betraying its tradition of meritocracy. It was usually presented in terms of cartoons about the 'joy train', the 'shame train' or an animal circus, which highlighted managerial nepotism, favoritism and self-serving. While the military management had been portrayed as a rigid but ethical organization, these metaphors now depicted a politically inclined and corrupt organization.

These metaphors were used to criticize managers' claims that the familial and technocratic elements of the founding corporate identity were being maintained. The 'Open Door' metaphor, which appeared particularly frequently after the fall of the military government, ridiculed management's claim that it was creating a more participative and pluralist organization. The use of the metaphor suggests that the putative open door to management remained closed in the perception of employees. Thus, while top management claimed that Telemig was becoming a more pluralist and open organization, this was contested by the 'Open Door' and the 'Flying Train' metaphors. These suggested instead that Telemig had gone off the rails when it abandoned the technical rationalism of the military and succumbed to political interests instead. The following statement by a middle manager provides an illustration of reflection on this change:

> After 1985 the board became more political with all sorts of people trying to influence the company and take advantage of it. The relationships between the organization and employees became much worse. The company has been criticized as a 'Flying Train'. We do not trust top management. The idea of a career in the company is no longer plausible. Political criteria are increasingly overriding those of technical competence. (Manager)

The family metaphor appeared more frequently in the form of a text accompanying the label. As table 9.2 indicates, the meanings associated with the 'Family' metaphor changed from a 'cooperative and friendly environment' during the first phase of Telemig's corporate identity development to a parody in the second. In the third phase, the 'Family' metaphor became a symbol of the 'good old times', now lost but still present in the collective memory. Both the 'Family' and the 'Mother' metaphor systems appeared more frequently during periods of crisis. These were mainly evoked when employees' interests and personal identity were under threat from a change in leadership and ownership that affected employment security. The family image appeared most frequently from 1986 to 1993. At this time, employees felt threatened by the introduction of redundancies, and the metaphor was used primarily to claim that the founding identity of Telemig as a family was now merely propaganda. As one engineer reflected, 'A relative, a mother, or a father. It's the same feeling when you lose them. People here feel abandoned.' Comparison of data from the newspaper with those from interviews leads to the conclusion that the 'Family' metaphor appeared so frequently during the 1986–93 period because of the fear that its traditional meaning was being eroded by the company's first serious breach of the employment relationship. The following statement from an interview with a director illustrates this point:

> The government had demanded that telecoms companies cut costs. We then called all the managers in on a Sunday and asked them for a list of employees to be dismissed. This was kept most secret inside the organization. Each manager had a number of people to cut. On Monday afternoon we provided the employees in the list with a dismissal letter. The union tried to shout, but they did not have prior information about this.

The following extracts, both from engineers interviewed in the late 1990s, further indicate the perception that management had breached the norm of secure employment, which in earlier times had given credibility to the family metaphor:

> Today there is terrorism in the organization. Management has dismissed people, but they did not convince us about the reason why they did that.

> There is no loyalty in this organization. What management has done was a betrayal of our notion of a big family in Telemig.

A manager said at the time that 'You have to sacrifice the family when you dismiss people.'

Other signs of a perceived breach in the core terms of the employment relationship were evident in the union newspaper during critical periods when jobs were threatened. The passage below is an example of how this undermined the idea of a big family:

> The image of Telemig as 'one big happy family' is no longer credible. The ossified technocrats who run the organization have shown how well they can follow instructions from Brasília. They've kept their privileges while scapegoating their employees and then dispensing with them. This proves that the ethical principles that had defined the company's identity are no longer worth the paper they're written on. (*O Bode*, July 1990)

Another metaphor conveying a similar meaning was quite frequently used during the second period of Telemig's history. This was the 'Mother' metaphor, which reflected the paternalism and protective policies of the then state-owned company. We analysed this metaphor separately from that of the family because it was mostly evoked when continuity of the firm's 'maternal duties' was threatened by changes in the institutional and economic environment. Its frequency was particularly high during the second phase of Telemig's corporate identity development, between 1986 and 1993. Triangulation (Todd, 1979) with interview data suggests that a sense of grievance arose because Telemig was losing aspects of its maternal identity that employees valued. For example, an engineer suggested that the organization was in a state of bereavement with the loss of the 'Telemig Family' and its maternal protection:

> I understand that we have to start all over again. Telemig was like a mother and when you bury your mother you cannot keep thinking about her. You have to move on. 'Mother Telemig' is dead. Before they introduced the new identity card, every one of us wore a black badge. This was a way to show the world that the old company was dead, and that nothing could replace it. It was like burying your own mother.

By the late 1990s, the 'Mother' metaphor was becoming replaced by that of the 'Stepmother' (for an example, see figure 9.5). This metaphor was used most in the period just before and after privatization, from 1997 to 1999. It depicted dissatisfaction and disappointment with what Telemig had become, and conveyed a sense of harsh treatment. It also expressed grievances at demands that were perceived as unfair and destructive of organizational activities that employees valued, such as attention to good human relations. The following reflections from interviews are illustrative:

> Some people started to work like crazy, beyond normal working hours, because they were foolish. This is a dangerous way to behave as it gives the impression that you will put up with anything. . . . If this is the case, they will demand even more. (Manager)

> I am very sad because of what is happening to relations within the company. The situation is deplorable. I am suffering like hell because I know what is happening. I can't see where the organization is going and I don't know what we stand for any more. (Engineer)

> Telemar [name of the newly privatized company] is like a stepmother. The more you do to please, the more it demands from you. Everything is confused, disorganized and without orientation. We work much more now, but we do not know for what. We do not know what the shareholders want and how we are going to benefit. (Engineer)

Textual material published by the newspaper suggests that for the union at least, a dramatic breach of the core employment relationship was now occurring in this third phase, particularly through implied or actual threats to security of employment and management's generally aggressive stance. For example:

> The company has damaged its relationship with employees to such an extent that its behavior is now tantamount to 'psychological torture', inflicted through threats of dismissal. The employees would now prefer an immediate execution of the sentence rather than going through this nightmare any longer. (O Bodim, 26 November 1998)

> By imposing a new code of conduct, Telemig does not allow employees to apply for legal recognition of their rights, something that would be taken for granted in any democratic country. This new code can be expressed in the following way: 'either you agree with everything I say or you are out of the job'. (O Bodim, 9 December 1998)

The union contested the new managerial discourse of flexibility, aimed at giving Telemig 'the lightness of a bird', to quote one director. By contrast, the union newspaper depicted Telemig as a dark cave. The 'Cave' metaphor expressed feelings of anomie, alienation and rejection from the company (for example, figure 9.6), and again focused primarily on lack of security. This metaphor appeared during the pre-privatization period, especially in 1995 when the privatization of

Figure 9.6   The cave.
Source: Bodim Semanal, n°12. 25/Mar/1994.

telecommunications companies was formally announced. The image of insecurity and demotivation expressed by the 'Cave' metaphor reflected how employees felt. For example:

> We do not know what is going to happen. Competition has increased our stress. We don't work with any pleasure anymore. The Board has not told us where we are going. We don't know why. (Engineer)

> People started to analyse the changes and raise questions. I've given 30 years of my life to this organization and what have I got out of it? Only uncertainty about my future. (Manager)

When interviewed, the architect of the 'Cave' metaphor, who was a Telemig employee seconded to work for the union, explained that:

> We invented a character with big eyes in a dark cave, in order to encourage the employees to reflect upon the current situation and how it could affect them. Our idea is that this should be a reflexive character. The goal was to make the workers think about the consequences of the changes for us.

Another significant metaphor is the 'Vampire', which also appeared only in the last period (see figure 9.7 for an example). Here the company is presented as a bloodsucker, as exploitative of employee fragility and as 'stealing' money and jobs from employees. This imaging was predominant in the period before and just after privatization. It seemed to be a reaction to the managerial discourse that stressed employee self-reliance and shareholder value. These aspects of corporate identity were associated with asymmetry in the exchange between inducements and contributions as the employees now perceived themselves as giving too much for too

GREED IS DEVOURING ALL OUR JOBS

Figure 9.7   The vampire.
Source: Bodim. Special Edition: CNL 98/99. 01/Dec/1998.

little. As one engineer reflected, 'The company wants everything from us, including our honour; it even pressurizes employees to betray their colleagues in court. Meanwhile, it is cutting back on even the smallest things, like free coffee.'

In short, the analysis of metaphors used in the union newspaper and employees' own expressions suggests that the metaphors expressed the widespread reflection by employees that as events moved into the 1990s there was an increasing breach of the trust in management's commitment to maintaining the previous employment relationship in terms of job security. The factors behind this change were management's destruction of valued features in the organizational culture, the downgrading of the status of previously powerful groups such as engineers, the new managerial emphasis on the conditionality of employees' jobs and the growing priority given to shareholder value.

This conclusion is supported by evidence from the interview data. As mentioned in the 'Method' section, interviews conducted in the first and second rounds of research permit a comparison of expressions indicating how the employees perceived changes in the employment relationship with reference to the last two of the three phases in Telemig's corporate identity development (1986–93 and

Table 9.3   Indications of breaches of the employment relationship

Items associated with changes in the employment relationships	Frequency with which each item was evaluated negatively		
	1986–93	1994–2000	Total
Core aspects			
Salary and benefits	26	46	72
Employment security	37	154	191
Career advancement	68	6	74
Changes in workload	8	119	127
Total	139	325	464
Average	2.4	5.7	4.1
Peripheral aspects			
Company's goals and missions, company ethics	91	179	270
Relationships between the company and the union	5	39	44
Relations among employees	39	44	83
Employees autonomy and voice	105	209	314
Total	240	471	711
Average	4.2	8.3	6.2
Overall total	379	796	1,175

Source: 57 staff outside top management in each period. Since the table focuses on perceived breaches of the employment relationship, only persons expressing *negative* evaluations of the above items were included. They constitute 79 per cent of those interviewed.

1994–2000 respectively). Table 9.3 presents the number of negative evaluations expressed by interviewees with reference to each of these two phases. The average number of negative evaluations per interviewee relating to core elements of the employment relationship was 2.4 for the former period, and more than doubled to 5.7 mentions in the latter phase – a rise of 138 per cent. The corresponding figures for change in the organizational culture were 4.2 for the former phase and 8.3 for the second phase, an increase of 98 per cent. These figures suggest that the employees interviewed tended to perceive a increasing breach in the employment relationship over time.

Reflective Imaging as a Force for Corporate Evolution

The architect of the 'Cave' metaphor quoted earlier said that the intention behind it was to raise consciousness among the workers about the meaning for them of the changes that management had initiated. When expressed forcefully and dramatically, as in the union newspaper, a heightened collective consciousness may cause management in turn to reflect upon and perhaps reconsider its actions. Some clues are available that permit a tentative assessment of whether this took place. Following the demise of the military government, the strong mobilization and series of industrial actions by the trade union appeared to contribute to such a process. This was recognized in interviews with directors. Their responses suggest that employee and union criticism through reflective imaging did lead management to reflect upon its practices. For example, one of the directors said:

> We were shaken many times by the trade union. When I entered Telemig I found a very strong union. They had a very well structured and aggressive language. They released their newspaper very quickly and caught us by surprise. . . . Their language was colloquial, humorous, based on slang and grounded on daily problems.

We also asked the union about the effectiveness of the images its newspaper portrayed at different points in time. A union official said the following about the period 1980–90:

> The images of the little chief were very effective because everyone knew whom the story was about. In many cases top management replaced the supervisor or manager who was accused of abusing his power. There was a time at which the employees were eager to receive our newspaper to know who our next 'victim' would be.

However, with the weakening of the union's power as the 1990s progressed, it appeared that, despite the ingenuity of the imaging it produced, this did not have a significant influence on preventing or mitigating the negative effects of the company's evolutionary path. The union now found it difficult to convince its members that they had any ability to change what was in progress. The current union head said the following about the period from 1990 to 2000:

> By using photos and cartoons we tried to mobilize the attention of what we considered to be a demotivated and detached workforce. We needed to show them what was happening to the company. They did not seem to believe that we could prevent the government from going ahead with privatization, and unions were already losing power at that time.

Discussion

One of aims of this chapter is to illustrate and extend the role of metaphors in organizational analysis. As table 9.1 indicates, organizational metaphors change with the changing dynamics of the outer and inner contexts and so does their meaning. The production of metaphors follows the dynamics of organizational change.

The concept of reflective imaging provides an insight into this process. Reflective imaging involves judgements as to whether ongoing organizational changes are relatively peripheral to collective interests or central to them and therefore reveals political and identification issues behind group divisions. The evidence suggests that organizational changes that are central to employees' interests, such as those that threaten employment, encouraged a particular type of reflective imaging by the trade union and its members. The Telemig experience therefore confirms the framework presented in figure 9.1, as well as suggesting certain elaborations to it.

What happened in Telemig indicates that reflective imaging can take two forms. The first was evident from the mid-1980s to the beginning of the 1990s. This appeared as a response to changes in those core *values* of the organization that its members cherished (Gagliardi, 1986). At that time reflective imaging reveals a dispute concerning the legitimacy of the management that replaced the military regime, and of its practices. The metaphors conveyed criticism of the perceived replacement of professional criteria by political considerations in the appointment of key positions. It also reveals an underlying power struggle between the engineers, until that time the key group in the organization, and the group of new political appointees. The 'Flying Train' and 'Circus' metaphors, which appeared more frequently at that time, had a strong moral content and directly accused top management of malfeasance. In this period reflective imaging captured other types of inconsistency between top management discourse and practice. Though management formally and widely announced its intention to transform the previous authoritarian and bureaucratic company into a more participative and democratic one, it did not extend this to lower levels in the company. The military metaphor therefore remained the most recurring one during this period, expressed mainly through cartoon and stories of the 'Powerful Little Chief' and the 'Telephonist'. These stories personally accused some managers of being authoritarian and harsh with employees. Though they did not indicate names, they contained sufficient information to identify who the 'villains' were. Evidence from the interviews suggests that the military metaphor system was successful in provoking shame in the managers concerned, by making their abuses public. This was also the case with the 'Flying Train', 'Circus' and 'Pig' metaphors, which exposed the faults of top management and questioned its legitimacy.

An important characteristic of reflective imaging at that time was its embeddedness in humour. Humorous metaphors can be appropriate in an authoritarian environment, where there is no room for subordinate participation and voice. Humour introduces ambiguity into the message, allowing for a negotiation of meanings. As messages conveyed through humour are not expected to be taken personally and seriously, the possibility of reprimand is less likely to occur (Rodrigues and Collinson, 1995).

The outer and the inner contexts were very important for the kind of reflective imaging that took place during this period. As Brazil returned to democracy, social pressures to extend the participation of citizens in all spheres of life, together with employee interest in having a voice in the company's affairs, legitimized mobilization by the Telemig union. At this time, the Brazilian unions became very powerful and unified nationally, while maintaining strong links with the PT (Workers Party). Union power was frequently mobilized through strikes in the telecommunications and other industries. Labour legislation required compulsory union membership until the mid-1980s, and at the time Telemig union represented about 95 per cent of Telemig's employees outside top management.

The kind of reflective imaging that occured in the early 1990s, when the Telemig began to prepare for privatization, was of a different nature. During this later period government policy became more market-oriented. This encouraged Telemig's management to develop a new corporate identity emphasizing the company's need to compete and the associated need for employees to be self-reliant. Top managers continued to be appointed by the Ministry of Telecommunications, but these were now professional managers who could make the company more attractive to private investors. They started a programme of downsizing that became more aggressive as the prospect of privatization became more definite. The type of reflective imaging that is apparent from 1994 onwards refers to these changes and their impact on the employment relationship. These new changes were more than just an affront to the organization's inherited core values. Besides altering the basis of exchange between the company and employees they directly threatened employees' *interests*. Senior managerial discourse about employability and self-sufficiency undermined the paternalism that had been nourished for years in Telemig as a state enterprise. Paternalism is a way of committing employees to the organization through use of the logic of the gift to create dependence (Mauss, 1990). The reciprocity is based on the honour of the giver and the loyalty of the receiver (Bourdieu, 1991). The discourse of competence and efficiency, by contrast, emphasizes independence and dispenses with loyalty. The 'Cave' metaphor depicts how employees were mesmerized by this change, and felt powerless to fight against it.

The 'Cave' metaphor was the main conveyor of messages about anomie and deidentification with the company and its management. These messages were also intended to serve as a wake-up call from the union, while at the same time expressing its growing loss of power. For example, in 1995 alone there were ten attempts to organize strikes in the telecommunications sector, but these failed to change the government's intention to proceed with privatization. Moreover, the membership of Telemig's union was now declining rapidly. Deprived of its power to mobilize effectively, the most the union could do was to reflect upon change. The privatization of the company led to the creation of more strident metaphors, such as the 'Vampire'. These reflected the perceived heartlessness of the downsizing associated with privatization, and accused managers of letting the company become a victim of the ideological forces of neoliberalism.

The differences in the type of reflective imaging prominent in these two periods furnish several insights into the phenomenon and its context. One concerns how the nature of reflective imaging by the union related to the impact that ongoing changes had on different aspects of the employment relationship. In the first period, reflection focused on the ways that new corporate management was deviating from central aspects of the organization's cultural *values*. It therefore questioned the legitimacy of managerial *behaviour*. By contrast, in the second period, reflection focused on the consequences of new owners breaking the very foundations of the employment relationship. It therefore questioned whether managers could any more be *trusted* to honour employees' *interests* against those of the new private owners.

A related insight is that the tone of organizational metaphors articulated by employees as an interest group varies with the ability of their organized body – the union – to mobilize in protection of their concerns and interests. In the first period, institutional provisions guaranteed employment security. The union could extend and invent ways of exercising its voice without fear of undue reprisal against its members. In the second period, the institutional environment no longer afforded such protection, and indeed conveyed policies informed by a neoliberal ideology that induced insecurity of employment. The main institutional factors prevailing from the mid-1980s to the early 1990s, such as a strong and militant political labour party and the social legitimacy accorded to a pluralistic and inclusive model of management, were no longer present by the second half of the 1990s. The decline in union membership and climate of fear among employees undermined the union's ability to mobilize effectively, and induced the use of increasingly desperate and hostile metaphors. The articulation of such metaphors not only expressed a growing sense of powerlessness, but may also have been intended to serve as a substitute for direct union action. Sandoval's (2001) study of the mobilization capacity of the Brazilian trade union movement supports the conclusion that the most unions could do as the 1990s progressed was to inform their members about the implications of current events.

The study of the metaphors applied to Telemig and its management points to two main features of the reflective images they expressed. The first is that they convey multidimensional meanings. They addressed multiple audiences, including politicians, managers and union members. The production of metaphors had the double function of coalescing collective consciousness and generating the political will to resist unwanted change. It reaffirmed the union's identity by clearly delineating workers from managers. The discourse of 'us and them' was frequently presented by portraying managers as villains and employees as saviours of the company and the guardians of its ethics and morality. The second feature is that although some metaphors discourse on the same theme, the meanings underlying a particular theme change as the situation evolves. For example, the 'family' metaphor was an affirmation of a cherished feature of Telemig's founding culture in the military period, but later it was increasingly used to denote that the ethos of care for the employees and dependents was being eroded. Eventually it was almost wholly replaced by the 'Stepmother' metaphor.

Conclusion: Organizational Metaphors
and Co-evolution

This chapter offers new insights into the role of metaphor and reflective imaging. It demonstrates how an analysis of metaphors can help to expose the nature of organizational evolution over time, including its dynamic features, such as the influence of different actors in the change process. The approach offered here uncovers not only the issues of identity surfaced by most studies of organizational metaphors, but also issues of power, conflict and resistance to change. It indicates one path towards a more politically oriented analysis of corporate evolution.

The chapter also adds to co-evolutionary understanding by illustrating the way in which metaphors are informed by their contexts and thus change over time. In so doing, it has developed a methodology that extends the use of metaphors in organization analysis. Going beyond their mere linguistic meaning has shown how metaphors, by serving as conduits of reflective thinking on change, can also be a political activity intended to influence the process of transformation. Metaphors are used in the 'game' of organizational politics and reflective imaging contains judgements as to whether organizational changes are central or peripheral to employees' interests.

The political role of organizational metaphor raises the question for further research as to the effectiveness of reflective imaging by employees and their unions in influencing management practices and policies. Circumstantial evidence from the Telemig case suggests that two conditions are relevant to this question. The first involves the content and form of reflective imaging. Thus reflective imaging based on humour is unlikely to provoke strong reprimand, but may be effective through shaming. Second, the case study suggests that the ability to mobilize opposition supports the effectiveness of reflective imaging. The more the outer context offers institutional protection for the organizational actors involved in reflective imaging, the more likely it is that they will be able to mobilize action strong enough to translate that imaging into a force of some consequence. If such protection is not available, reflective imaging is likely to function merely as an 'escape valve' (Rodrigues and Collinson, 1995).

A third contribution concerns methodology. Instead of just focusing on single metaphors that arise in a particular point in time, the methodology we employ focuses on systems of metaphors and how these changed. Moreover, rather than examining only rhetorical metaphors, we have examined multiple modes of metaphorical expression, such as cartoons, figures, pictures and text. The application of this methodology to the Telemig case suggests that metaphors offer more as tools for understanding organizational life than has normally been recognized. The examination of organizational metaphors in their outer and inner contexts enhances our understanding of how, within organizations, a unique dynamic is created in response to external and internal pressures, which may sometimes assist members to cope with such pressures and mitigate them when they have the power to do so.

References

Alvesson, M. and Willmott, H. (2002) Identity regulation as organizational control: producing the appropriate individual. *Journal of Management Studies*, 39, 585–618.

Blair, M. (1995) *Ownership and Control: Rethinking Corporate Governance for the Twenty-first Century*. Washington, DC: The Brookings Institution.

Bourdieu, P. (1991) *Language and Symbolic Power*. Cambridge, MA: Harvard University Press.

Carrieri, A. P. (2001) O fim do mundo Telemig: A transformação das significações culturais em uma empresa de telecomunicações. Doctoral Thesis, UFMG–CEPEAD.

Cascio, W. F. (2002) *Responsible Restructuring*. San Francisco: Berrett-Koehler.

Cazal, D. and Inns, D. (1998) Metaphor, language and meaning. In D. Grant, T. Keenoy and C. Oswick (eds), *Discourse and Organizations*. London: Sage, pp. 258–78.

Child, J. (2000) Theorizing about organization cross-nationally. *Advances in Comparative International Management*, 13, 27–75.

Child, J. and Rodrigues, S. B. (2004) Repairing the breach of trust in corporate governance. *Corporate Governance: An International Review*, 12, 143–51.

Collinson, D. L. (1992) *Managing the Shopfloor: Subjectivity, Masculinity and Workplace Culture*. Berlin: Walter de Gruyter.

Chreim, S. (2005) The continuity–change duality in narrative texts of organizational identity. *Journal of Management Studies*, 42, 567–93.

Fairclough, N. (1995) *Critical Discourse Analysis*. London: Longman.

Gagliardi, P. (1986) The creation and change of organizational cultures: a conceptual framework. *Organization Studies*, 7, 117–34.

Gibson, C. B. and Zellmer-Bruhn, M. E. (2001) Metaphors and meaning: an intercultural analysis of the concept of teamwork. *Administrative Science Quarterly*, 46, 274–303.

Glazer, B. and Strauss, A. (1965) Discovery of substantive theory: A basic strategy underlying quantitative research'. *American Behavioral Scientist*, 8, 5–12.

Hardy, C., Thomas, L. B. and Grant, D. (2005) Discourse and collaboration: the role of conversations and collective identity. *Academy of Management Review*, 30, 58–77.

Hatch, M. J. and Schultz, M. (2002) The dynamics of organizational identity. *Human Relations*, 55, 989–1018.

Hemming, E. and Unnithan, N. P. (1996) Determinants of privatization in developing countries. *Social Science Quarterly*, 77, 434–44.

Katz, H. (ed.) (1997) *Telecommunications. Restructuring Work and Employment Relations Worldwide*. Ithaca, NY: ILR Press.

Keefe, J. H. and Batt, R. (1997) Restructuring of telecommunications in the United States. In H. Katz (ed.), *Telecommunications: Restructuring Work and Employment Relations Worldwide*. Ithaca, NY: ILR Press, pp. 31–88.

Koller, V. (2003) Metaphor clusters in business media discourse: a social cognition approach. PhD thesis submitted to the Department of English, University of Vienna.

Kovecses, Z. (2002) *Metaphor: A Practical Introduction*. Oxford: Oxford University Press.

Lakoff, G. and Johnson, M. (1980) *Metaphors We Live By*. Chicago: University of Chicago Press.

Lee, G. (2001) Towards a contingent model of key staff retention: the new psychological contract reconsidered. *South African Journal of Business Management*, 32, 1–9.

Lieberman, M. D. (2003) Reflective and reflexive judgment processes: a social cognitive neuroscience approach. In J. P. Forgas, K. R. Williams and W. von Hippel (eds), *Social Judgments: Explicit and Implicit Processes*. New York: Cambridge University Press, pp. 44–67.

Littler, C. R. (2000) Comparing the downsizing experiences of three countries: a restructuring cycle? In R. J. Burke and C. L. Cooper (eds), *The Organization in Crisis*. Oxford: Blackwell, pp. 58–77.

Marshak, R. J. (1993) Managing the metaphors of change. *Organizational Dynamics*, 22, 44–56.

Mauss, M. (1990) *The Gift*. London: Routledge.

Morgan, G. A. (1986) *Images of Organizations*. London: Sage.

Morgan, G. A. (1993) *Imaginization*. Newbury Park, CA: Sage.

Oswick, C. and Grant, D. (eds) (1996) *Organization Development: Metaphorical Explorations*. London: Pitman.

Pettigrew, A. M. (1985) *The Awakening Giant: Continuity and Change in ICI*. Oxford: Blackwell.

Rodrigues, S. B., Child, J. and Carrieri, A. (2006) Corporate identity and reflective imaging through metaphors. Unpublished working paper, Birmingham Business School, University of Birmingham.

Rodrigues, S. B. and Collinson, D. L. (1995) 'Having fun?' Humour as resistance in Brazil. *Organization Studies*, 16, 739–68.

Sackman, S. (1989) The role of metaphors in organization transformation. *Human Relations*, 42, 463–85.

Sandoval, S. A. M. (2001) The crisis of the Brazilian labor movement and the emergence of alternative forms of working-class contention in the 1990s. *Revista Psicologia Politica*, 1(1), 173–95.

Schneider B. R. (2004) Organizing interests and coalitions in the politics of market reform in Latin America. *World Politics*, 56, 456–79.

Scott, W. R. (1995) *Institutions and Organizations*. Thousand Oaks, CA: Sage.

Sims, R. R. (1994) Human resource management's role in clarifying the new psychological contract. *Human Resource Management*, 33, 373–82.

Sirico, R. A. (2001) The culture of value, the culture of the market. In Brian Griffiths, Robert A. Sirico and Frank Field (eds), *Capitalism, Morality and Markets*. London: Institute of Economic Affairs, pp. 41–56.

Schneider Ross, B. (2004) Organizing interests and coalitions in the politics of market reform in Latin America. *World Politics*, 56, 456–79.

Sødeberg, A. (2006) Sensegiving and sensemaking in integration processes. In B. Czarniawska and P. Gagliardi (eds), *Narratives We Organize By: Narrative Approaches in Organization Studies*. Amsterdam: John Benjamins.

Suddaby, R. and Greenwood, R. (2005) Rhetorical strategies of legitimacy. *Administrative Science Quarterly*, 50, 35–67.

Todd, J. (1979) Mixing qualitative and quantitative methods: triangulation in action. *Administrative Science Quarterly*, 24, 602–11.

Tsoukas, H. (1991) The missing link: a transformational view of metaphors in organizational science. *Academy of Management Review*, 16, 566–85.

Vaara, E., Tienari, J. and Säntti, R. (2003) The international match: metaphors as vehicles of social identity building in cross-border mergers. *Human Relations*, 56, 419–51.

Weick, K. (1995) *Sensemaking in Organizations.* Thousand Oaks, CA: Sage.

Weick, K. and Quinn, R. (1999) Organizational change and development. *Annual Review of Psychology,* 50, 361–86.

Wilson, F. (1992) Language, technology, gender and power. *Human Relations,* 45, 883–904.

Winsor, R. D. (1996) Military perspectives of organizations. *Journal of Occupational Change Management,* 9, 34–42.

CHAPTER TEN

The Politics of Learning at a Time of Restructuring

This chapter focuses on the process whereby during the 1990s the tenets of neoliberal ideology were applied within Telemig through a programme of restructuring and re-education at both organizational and individual levels. As chapter 6 has described, the reconstruction resulted in a co-evolutionary manner from a combination of change within the company and externally. The initiative for this programme came from the company's own senior management, but it was informed and influenced by the government's clear intention to institute neoliberal reform so as to prepare Telemig for privatization. Although it is argued that organizations are infused with ideology (Simons and Ingram, 1997), there is as yet little understanding about how organizations import and apply it through a process of learning. Studies of managerial workplace control have drawn attention to the connection between ideology and learning (Knights and Willmott, 1987; Alvesson and Willmott, 2002), but with little reference to the potential influence of external factors. There has been little investigation into how learning within organizations can be a reflection of ideologies that justify particular distributions of power and benefit, and provide a means to forge new organizational arrangements consistent with such distributions.

Studies of what is commonly called 'organizational learning' have for the most part adopted a social-psychological perspective. Two focuses within this perspective have been on the association of learning with changes in intersubjective meaning and identity (Gherardi and Nicolini, 2001; Corley and Gioia, 2003), and on the creation and diffusion of new competencies in organizations (March, 1991, 1994). Many of these analyses have assumed, at least implicitly, a consensus between top management and employees concerning such changes. They have therefore not given much attention to how learning might be motivated by sectional interests within a broader context of political and organizational change, and hence a contentious character. Some attention has been given to the association between organizational learning and organizational change in general (e.g. von Rosenstiel and Koch, 2001), but only a few studies have gone further (LaPalombara, 2001;

Merkens et al., 2001) in articulating how organizations absorb views and beliefs that are ideologically and institutionally embedded and transform them into new practices and routines.

This chapter locates learning in relation to the programme of radical change that took place within Telemig during the 1990s. This programme was outlined in chapter 6, and it represents a particularly discontinuous phase of the company's evolution. We describe how the competencies emphasized by Telemig's leaders in connection with the company's restructuring mirrored the then current ideological conceptions at the macro level of the political economy. Essentially, neoliberal ideas of economic good were reflected in what were defined as appropriate organizational competencies and practices. These developments speak for a political perspective on organizational learning.

Theoretical Perspective

1 Learning as a political enterprise

Organizational learning and knowledge-creation have been regarded as conducive to 'development' and 'innovation'. In other words, they have been associated with levelling up from an inferior, less sophisticated capability to superior and complex skills that enhance the subject's behavioural repertoire, and improve his or her capacity to solve problems (Skinner, 1974; Sutherland, 1992). Thus, learning has been usually conceived as a good thing, and even emancipatory (Fiol and Lyles, 1985; Senge, 1997). In this perspective, learning is assumed to benefit all employees, and this is one of the reasons why their role as agents in the process has been perceived as unproblematic. Likewise, it is widely assumed to be a good thing for learning by the organization members to be shared so as to become an organization property – for instance, converting their tacit knowledge into explicit knowledge (Nonaka and Takeuchi, 1995).

This benign view of 'sweetness and light' ignores conflicts of interest between management and employees, and the possibility that organizational learning can become the servant of policies that are not in the interests of the collective (Knights and Willmott, 1987; Alvesson and Willmott, 1996). The consequence is that organizational learning may create a breach of trust between management and employees, rather than strengthening trust between them.

Different perspectives highlight distinctive dimensions of this problem. Studies of ownership and control concerned with corporate governance indicate that managers may be politically engaged with adopting a self-serving view of their companies that fails to meet employees' expectations and needs. Blair (1995, 1996) suggests that some managerial strategies leading to organizational restructuring tend to transfer wealth to shareholders at the expense of employees. Organizational studies of management and control indicate that learning strategies can be a powerful weapon of organization change, and of service to the interests of the dominant coalition.

Managers can advance their ideas through various means, such as educational programmes and organization restructuring, or through more subtle ways such as by
creating a new organization culture. There is also plenty of evidence about how
managers can use organizational culture as a mechanism to control employees and
achieve their goals (Collinson, 1992; Thompson and McHugh, 2002; Child, 2005;
Rodrigues, 2006). Learning can be a powerful weapon of change because it can
be used to stimulate the development of work orientations and 'work identities'
that are congruent with management's goals (Alvesson and Willmott, 2002, p. 622).
These authors suggest that managing the worker's identity has become a critical
tool for managers because they can help employees to 'swallow' unpalatable
changes, such as restructuring and downsizing.

Environmental change entails ideological repositioning by dominant coalitions,
with consequences for the type of institutional demands that impinge upon organizations. A change of government, for example, can generate pressures for changes
of ownership and control, especially through privatization, that tend to trigger new
organizational policies with implications for organization forms and identity
(Rodrigues and Child, 2003). In such ways, political ideology can impact organizations by informing decisions about organization forms (hierarchy and structure)
and strategy (Simons and Ingram, 1997).

Ideology, however, is not simply an autonomous, exogenous force. Managers
espouse it and bring it into organizations, as a rationale to justify and inform programmes of learning and retraining. Such programmes can be ideal conduits of
ideology because they embody ideas about organizational forms and strategies and
also define the place that is reserved for the employee in the organization. These
ideas are channelled to employees in subtle ways, such as through corporate cultures. Managers articulate and channel corporate cultures to supply workers with
strong values (Pettigrew, 1979, 1987; Ray, 1986). Restructuring leading to changes
in the social contract with employees can be presented in a positive light as representing 'more advanced modes of organizing' or empowerment (Kelly, 1998). If
effectively implemented, learning leads to the internalization of values and norms,
accompanying the acquisition of new competencies.

The literature on organizational learning suggests the kind of values that free
market organizations are likely to inculcate. One of its prime concepts is that of
acquiring competencies (Doz, 1997). Developing core competencies has meant being
able to do key tasks better than others (Prahalad and Hamel, 1990). Insofar as core
competencies represent the addition of value, companies have been encouraged to
get rid of activities and people that do not meet this criterion (Cascio, 2002). The
concept of core competencies was accompanied by the model of lean and mean
structures, and the view that managers' and employees' qualities had to be reshaped
in a way that was congruent with building the organization's key competencies
(Doz, 1997).

The analysis of organizational learning theories reveals the ideological tone of
the concepts they embody. They suggest that the development of new competencies depends on the organization's capacity to align individual competencies to

intended strategies. It is assumed that strategic competencies can only be acquired when the organization is able to associate thinking and behaviour with a certain type of mentality (Doz, 1997). 'Knowing how to be' (Levy-Leboyer, 1993) in terms of attitudes and values is seen as constituting the possible link between individual qualities and the competencies management wishes the organization to acquire. The concept of competencies also implies an externalization of the tacit knowledge and skills that individuals hold. It refers to skills that are applicable to particular contexts, with flexibility being a prime consideration (Bartlett and Goshal, 1997).

When a learning programme is applied to connect knowledge, skills and organization-related competencies with views that are externally and institutionally articulated, it ceases to be just an educational device (Skinner, 1974). It becomes a political instrument that ties the self-regulating capacities of individuals to programmes at the institutional level (Rose, 1992). This draws attention both to the way in which managers can be agents for implementing ideas conceived at the macro level, and to the role of ideology itself in reconciling individual subjectivity to institutional aspirations.

2 The role of ideology: neoliberalism as motivation and content for learning

Liberalism was the most important ideology elaborated in western society through the nineteenth century up to the First World War. Though it retained a following in the USA and the UK, and was rearticulated in the 1940s as an antidote to totalitarianism by authors such as Hayek (1960) and Popper (1962), it became a dominant global force only by the beginning of the 1990s. At that time, the governments of most emerging economies were opening their markets to international competition and undertaking privatization, so creating a political and economic environment that allowed for neoliberal ideas to be applied to organizations and their members.

Neoliberalism conveys three interlinked sets of ideas that are relevant to the subject of this chapter: ideas on ownership, on the free market and on individualism. The persuasiveness of neoliberalism derives from its capacity to link conceptions about institutions (the market as an institution), organizations (competitiveness) and individual self-reliance. In the UK these ideas were transmitted to organizations and individuals through Margaret Thatcher's idea of the 'enterprise culture' (Hellas and Morris, 1992). This advocated the creation of a free market by reducing the power of the state and returning it to individuals and families. The concept was to expand market forces so that people would increase their autonomy both as consumers and as individuals in society. According to this view, individuals should free themselves from an overbearing state and strive for self-development. People could then rely on their own competencies to compete in the free market and use the wealth they created to invest in their own capabilities and needs, such as in health and education. Self-reliance would provide them with self-respect.

The enterprise culture therefore perceives state interference to be an impediment to organizational efficiency and individual achievement. It regards state organizations as villains (Carrier, 1997); they are to blame for economic failures as well as for constraining the freedom of organizations and individuals. It claims that the market is superior to the state in coordinating the production and distribution of products and services, both in terms of efficiency and morally in terms of wealth distribution (Hayek, 1960; Friedman, 1962). Private organizations are seen to be the ideal economic unit because they are based on an ownership structure that lends them the characteristics essential for market success, such as flexibility in moving their activities to wherever is more advantageous, and flexible contractual arrangements so as to adjust their operations in ways that maximize wealth.

The enterprise ideal offered an ethical model for organizations in which emphasis is placed on the sovereignty of the client and on competition. The logic was one of the survival of the fittest: enterprises should achieve through 'competitiveness, strength, vigour, boldness, outwardness and the urge to succeed' (Rose, 1992, p. 149). The enterprise culture borrowed from Schumpeter's (1939) vision of dynamic innovation. It emphasized managerial virtues with its stress on efficiency and the relevance of risk, and with its attention on profits (Marquand, 1992). It was not surprising, therefore, that ideas about competitive advantage, the 'knowledge-creating company' and core competencies became the leading paradigms in strategic management in the 1990s.

The enterprise culture was based on the neoclassical assumption that self-interest is the stimulus that motivates human behaviour. In their writings, Friedman (1962) and Hayek (1960) suggest that the well-being of individuals can be achieved if they can create their own wealth by participating freely in market activities. The state not only restricts individual rationality, but also creates dependency. The new moral order involved a withering away of the social policies that encourage dependency and accommodation. Yet, paradoxically, neoliberalism assumes that both organizations and individuals could learn to be what government expected from them. Hellas and Morris (1992) criticized the enterprise culture for its assumption that individuals should learn what neoliberal governments assumed was appropriate for them.

Neoliberalism, therefore, provides clear ideas about the kind of organizations and employees that suit the free market. Governments expected managements to take these precepts on board and implement them in their organizations. This was to be done through the creation of new competencies by and within organizations (Marquand, 1992; Rose, 1992). Because learning deals with intersubjective meanings (Corley and Gioia, 2003), it becomes a technology of the self, not only shaping aspects of private life but also affecting an individual's identity. This means that learning can be used as a political instrument capable of articulating new conceptions of the employee.

On the other hand, people are not necessarily passive beings simply subject to external forces or to the managerial will (Littler and Salaman, 1982; Alvesson and Willmott, 2002). They also enjoy a degree of personal autonomy. Consequently, learning is a field of political and social engagement in which actors are cognitively informed by the past (such as their earlier experiences in the workplace), by the present (their capacity to contextualize past experience and ongoing projects within the contingencies of the moment) and by their orientation to the future (their capacity to envisage alternatives). In situations where change is forced upon them – and they are presented with an alternative of either 'learn or perish' – this may give rise to *contested learning*.

Contested learning refers to disputes concerning its legitimacy and purpose. It involves conflict over the fairness of the balance between contributions and benefits, including the destribution of returns between stakeholders and different occupational groups (Child and Loveridge, 1990). When there is contested learning, management may be unable to construct intersubjective meanings that are congruent with the projected organization identity (Corley and Gioia, 2003). As Brown and Starkey (2000) point out, participants may refuse to learn what threatens their idealized image of the organization, and therefore what increases their fears for the integrity of their own identity. Instead of encouraging emancipation, learning then creates more insecurity and frustration concerning the future. Employees may realize that changes that were supposedly positive bring about a breach in their implicit social contract with management.

A breach of the social contract can be felt along cognitive, emotional and economic dimensions. It reflects the resentment that comes from comparing the organization as it was with what it has become in terms of the elements affecting the employee's identity. The new situation may cause employees to suffer a reduction of status, financial deprivation and restricted choice. The choice now might be between uncommitted adaptation and exit. In the former, employees go along with managerial discourse without buying into it; in the second they may opt for earlier retirement or find another job. In other words, if they feel trapped in an organizational system with which they do not agree, they are likely to withdraw, either passively or actively.

3 Learning and the breach of trust

Although learning can be a powerful tool of organizational change, there is already plenty of evidence that recent organizational restructurings can lead to alienation and extend conflict between management and employees in ways that reverse the objectives of learning (Cascio, 2002). When investment in learning follows on from changes in ownership or from acquisitions, it is usually accompanied by restructuring (Blair, 1995, 1996; Bowman et al., 1999; Weston et al., 2001). Such restructuring, especially when accompanied by downsizing, often gives rise to a breakdown in trust, with learning consequently becoming contested between winners and losers in the restructuring process (Littler, 2000). In some cases, as with Telemig, when a company is being prepared for privatization restructuring may anticipate the change of ownership. In other cases, when restructuring follows a change of ownership, the incoming management is unlikely to feel committed to contracts previously agreed by the outgoing management. This then provokes a breach of trust between employers and employees (Shleifer and Summers, 1988; Blair, 1995, 1996; Deakin et al., 2003; Child and Rodrigues, 2004). The incoming management may claim that it does not have a 'moral' obligation to maintain the implicit contracts made by previous managers. This breach of trust argument is born out by studies of company restructuring that indicate how it has benefited shareholders and senior management at the expense of employees (Shleifer and Summers, 1988; Blair, 1995, 1996). There are indications that employees who are forced to find new jobs often lose between 15 and 20 per cent in wages plus the value of benefits that do not move with them (Osterman, 1999).

This claim is consistent with an economic perspective that views the organization simply as a nexus of contracts. Blair (1995) and others have argued that if the organization is understood in terms of a bunch of contracts, it is impossible to specify every instance where a breach of the social contract in employment relationships may occur. This is because many of the mutual expectations between employees and employers remain largely implicit. Consequently, when employees invest in training and learning that provide them with skills oriented to the enhancement of their firm's specific advantages rather than skills that they can use in the general labour market, they tend to expect that managers will in return provide them with employment, security and pensions.

Sources of Information

In addition to the main body of interviews and documents used for this book, primarily from the second round of the research, two additional sources were used to investigate organizational learning and restructuring during the 1990s. The first consisted of interviews with 52 staff who comprised approximately one-fifth of the managerial hierarchy. Those interviewed included a chief executive, six executive directors, 13 departmental heads, 19 team leaders and 13 section heads. While this distribution overrepresents directors and departmental heads and somewhat underrepresents section heads, it does cover all the main categories in the managerial hierarchy. Most of these interviews were conducted in 1998. They addressed the restructuring under way within the company and also included questions relating to the acquisition of new organizational competencies, individual skills and qualities. As with the other interviews we conducted, all were tape-recorded and subsequently transcribed.

The second additional source of information was a structured questionnaire sent by e-mail to everyone holding Telemig's 251 managerial positions in 1999. Forty-eight usable questionnaires were returned, giving a response rate of 19.1 per cent. The respondents were two directors, ten departmental heads, 28 team leaders and eight section heads. This distribution overrepresents team leaders and underrepresents section heads, but again includes respondents from each main managerial category. The questionnaire specifically addressed changes relating to competencies and learning perceived to have occurred since Telemig's privatization in 1998, including organizational learning methods, organizational competencies and individual skills and qualities.

Learning New Competencies

By 1993 employees already knew that the company would be privatized in the foreseeable future. As described in chapter 6, a neoliberal approach to the economy engendered a change of emphasis from engineering to service provision. To support this change, Telemig introduced a programme of early retirement and increased its investment in training. The message being conveyed was that the company needed to become a more proactive and agile organization that possessed detailed knowledge of the telecommunications market. Terms such as creativity, flexibility, motivation and optimization became part of the company's vocabulary.

The learning that took place from 1993 was thus oriented towards the incorporation of a new organizational culture and identity (see chapters 8 and 9). These were to be reflected more tangibly in a new structure, modes of working and conditions of employment. From 1993 to 1998, top management's objective was the construction of a 'market organization'. After privatization in 1998, the intention was to reconstruct the company into a 'private organization' oriented to the maximization of shareholder value.

Management understood that the capacity of Telemig to put the idealized image of a 'free market organization' into practice depended on introducing a learning process involving a programme of re-education. The ultimate goal was to prepare the employees for a major change of ownership – from a state to private organization. This meant not only having visible owners, but also working for them. Reflecting upon the changing conception of employees that this involved, some managers mentioned that 'the value of employees is what they produce' and that 'they are expected to behave as if they were the owners' because 'what counts nowadays is how we are able to generate profits, not the company's contribution to society as in past'. According to one of the company directors, this required a change in the 'employees' personality'. There was an understanding that building this new organization involved renewing and constructing a shared conceptualization of employees' identity: the way they perceived themselves and were perceived by others (Tajfel, 1982).

A specific language was used in the re-education programme to neutralize and justify its negative impact and to enlighten its positive side (see Kelly, 1998). As noted in chapter 7, the key concepts in this new language were *the employable employee, the renewable employee* and *the competitive employee*. Another metaphor that management used was that of *multifunctionality*. A director mentioned that 'the world is created from conflict. Therefore, not only the organization, but also the employee must now learn how to kill his competitor with his own "nails".' This set of expectations was clearly of potential benefit to management because it involved preparing employees for the downsizing that was to follow privatization. It was also highly consistent with the broader neoliberal ideology behind marketization and privatization, namely that both organizations and individuals had to rely for survival more on their own skills and resources.

Tables 10.1 and 10.2 summarize the views expressed by managers on the competencies that it was necessary for Telemig to acquire. Table 10.1 reports the total number of times that new areas of organizational competence were mentioned. Table 10.2 describes the specific job-related and personal competencies that the incumbents at different levels of the management structure viewed as relevant for carrying out their particular function. In compiling table 10.1, a team of three researchers allocated interviewees' statements to the categories used in the tables. Thus expressions such as 'gaining market experience', 'knowledge of the market' and 'understanding the market of both today and the future', were classified under 'market knowledge'. Table 10.2 categorizes the respondents' replies about competencies into those concerned with knowledge relevant to aspects of management and those concerned with more intrinsically personal skills.

The questionnaire survey of 48 personnel provides further insights into the individual and organizational learning pursued by Telemig following its privatization in 1998. The survey, administered in 1999, asked respondents to assess the nature and direction of change that had taken place in different aspects of learning and competences since privatization, using seven-point scales that ranged from −3 for a considerable reduction to +3 for a considerable increase in each variable, with 0 indicating no change.

Telemig was reported to have increased its emphasis on programmes of knowledge management and total quality management following privatization, but those of re-engineering to a lesser extent (table 10.3). Table 10.4 provides a more detailed

Table 10.1 New organizational competencies required

Competency	Times mentioned	Percentage of total mentions
Strategic thinking	37	4.9
Market knowledge	222	29.3
Awareness of competition	102	13.5
Flexibility	94	12.4
Improved human resources	159	21.0
Technological knowledge	144	19.0

Source: interviews with 52 managers.

Table 10.2 Work-related and personal competencies as perceived by respective levels

Level	Competencies (work-related and personal)	
	Know how to do	Know how to be
Directors (n = 7)	• Knowledge of technology and of the business • Knowledge of information technology • Ability in at least three languages • Capacity for broader vision • Understanding the future • Understanding cutting edge technology • Capacity to bring new knowledge to the organization	• Multifaceted manager • Capacity to learn • Proactive • Eclectic • Adaptability • Open minded • Negotiation skills
Department heads (n = 13)	• Knowledge of marketing communications, economics, on information technology, of planning and about the business • Major in engineering • Evaluation of projects • Know how to choose his subordinates • Knowledge in different languages • Experience in telecommunications	• Interpersonal skills • Capacity to work under pressure • Adaptability • Feet on the ground • Know how to listen • Negotiation skills • Flexibility • Capacity for continuous learning • Proactive • Problem-solving capacity
Team leaders (n = 19)	• Technical knowledge • Capacity to evaluate the scenario • Knowledge about the market and finance • Know how to deal with people • Teamwork and organize teamwork • Motivate people • Emotional balance • Holistic vision of the organization	• Acceptance of changes • Reliability • Respect for people • Learn from each experience • Maintain calm and good humour • Not being distressed by the company's changes • Creativity • Capacity for continuous learning
Supervision (n = 13)	• Market vision • Knowledge of information technology • Knowledge of HR • Know how to operate new technology • Knowledge of accountancy and budgeting • Systemic vision of the organization	• Know to listen • Initiative • Perspicacity • Self-confidence • Flexibility • Sensitiveness

Source: interviews with 52 managers.

Table 10.3 Perceived change since privatization in programmes intended to support organizational change

Programme	Mean change	Standard deviation
Total quality management	1.23	1.60
Knowledge management	1.17	1.52
Re-engineering	0.87	1.55

Higher score indicates greater perceived change; $n = 48$ respondents.

Table 10.4 Perceived change since privatization in the use of methods and systems of organizational learning

Method or system of organizational learning	Mean	Standard deviation
Demonstration projects using multifunctional teams	2.12	1.18
Programmes to promote standardization	1.98	1.24
Incremental improvement	1.89	1.14
Use of intranet	1.89	1.24
Use of university consultants or other specialists	1.83	1.44
Problem-solving	1.81	1.49
Contracting professional services from other companies	1.80	1.17
Feedback from customers	1.79	1.18
Direct contact with customers	1.72	1.29
Policies for knowledge transfer	1.68	1.37
Learning from other organizations	1.65	1.28
Improvements in projects from study of specific cases	1.64	1.24
Development of strategic alliances	1.63	1.34
Use of Internet	1.62	1.61
Knowledge transfer and dissemination	1.50	1.27
Experimentation	1.40	1.55
Benchmarking	1.19	1.61
Use of audio–visual reports	1.19	0.95
Learning from past mistakes	1.09	1.91
Staff rotation	1.08	1.25
Use of data based projects	0.89	1.37
Technical visits	0.64	1.43
Use of oral reports	0.60	1.61
Continuing education programmes	0.35	1.53
Use of written reports	−0.11	1.85
Training programmes	−0.15	2.10

Higher score indicates greater perceived change; $n = 48$ respondents.

assessment of changes in Telemig's use of methods and systems to promote organizational learning. The company was seen to have placed substantially greater emphasis on activities directed towards three main areas: (a) internal integration (demonstration projects to foster the use of multifunctional teams, a greater use of programmes to promote common standards, increased use of the internal IT network); (b) sensitivity to the market (more attention to feedback from customers, and more direct contact with them); and (c) the use of external contractors and partnerships (use of university consultants and other specialists, contracted services from other companies, policies for knowledge transfer, learning from other companies and development of strategic alliances). All three of these learning initiatives – towards internal integration, sensitivity to the market and the use of external contractors – constituted moves away from Telemig's old culture of a largely self-sufficient state bureaucracy that relied heavily on its own knowledge generation, primarily by a high-status and relatively self-contained telecommunications engineering function.

The company's investment in organizational learning in the years leading up to, and accompanying, privatization was seen to have produced results. There was a reported increase in organizational competencies, especially those that were consistent with implementing its transformation into a market-oriented and private firm. Table 10.5 shows that Telemig was seen to have acquired substantially more competence in entrepreneurship, the ability to adapt to change, and the weakening of former internal functional boundaries through team working and innovation.

The application of neoliberal principles, stressing the importance of firms being competitive and agile, is not limited to attributes of the organization as a whole. It also calls for complementary moves towards enhancing the contribution of individual employees, including making them more self-reliant. Table 10.6 indicates that its managerial and supervisory staff interpreted Telemig's investment in organizational learning as meaning that the company required such changes in the

Table 10.5 Perceived change since privatization in organizational competences

Organizational competence	Mean	Standard deviation
Entrepreneurship	2.06	0.91
Ability to adapt to change	1.94	1.09
Multifunctional teamworking	1.87	0.96
Innovation	1.77	1.25
Learning to adapt	1.50	1.56
Planned learning	1.34	1.63
Access to information	0.76	1.65
HRM incentives and support for organizational learning	0.40	1.45
Decision-making initiative	0.07	1.89
Ability to exchange information	−0.08	1.45

Higher score indicates greater perceived change; $n = 48$ respondents.

Table 10.6 Personal qualities and skills required by the company since privatization

	Mean	Standard deviation
Personal qualities		
Ability to adapt to new situations	2.83	0.42
Ability to cope with stress	2.65	1.08
Flexibility	2.52	0.70
Creativity	2.28	0.81
Sensitivity	1.89	1.24
Judgement	1.85	1.34
Respect for the customer	1.85	1.54
Reflection	1.81	1.35
Honesty	1.30	1.49
Skills		
Dealing with uncertainty	2.70	0.82
Commitment to organizational change	2.66	0.76
Ability to negotiate	2.40	0.86
Ability to manage conflict	2.33	0.91
Teamwork	2.33	0.93
Social skills	2.31	0.93
Communication	2.28	0.90
Professional experience	2.11	1.11
Cooperativeness	2.11	1.25
Capacity to listen	1.81	1.33
Foreign languages	1.22	1.22

Higher score indicates higher skill requirement; $n = 48$ respondents.

qualities and knowledge they brought to their jobs. The table reports respondents' assessments concerning the personal qualities and skills the company required of them since its privatization. High on the list are the ability to adapt to new situations, cope with stress and be flexible and creative, and skills to deal with uncertainty, negotiate, manage conflict and work in teams. These are all qualities and skills oriented towards organizational adaptation and innovation. The company was also seen as now requiring its staff to be more committed to organizational change. Yet at the same time, these attributes reflect a personal cost to the employee. They reflect the strain placed on individuals by the new corporate policies, such as stress and having to manage conflict, which were also qualities that the company as a whole was now seen to require. They are also attributes of the employee who has been 'renewed' so as to become more 'employable' in the external labour market and is therefore easier to dispense with should the company seek to downsize – which, as we have seen, it did. Thus at least some of Telemig's investments in learning were oriented towards providing a basis for the potential weakening of the employment contract in both its explicit and implicit forms. In this way the company's learning programme facilitated a breach of trust.

Learning and the Breach of Trust

As Sisson (1994, p. 15) pointed out, organizations no longer fire employees, they 'downsize', they do not control employees, they 'empower them'; total quality management and re-engineering actually mean 'doing more with less'. Telemig's privatization changed not only the employment contract, but everything that had defined its distinctiveness as a company to work for. As a state organization it had provided security of employment, and had been viewed as a family and as a mother because of the benefits it provided. Employees were proud of the organization's friendly atmosphere. Telemig was a company that had previously had a good reputation for its services and the quality of its professionals.

The employees could not understand why the previous emphasis on an internal career was being replaced in top management discourse by the possibility of building a career outside the company. They identified what appeared to them to be inconsistencies in management's policies. One middle manager mentioned: 'This new equation does not square up. The company has now reduced the number of employees, cut payment for extra hours, and increased the amount of work for the employees significantly.' It seemed inconsistent to change symbolic ties that were a source of identification with the company. Managers referred to the substantial reduction of autonomy in favour of the head office, and the movement to that office of key staff, as the 'domestication of Telemig', and as 'the milch cow effect', to indicate how Telemig was now obliged to provide skilled human resources to the other parts of the group. In the words of one manager, 'Telemig was good while it lasted. For all of us, it meant that we were protected. The change was so drastic that employees compare it with a situation in which one enters one company and goes out from another.'

The notion of a breach of trust has been treated in the literature primarily as a breakdown in the economic, albeit implicit, dimensions of the employment contract. What happened in Telemig shows that it impacted on non-economic dimensions, such as the cognitive, emotional and social ties that employees had to the organization. It suggests that the breach of trust also involved a deprivation of the symbolic signs that made Telemig a leader in the sector. Interviews with managers in particular uncover a deep resentment against a restructuring that took away the symbols that had given Telemig a distinct status within its sector. The breach of trust after privatization injured employees' self-esteem. One manager referred to this in the following way: 'Today there is a wound to our self-esteem. People resent the lean organization that has been created as a result of privatisation.' According to another manager, 'the "best heads" have been transferred to the head office, and those who have stayed resent not having been chosen to move'. A third manager said that 'the reduction of autonomy represents a punishment to the region

[Minas Gerais] and to our customers'. Another thought that the centralization following privatization 'is killing creativity, initiative and people's sense of achievement'.

The underlying political process that took place concerned the change of ownership, which brought about a rearrangement of the company's relations with its stakeholders. This in turn led to radical adjustments in its employment rules. These appear to have been the most important reason for the breach of trust that followed privatization. The rearrangement in stakeholder relations triggered a reappraisal of the system of contribution and redistribution in which managers, and employees even more so, were now expected to contribute more in return for less. The new top management justified this redistribution by defending the idea that, in the words of one director, 'subordinates are expected to do more for the company than it does for them, a reverse of what happened when Telemig was a state organization'. Or, as a manager observed, 'nobody should adopt the position that it is the organization's obligation to provide the means for employee's development; we have to do this ourselves'. However, while the change in the company's situation – that of ownership – triggered and justified the redistribution of costs and benefits in the employment relationship, the way this was applied was decided by the new holding company's top management.

Conclusion

What transpired in Telemig illustrates how ideology can be a tool that ties learning in organizations to essentially political aims concerning the restructuring of an organization so as, inter alia, to effect a redistribution of benefits. It shows how management's educational and training programmes were intentionally designed to change employee mentality and to create new competencies that would fit the new profile of organization it intended to build. More flexible, adaptable and proactive employees would contribute to achieving a more flexible, fast and proactive organization. These remodelled employees could also more readily fend for themselves if they were forced into the labour market as part of the company's downsizing.

Neoliberalism helped to put these changes into context; in other words it provided justification for them at the organizational and individual levels. It provided a framework that integrated an ideal 'work identity' (Alvesson and Willmott, 2002) with an ideal type of organization. Moreover, it helped to present change as inevitable. Globalization and the opening of markets were worldwide events that have been affecting people everywhere. Telemig's condition was portrayed as one of organization fragility in the increasingly hypercompetitive environment of the telecommunications sector. Firms therefore have to contract and move location and ownership at a faster pace in order to cope with greater environmental uncertainty. The implication of portraying this kind of environment was that it required a different profile of employee: one who was more adaptable, and less attached to the organization as a source for his or her survival and personal satisfaction. The new management encouraged a rejection of the company's historical culture and identity. The friendly, familial and particularistic organization was to be replaced by one that valued individualism and cost conscientiousness. Self-reliance and autonomy were to be encouraged as individual attributes in similar terms to the neoliberal enterprise culture (Hellas and Morris, 1992). This kind of mentality was not only supposed to exempt the organization from its special responsibilities towards the employee; it would in addition serve to encourage individuals to find their own alternatives by investing in their own education.

Learning served the purpose of presenting the application of neoliberal ideals as a positive development. Discourses of liberation and self-actualization usually express changes in seductive ways so as to secure commitment to management goals and a transition without social unrest and resistance (Alvesson and Willmott, 2002). As these authors point out, terms now used within Telemig, such as empowerment, team leader and project coordinator, sell a positive image of the organization to the employee. At the same time, their connotations of emancipation discourage organized resistance.

Ideology was also a tool to prepare employees for the breach of trust that was about to accompany change of ownership. With privatization, the new owners were exempt from the obligation to maintain the social contract that prevailed under state ownership. The new management expected employees to work harder, without offering any assurances about their security of employment. Telemig's employees were well aware of the contraction between the loyalty they were expected to give to the organization and its failure to offer any grounds for them to identify with it. It required loyalty without undertaking the responsibility that this implied. It sought to take without giving.

The breach of trust nevertheless had a much wider impact. As well as affecting the employment contract, it undermined the company's positive traditional identity as a caring and mothering organization. The changes that were introduced carried negative implications for the status, power and prestige of staff. Managers and engineers were relocated to subsidiaries in different parts of the country. Many of those who did not lose their jobs had their status reduced from managers to mere project coordinators – a position for which pay was variable rather than fixed.

Learning was a way of preparing employees either to accept the terms of the new implicit social contract that was about to be established or to quit the company. The breach of trust led to changes in the material, cognitive and political dimensions of employee identity that undermined it. What happened in Telemig illustrates how identity change can be one of the targets for learning programmes within organizations. Such programmes aim to change the profile of an organization's human resources so as to facilitate its adjustment within the co-evolutionary process, but their implementation can be politically highly charged.

Note

This chapter draws from Luz (2001) and is also informed by Cabral (2001).

References

Alvesson, M. and Willmott, H. (1996) *Making Sense of Management. A Critical Analysis.* London: Sage.

Alvesson, M. and Willmott, H. (2002) Identity regulation as organizational control: producing the appropriate individual. *Journal of Management Studies,* 39, 619–44.

Bartlett, C. A. and Goshal, S. (1997) The myth of the generic manager: new personal competencies for new management roles. *California Management Review,* 40, 93–116.

Blair, M. (1995) *Ownership and Control. Rethinking Corporate Governance for the Twenty-first Century.* Washington, DC: The Brookings Institution.

Blair, M. (ed.) (1996) *Wealth Creation and Wealth Sharing. A Colloquium on Corporate Governance and Investments in Human Capital.* Washington, DC: The Brookings Institution.

Bowman, E., Singh, H., Useem, M. and Bhadury, R. (1999) When does restructuring improve economic performance? *California Management Review,* 41, 33–55.

Brown, A. D. and Starkey, K. (2000) Organizational identity and learning: a psychodynamic perspective. *Academy of Management Review,* 25, 102–20.

Cabral, A. C. de A. (2001) Histórias de Aprendizagem: um estudo de caso no setor de telecommunicações. Thesis submitted for the title of Doctor in Administration at Universidade Federal de Minas Gerais, Brazil.

Carrier, J. (1997) *Meanings of the Market.* Oxford: Berg.

Cascio, W. F. (2002) *Responsible Restructuring.* San Francisco: Berrett-Koehler.

Child, J. (2005) *Organization: Contemporary Principles and Practice.* Oxford: Blackwell.

Child, J. and Loveridge, R. (1990) *Information Technology in European Services.* Oxford: Blackwell.

Child, J. and Rodrigues, S. B. (2004) Repairing the breach of trust in corporate governance. *Corporate Governance: An International Review,* 12, 143–51.

Collinson, D. (1992) *Managing the Shopfloor: Subjectivity, Masculinity and Workplace Culture.* Berlin: Walter de Gruyter.

Corley, K. and Gioia, D. (2003) Semantic learning as change enabler: relating organizational identity and organizational learning. In M. Easterby-Smith and M. A. Lyles (eds), *Handbook of Organizational Learning and Knowledge Management.* Oxford: Blackwell, 623–38.

Deakin, S., Hobbs, R., Nash, D. and Slinger, G. (2003) Implicit contracts, takeovers, and corporate governance: in the shadow of the City Code. ESRC Centre for Business Research, University of Cambridge, Working Paper 254, December.

Doz, Y. (1997) Managing core competency for corporate renewal: towards a managerial theory of core competencies. In A. Campbell and K. Luchs (eds), *Core Competency-based Strategy.* Boston: International Thompson Business Press, pp. 53–81.

Fiol, C. M. and Lyles, M. A. (1985) Organizational learning. *Academy of Management Review,* 10, 803–13.

Friedman, M. (1962) *Capitalism and Freedom.* Chicago: Chicago University Press.

Gherardi, S. and Nicolini, D. (2001) The sociological foundations of organizational learning. In M. Dierkes, A. Antal, J. Child and I. Nonaka (eds), *Handbook of Organizational Learning and Knowledge.* Oxford: Oxford University Press, pp. 35–60.

Hayek, F. A. von (1960) *The Constitution of Liberty.* London: Routledge.

Hellas, P. and Morris, P. (1992) *The Values of the Enterprise Culture.* London: Routledge.

Heller, F., Pusic, E., Strauss, G. and Wilpert, B. (1998) *Organizational Participation: Myth and Reality.* Oxford: Oxford University Press.

Kelly, J. (1998) *Rethinking Industrial Relations*. London: Routledge.

Knights, D. and Willmott, H. (1987) Organizational culture as management strategy: a critique and illustration from the financial services industry. *International Studies of Management and Organization*, 17, 40–63.

LaPalombara, J. (2001) The underestimated contributions of political science to organizational learning. In M. Dierkes, A. Antal, J. Child and I. Nonaka (eds), *Handbook of Organizational Learning and Knowledge*. Oxford: Oxford University Press, pp. 137–61.

Levy-Leboyer, C. (1993) *Le billan de compétences*. Paris: Les Áditions d'Organisation.

Littler, C. R. (2000) Comparing the downsizing experiences of three countries: a restructuring cycle? In R. J. Burke and C. L. Cooper (eds), *The Organization in Crisis*. Oxford: Blackwell, pp. 58–77.

Littler, C. R. and Salaman, G. (1982) Bravermania and beyond: recent theories of the labour process. *Sociology*, 16, 251–69.

Luz, T. (2001) Telemar-Minas: competências que marcam a diferença. Thesis submitted for the title of Doctor in Administration at Universidade Federal de Minas Gerais, Brazil.

March, J. G. (1991) Exploration and exploitation in organizational learning. *Organization Science*, 2, 71–87.

March, J. G. (1994) *A Primer on Decision-Making: How Decisions Happen*. New York: Free Press.

Marquand, D. (1992) The enterprise culture: old wine in new bottles? In P. Hellas and P. Morris (eds), *The Values of the Enterprise Culture*. London: Routledge, pp. 61–72.

Merkens, H., Geppert, M. and Antal, A. (2001) Triggers of organizational learning during the transformation process in Central European countries. In M. Dierkes, A. Antal, J. Child and I. Nonaka (eds), *Handbook of Organizational Learning and Knowledge*. Oxford: Oxford University Press, pp. 242–63.

Nonaka, I. and Takeuchi, H. (1995) *The Knowledge-Creating Company*. New York: Oxford University Press.

Osterman, P. (1999) *Securing Prosperity*. Princeton, NJ: Princeton University Press

Pettigrew A. M. (1979) On studying organizational culture. *Administrative Science Quarterly*, 24, 570–81.

Pettigrew A. M. (1987) *The Awakening Giant: Continuity and Change in ICI*. Oxford: Blackwell.

Popper, K. R. (1962) *The Open Society and Its Enemies*, 4th edn. London: Routledge and Kegan Paul.

Prahalad, C. K. and Hamel, G. (1990) The core competences of the corporation. *Harvard Business Review*, 68, 79–91.

Ray, C. A. (1986) Corporate culture: the last frontier of control? *Journal of Management Studies*, 23, 287–97.

Rodrigues, S. B. (2006) The political dynamics of organizational culture in an institutionalized environment. *Organization Studies*, 27, 537–57.

Rodrigues, S. B. and Child, J. (2003) Co-evolution in an institutionalized environment. *Journal of Management Studies*, 40, 2137–62.

Rose, N. (1992) Governing the enterprising self. In P. Hellas and P. Morris (eds), *The Values of the Enterprise Culture*. London: Routledge, pp. 141–64.

Schumpeter, J. A. (1939) *Business Cycles: A Theoretical, Historical and Statistical Analysis of the Capitalist Process*. New York: McGraw-Hill.

Senge, P. (1997) Through the eye of the needle. In R. Gibson (ed.), *Rethinking the Future*. London: Nicholas Brealey, pp. 123–45.

Shleifer, A. and Summers, L. H. (1988) Breach of trust in hostile takeovers. In A. J. Auerbach (ed.), *Corporate Takeovers: Causes and Consequences*. Chicago: University of Chicago Press, pp. 33–56.

Simons, T. and Ingram, P. (1997) Organization and ideology: kibbutzim and hired labor, 1951–1965. *Administrative Science Quarterly*, 42(4), 784–814.

Sisson, K. (1994) In search of HRM. *British Journal of Industrial Relations*, 31, 201–10.

Skinner, B. F. (1974) *About Behaviorism*. New York: Knopf.

Sutherland, P. (1992) *Cognitive Development Today. Piaget and His Critics*. London: Paul Chapman.

Tajfel, H. (ed.) (1982) *Social Identity and Group Relations*. Cambridge: Cambridge University Press.

Thompson, G. and McHugh (2002) *Work Organizations*, 3rd edn. New York: Palgrave.

von Rosenstiel, L. and Koch, S. (2001) Change in socioeconomic values as trigger of organizational learning. In M. Dierkes, A. Antal, J. Child and I. Nonaka (eds), *Handbook of Organizational Learning and Knowledge*. Oxford: Oxford University Press, pp. 198–220.

Weston, F., Siu, J. and Johnson, B. (2001) *Takeovers Restructuring and Corporate Governance*, 3rd edn. Englewood Cliffs, NJ: Prentice Hall.

PART IV

Conclusion

CHAPTER ELEVEN

A Political Interest Theory of Corporate Co-evolution

Parts II and III of this book have illustrated how during the life history of Telemig both the company and its environment evolved in ways that impacted each on the other. While Telemig's environment, especially governmental institutions, undoubtedly played a major role in shaping the company's development, this does not tell the whole story. To ignore the influence of the company's founders on the formation of Brazil's telecommunications sector, or the leading role that Telemig played in the sector's preparation for privatization, would be to present an incomplete and misleading analysis. Moreover, Telemig's status as a state enterprise during most of its lifetime created a relational framework that permitted a continuous process of interaction and mutual influence between company, sector holding company and federal government. This process was essentially a political one concerned with mobilizing resources for the company's expansion and securing governmental and social legitimacy for its leaders' intentions.

For these reasons, we consider the *co*-evolutionary perspective to be the most apposite for analysing the Telemig case, and corporate evolution in general. Chapter 1 introduced this perspective and the theories that inform it. In this concluding chapter, we endeavour to develop the co-evolutionary perspective further, starting with a recognition of its present limitations. We consider that its most serious limitation stems from its overly functionalist orientation. This limitation can be traced back to the biological origins of the evolutionary concept, which encourage an organic view of organizations. This organic orientation overlooks the nature of organizations as social constructions that inherently contain different sectional interests. To correct this limitation, it is necessary to incorporate a political perspective that appreciates how co-evolutionary processes have an inherently political aspect. Previous chapters have provided ample evidence of how political forces played an intrinsic part in Telemig's evolution. This chapter, building upon that foundation, offers a co-evolutionary analysis that explicitly incorporates the missing political interest perspective.

The chapter begins with a reminder of the case in favour of adopting a co-evolutionary approach for understanding corporate development. It then notes the limitations of current co-evolutionary thinking. Building on this groundwork, the remainder of the chapter is devoted to developing a political interest theory of co-evolution between organizations and their environments, informed by the Telemig case study. We first set out a framework that locates organizational and institutional interactions within broader ongoing processes at the macro, meso and micro levels. The framework links together the evolution of Telemig's culture, corporate identity, internal differentiation and learning, discussed in chapters 7 to 10. While the content of this framework has been informed by our case study of a public infrastructural company closely linked to an institutional regime, we believe that with suitable modifications it has a more general application. The interactions between micro (company) and other levels are the central drivers of the co-evolutionary process. Their essentially political nature requires an appropriate theory to account for them. With this in mind, the chapter then proceeds to offer a political interest theory of corporate co-evolution that incorporates the twin dynamic forces of mobilization and legitimation already introduced in chapter 8.

The Co-evolutionary Approach and its Contribution

The idea of co-evolution has its roots in the recognition by some biologists over a hundred years ago that human beings do not evolve simply through a process of natural selection by their environments, but that their capacity to learn can moderate environmental impacts (Baldwin, 1896). In a similar vein within economics, Schumpeter (1934) maintained that entrepreneurs can create opportunities for firms through their insights and purposeful actions. This means that the development of firms is not simply determined by their environments. The scope for leading organizational groups to shape environmental conditions, and even select environments, through purposeful actions also came to be appreciated within organization theory, somewhat later on, as it broke free from the assumptions of contextual determinism (Child, 1972).

These insights permit us to appreciate that while environments have an existence over and above particular organizations, they can be open to intervention by organizational leaders. Moreover, the relevance of environments depends on the specific identities and purposes attached to an organization. For these denote the ideational and material supports upon which an organization's continued existence depends (Child, 1988). The 'black box' to which neoclassical economists consign the firm in order to concentrate on external market processes is therefore as artificial as the tendency of some organizational analysts to ignore the interaction that actors have with the environment in order to concentrate on intra-organizational micro processes. The relationship of organizations to their environments is one that proceeds within a number of institutional arenas, ranging from arm's length market transactions to face-to-face negotiations within 'relational frameworks' (Scott and Meyer, 1983).

These considerations provide the fundamental justification for adopting a co-evolutionary framework. As chapter 1 noted, the co-evolutionary perspective 'considers organizations, their populations, and their environments as the interdependent outcome of managerial actions, institutional influences, and extra-institutional changes (technological, sociopolitical, and other environmental phenomena)' (Lewin et al., 1999, p. 535). It posits a framework of analysis, focusing on firms, in which there are ongoing recursive processes linking the evolution of institutional and extra-institutional environments with that of the firms themselves. These processes are mediated by managerial action, strategic intent, adaptation and performance achievement in each firm, as well as by the competitive dynamics established by the behaviour of all firms in a sector. By drawing attention to the continuing interdependence between context and organization, the co-evolutionary perspective offers a framework in which the development over time of firms and their populations can be better understood.

The co-evolutionary approach applied to organizations is based on the two assumptions that (a) there is a reciprocal relationship between organizations and their environments and (b) change results from joint effects arising from this relationship. In other words, the evolution of organizations is not an outcome of environmental selection or managerial adaptation alone, but also the joint outcome of environmental effects and 'intentional strategic adaptation' (Lewin and Volberda, 1999). As McKelvey (1997, p. 359) states, 'evolution is mostly *co*evolution'. Environments do not simply select the organizations that survive; organizations may also shape the environments in which to operate. Moreover, selection and shaping are achieved through human agency as organizational agents interact with other agents in their environments. Nevertheless, as Lewin and Volberda point out, the mutual and systematic influence of environments on organizations and of organizations on environments has not often been studied or multiple theoretical perspectives applied. Instead, 'most scholars in strategy and organization theory [consider] environmental change as an exogenous variable . . . [and] employ a single theme for describing how and why organizations tend to become isomorphic with their environments through processes or either adaptation or selection' (Lewin and Volberda, 1999, p. 520).

These shortcomings in previous work make the general case for adopting a co-evolutionary framework. There are also more specific reasons for so doing. First, co-evolutionary thinking avoids the respective limitations of environmental determinism and pure enactment, and the paradigm war between them (McKelvey, 1997). Instead, it regards environments as being simultaneously exogenous and endogenous. Thus, on the one hand, environments have an objective external reality and contain some dynamic forces, such as the 'hidden hand' of the 'free' market, that are beyond the control of any organizations including those of the nation state. To ignore this reality can incur the risk of organizational failure. Many organizations are, moreover, embedded in certain environments from which they cannot easily escape, at least not without incurring considerable cost. On the other hand, the environments to which the organizations respond, and in which they may attempt to create new opportunities or conditions, are understood only through sense-making by organizational decision makers. In this respect, they take on an endogenous character (Weick, 1979, 1995). Here the 'visible hand' of management plays an active role (Chandler, 1977).

Second, as Lewin and Volberda (1999) indicate in their prolegomena, a co-evolutionary framework embraces and integrates explanations from multiple perspectives. In so doing, it offers a multifaceted view of organizations and environments that has the merit of far more than just additional comprehensiveness. This is because the drivers for change and development can be lodged in the dynamics between these different facets. For example, if a firm's practices fail to match its proclaimed philosophy, there may be a hostile response among stakeholders such as customers and community groups. This inconsistency between two facets of the organization gives rise to a breakdown in legitimacy, which in turn may well oblige a change in the offending practices. In this example, while the organization evolves in relation to external groups, the process of evolution is triggered by an internal inconsistency between two key components of its identity.

This second advantage of a co-evolutionary approach is associated with a third contribution, namely the way in which its biological heritage encourages a holistic analysis. Just as organisms as wholes are comprised of a number of interdependent systems (cardiac, nervous, respiratory and so forth), so co-evolutionary thinking draws attention to interdependencies both within systems and between them. This is a strength to the extent that it encourages recognition of interdependencies between *differentiated* system components, but it can become a weakness if the bases of differentiation are overlooked. To do so encourages a neglect of internal strains and conflicts, or at least a view that these are pathological. As sociologists have long recognized, the organic analogy runs the risk of bracketing out the consideration of political contest within organizations as socially plural entities. A similar criticism applies to treatments of organizational environments in an undifferentiated manner, such as when they are assessed in terms of holistic characteristics such as 'uncertainty' and 'hostility versus munificence'. Moreover, given categories of collective social differentiation can apply to, and link together, both environmental and organizational levels, as with owners and their representatives on company boards, or labour unions and their employee members.

Fourth, a co-evolutionary framework accounts naturally for longitudinal development. Evolution denotes a development over time through changing forms, such as the process whereby a species develops from earlier forms. The idea of co-evolution in organizational studies endeavours to account for how organizations and environments develop together in time. It grants special attention to changes in non-natural or social environments, the social construction of which may to an extent be at the hands of organizational leaders themselves. Insofar as the evolution of both organizations and their environments follows a pattern of punctuated equilibrium (Gersick, 1991), with relatively long periods of steady state or smooth growth punctuated by more dramatic changes (Greiner, 1972), its investigation requires the adoption of lengthy time frames.

Lewin and Koza (2001, p. vii) distinguish empirical co-evolutionary research from that on longitudinal adaptation in that it incorporates the following features simultaneously. They amount to a very demanding set of requirements, though we have endeavoured to meet most of them in the present study:

1   A longitudinal time series of microstate adaptation events and the study of organization adaptations over a long period.
2   Organizational adaptation within the historical context of the firm and its environment.
3   Multidirectional causalities between micro and macro co-evolution, where the distinction between dependent–independent variables becomes indeterminate, and where changes in any one variable may be caused endogenously by changes in the other.
4   Mutual, simultaneous, lagged and nested effects.
5   Path dependence that enables and restricts adaptation at the firm and population level.
6   Changes to the institutional systems within which firms and industries are embedded.
7   Economic, social and political macro-variables that may change over time and influence the deep structure within which micro and macro co-evolution operate.

Co-evolutionary research goes beyond adaptation research in allowing for simultaneous organizational–environmental influence and a lack of distinction between dependent and independent variables. While typically relying on historical information, co-evolutionary research also differs from much historical investigation in that it is concerned with events not so much in their own right but as a means of uncovering underlying developmental processes.

The Limitation of Co-evolution's Origins

Co-evolutionary thinking has its roots in biology rather than in the social sciences. As well as providing insights, this can also impose certain limits on our understanding. One limitation stems from the focus of Darwinian biology on the variety–competition–selection–retention evolutionary process. Co-evolutionary studies follow this orientation in their tendency to focus on organizational survival within competitive environments (Aldrich, 1999). Such environments are conducive to high levels of selection among organizations. They have relatively low levels of institutionalization, or more precisely they have institutional rules aimed at securing open competition and low entry barriers rather than being characterized by much direct intervention by institutional bodies such as agencies of the state. However, there are many domains of business, let alone of public administration, that are highly regulated and subject to political intervention – domains such as health care, power and energy, public utilities, telecommunications and transportation. In these heavily institutionalized environments, selection among organizations may be low and the evolution of their strategies and forms governed as much by how well these meet political or social considerations as by competitive forces. The nature and extent of co-evolution in such environments deserves more attention than it has received to date.

Some co-evolutionary studies accord only a limited role to human agency. The Darwinian view is that the natural selection process proceeds on the basis of *selecting* out the organisms that happen to have the best fit to their environments, ignoring whether others have the capacity to *adapt* to their environments during their lifetimes. Applied to organizational analysis, this lends itself to treating *organizations* as the units of analysis at the expense of considering the *people* within them and their capacities to learn. This is particularly evident in the population ecology approach, which ignores or minimizes the role of human agency (Hannan and Freeman, 1989). The 'Baldwin effect' within biological discourse is, however, conducive to bringing organizational actors back into the picture. For it postulates that species (read 'organizations') have the capability of adjusting to their environments through the learning achieved by their individual members. They are consequently able to modify the selection processes acting upon them. This knowledge can be passed down to later generations through a process of 'social heredity'. In other words, the ability of individuals to learn can guide the evolutionary process (Baldwin, 1896; Kull, 2000).

Contemporary co-evolutionary thinking has taken on board the Baldwin effect to the extent that it allows for calculation and learning by organizational actors. It nevertheless retains the biological presumption that organizations are organic units. This presumption implies that intra-organizational learning is motivated by, and oriented towards, satisfying a common interest among all actors. Investigations, including the Telemig case, demonstrate that this is not necessarily the case. Learning can be contested in the sense that different organizational groups can frame knowledge in their own ways so as to draw contrasting recommendations for action. Since these recommendations serve conflicting interests, the learning from which they derive becomes contested (Child and Loveridge, 1990). Its biological heritage encourages co-evolutionary work to adopt an organic view of organizations that is naive to the way that organizations are constituted. For rather than being organic unities, most organizations are plural systems comprising different interest groups that compete for the returns from organized activities. The quality of their 'organic' cooperation is liable to depend on how well they perceive those interests to be satisfied and whether the implicit contract underpinning their commitment to the organization is being honoured. This inherited limitation in turn encourages co-evolutionary theorizing to look to an overly functionalist explanation of organization–environment adjustment.

The functionalist explanation sees organizational attributes and actions as being informed by the requirements for the performance of an organization as a whole. It assumes the organizational interest to be the key motivator of change, rather than attending to the ways in which organizational behaviour may be oriented towards the satisfaction of group or sectional interests. Thus an organization's stance towards its environment is usually conceptualized within co-evolutionary discourse in terms of its *strategy*. This implies a unitary set of agreed policies consonant with an agreed organizational identity. The possibility is ignored that different constituent groups may commit to that strategy only in a qualified way, with different ends in view to those of the organization's top management. Recent collections of co-evolutionary research indicate a common failure to take account of interest-based considerations such as these (*Organization Science*, 1999; *Organization Studies*, 2001; *Journal of Management Studies*, 2003).

Yet if organic and functionalist assumptions are discarded, the Darwinian notion of struggle can be applied just as well to competition for organizational control between the parties to an organization (its relevant interest groups) as it can to competition between organizations themselves. Organizations are social instruments that competing groups seek to capture or influence for their own ends, as is witnessed in the boardroom struggles of companies or in industrial conflicts. Organized interest groups frequently span system levels and this vertical boundary-spanning is integral to the interaction between environments and organizations. Thus the same interest groups can compete for control within organizations and for positions of influence over the institutional rules laid down for the operation of the markets within which organizations operate (Fligstein, 1996). For example, there was an identity of aims between efforts by Telemig's labour union to improve employment conditions within the company during the 1980s and action by the national union and the Workers Party to reshape some of the rules of the Brazilian economy such as employment protection.

An organization's capability to evolve with its environment depends importantly on the extent to which its management secures sufficient legitimacy for its policies and practices among its stakeholders and mobilizes necessary resources from them, not least the commitment of its employees. Without legitimacy and resource mobilization, there is the risk of collapse and closure. This indicates the ultimate dependency of any organization on securing social approval for both its ideational and its material characteristics – for its identity and its efficiency. Equally, the influence that organizational leaders possess within their environments is a function of their ability to secure legitimacy and command resources. The greater the legitimacy they enjoy, and the stronger the resource base they can secure for their organization, the more independence it is likely to have from environmental constraints and the more external influence its leaders are likely to enjoy (Pfeffer and Salancik, 1978).

The considerations point to the fundamental need for organizations to satisfy the expectations of the various interest groups on which their success depends. This is not to say that such groups enjoy equal power within or over an organization, but rather that their willingness to contribute to, or cooperate with, the purposes of the organization is vital to its continuation as a viable entity. If this willingness is absent, it could create dysfunctional alienation or confrontation at best, and withdrawal from the organization at worst – in other words 'voice' and 'exit' respectively, to use Hirschman's (1972) terms. The interdependence of organizations and environments therefore contains an intrinsically political dimension, which is concerned with the negotiation and exercise of power and influence. This has not been granted due prominence within the co-evolutionary project. It has been the aim of this book to set this right, and this chapter suggests some ways of doing so.

A Co-evolutionary Framework[1]

Figure 11.1 presents a model of co-evolving cycles of environment and organization. Its origins are both deductive and inductive. On the one hand, it reflects the basic co-evolutionary framework advanced by Lewin et al. (1999) and Lewin and Koza (2001), particularly in the form developed by Huygens et al. (2001). On the other hand, it draws inductively on the Telemig case to take account of its distinctive features discussed in this book. These are an institutionalized context, the relevance of events at both macro and meso (sector) levels of the environment level and the role of ideology as well as economic and technological factors of a material nature. The framework is organized in terms of the relationships between institutional regime, policies, political dynamics and performance.

The framework in figure 11.1 is informed by the following rationale. We can start with the macro and meso environments, which chapter 2 described for the case of telecommunications in Brazil, and which has also featured in other chapters. Within the macro environment of telecommunications companies, the institutional regime and its identifiable values, norms and regulations play a significant role in shaping the possibilities for co-evolution in a public infrastructure sector, at the meso level. First, the specific regulations applied to the sector, in respect of different market segments, tariffs and provision of new services, are laid down at the macro level. Second, governmental action affects the extent to which exogenous non-institutional forces can operate within the sector. Thus changes in the rules applied to the sector, allowing for new entrants to the market and the privatization of telecommunications companies, impact directly on the degree of competition experienced by individual companies. These changes in turn modify the pressures on companies to undertake evolutionary adaptation. The extent to which the global evolution of non-institutional features such as new telecommunications technologies impact on a particular national sector will also be influenced by the institutional regime that is applied to it (Saunders et al., 1994).

These factors give rise to the regime that prevails within the sector. The term 'regime' refers to the ownership permitted in the sector and its structure of competition, including factors such as ease of entry. A regime is likely to be reflected in the objectives and policies found within the sector, and that indeed will come to typify the sector the more that there are significant population ecology pressures (Hannan and Freeman, 1989). In turn, the policy norms of a sector will be

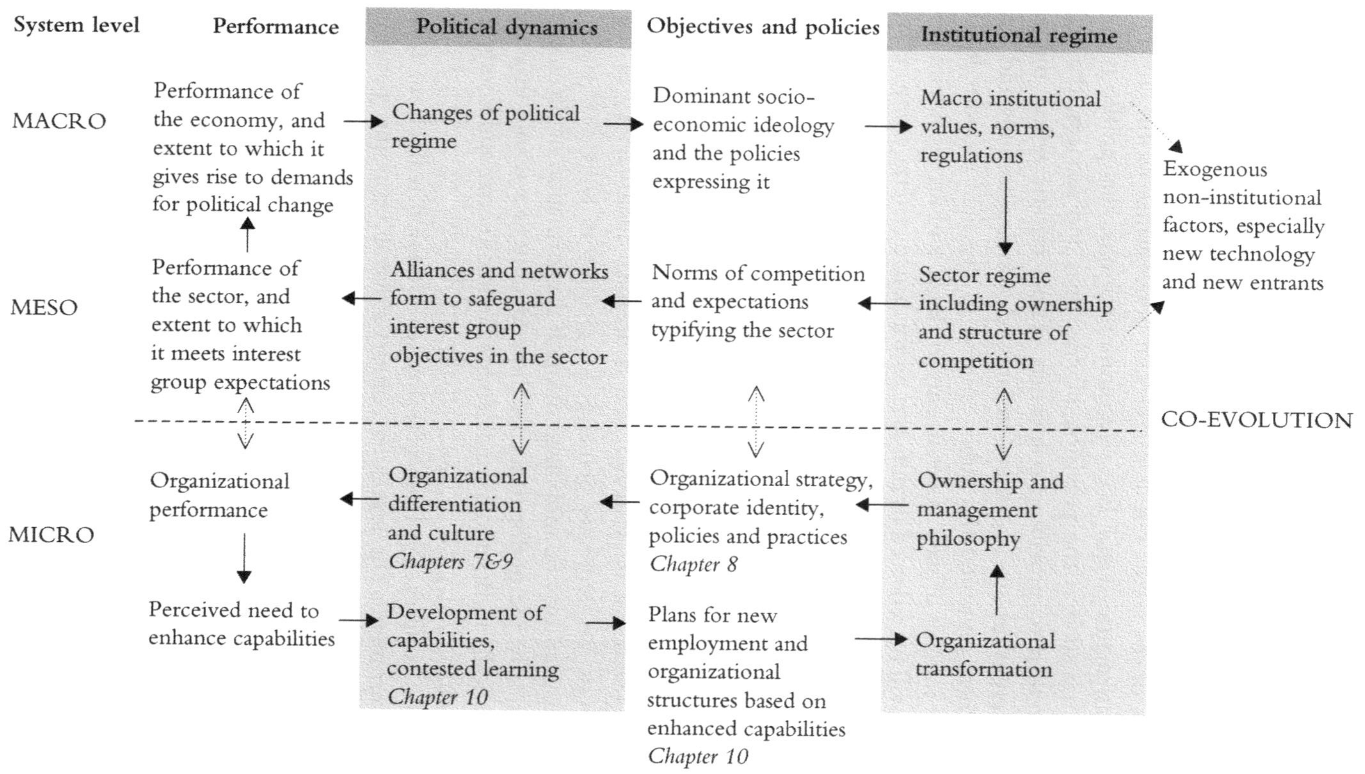

Figure 11.1 A framework of co-evolution for a public infrastructure organization.

Source: adapted from Rodrigues and Child (2003, figure 1).

System level	Performance	Political dynamics	Objectives and policies	Institutional regime
MACRO	Performance of the economy, and extent to which it gives rise to demands for political change	Changes of political regime	Dominant socio-economic ideology and the policies expressing it	Macro institutional values, norms, regulations
MESO	Performance of the sector, and extent to which it meets interest group expectations	Alliances and networks form to safeguard interest group objectives in the sector	Norms of competition and expectations typifying the sector	Sector regime including ownership and structure of competition
MICRO	Organizational performance	Organizational differentiation and culture *Chapters 7&9*	Organizational strategy, corporate identity, policies and practices *Chapter 8*	Ownership and management philosophy
	Perceived need to enhance capabilities	Development of capabilities, contested learning *Chapter 10*	Plans for new employment and organizational structures based on enhanced capabilities *Chapter 10*	Organizational transformation

Exogenous non-institutional factors, especially new technology and new entrants

CO-EVOLUTION

reflected in its political dynamics. The patterns of action prevalent within a sector will depend on how it is governed and structured. The more it is characterized by government monopoly, as has often been the case with telecommunications, the more likely it is that the dominant sector dynamics will involve various forms of political accommodation between interest groups rather than economic competition for custom in the market place (Davies, 1994). As in Telemig's history, political accommodation can bring alliances and networks into play and involve contest and negotiation.

The dynamics of the sector result in a certain performance profile. In the case of a public infrastructure sector like telecommunications, this profile is defined in terms of criteria such as the provision of new lines and services, the level of tariffs and the return to providing companies. These criteria reflect the policy priorities of different groups in society towards telecommunications and varying definitions of what constitutes the public interest in this field (Lundstedt, 1990). For instance, the interest of state governments in Brazil wishing to extend services to remote areas will be reflected in different performance criteria compared to the interest of investors who seek a high return on the capital they provide to companies through stocks or bonds.

At this point, the dynamics of the meso level impact upon those at the macro level. The performance of the sector feeds into considerations of how the economy as a whole is performing, both through the efficiency gains provided by improved telecommunications services and in terms of how far the sector is seen to be satisfying the expectations of different interest groups within the macro society. The performance of the sector is evaluated, and if deemed unsatisfactory in the eyes of powerful groups this generates demands for changes in policies regarding the sector. These demands may be mobilized through the formation of alliances across system levels. Equally, the performance of the economy as a whole may change, and did so dramatically in Brazil during Telemig's lifetime (Ferraz and Lootty, 2000). Although such change may be at least partially attributable to external developments outside the country, the blame for any deterioration is likely to fall upon the national government. The level of a country's overall economic performance can legitimate the prevailing socio-political ideology if it is satisfactory, or delegitimate it if unsatisfactory. In these ways, both meso and macro level performance can give rise to demands for changes of political regime. The regime in power articulates the social and economic ideology that dominates national policy. This ideology and the policies associated with it in turn give rise to the institutional regime that governs the sector. Thus the evolutionary loop in the environment of telecommunications companies is completed.

There are a number of critical points at which the evolution of the meso environment interacts with that of individual companies such as Telemig. These are shown in figure 11.1 by the double-headed arrows that cross the co-evolutionary 'frontier'. The interaction is two-way, so giving rise to co-evolution. On the one hand, the sector regime and norms of competition are likely to impact upon member companies through isomorphic effects (Powell and DiMaggio, 1991), although in an environment of limited institutional regulation firms have the option to formulate their own idiosyncratic strategies and organizational designs. Sector dynamics have an impact insofar as they provide the immediate context for firms with respect to operational specifics such as the securing of necessary resources. Similarly, conditions that affect the performance of the sector, such as scarcity of resources and new technologies, are also shared by its member firms. While firms can through their own policies and actions aspire to attain levels of performance that surpass the sector average, sector performance levels reflect conditions that set limits to firm performance and help to account for variations in the latter over time. Industrial organization economics, for instance, identifies sector conditions that can lead to monopoly rents such as concentration and restrictions on entry (Bain, 1956).

On the other hand, an individual organization retains the potential to influence sector conditions, especially under one or both of two circumstances. The first is that the organization is a dominant player in the sector. The second is that it has become a leader in the innovation and/or quality of its policies and practices, as Telemig was both in its formative years and in the mid-1990s. These circumstances enhance the capacity of senior executives to insert themselves into networks that link them to circuits of decision-making power (Clegg, 1989). There is in any case always some potential for major actors within the firm to shape its evolution, even, as we have seen with Telemig, under heavily institutionalized conditions. Child (1997) has conceptualized this possibility of exercising strategic choice in terms of a cycle of 'outer structuration' by which 'organizational actors seek to influence or reach an accommodation with specific environmental groups and more general environmental conditions. They are thereby simultaneously informed of the opportunities for action which environmental conditions present and of the constraints which external circumstances place upon their room for action' (p. 70).

The evolutionary cycle at the micro level − that of the firm − is thus seen to be partly stimulated by environmental changes and partly by internal developments including managers' mental models and strategic intentions. One part of the cycle involves a sequence whereby the ownership and management philosophy of an organization is reflected in its objectives, which then impact on its strategy and corporate identity, on its culture and internal processes, and ultimately on its performance. In a competitive environment, a company's superior performance will permit its managers' intentions to translate easily into new organizational forms and practices. This is partly because of the resource slack that is made available and partly because success is highly visible and enhances managerial legitimacy. A favourable standing may also permit the new forms and practices to become exemplars that trigger transformation within the rest of the sector as well. If a company's performance is inferior, leading to the perception that it needs to enhance its capabilities, its achievement of organizational innovation will probably depend on its first undertaking a process of development, including hiring new talent and acquiring new knowledge. The impact of organizational performance and associated environmental reactions on the ability of management to pursue its political interest within an organization is central to the co-evolutionary process, and is explored later in this chapter.

A highly constrained institutional environment, on the other hand, is likely to restrict options for management action and encourage managerial inertia (Oliver, 1992). In this situation, knowledge transference to the sector follows norms of top-down isomorphism rather than emerging from the competitive process. Changes are likely to originate from a cohesive internal culture or a leadership whose power derives from authority, coercion or normative identity. This characterized Telemig in its formative period when it was under military direction. While a high level of institutionalization can drive organizational transformation by virtue of the embeddeness of organizational leadership, it often bolsters resistance to change (Greenwood and Hinings, 1987) that may persist until the coalition sustaining the leadership collapses and a new coalition emerges. In highly institutionalized environments, the sources of changes derive largely from political forces rather than from differences in performance and capabilities. Thus, in the 1990s, governments informed by a neoliberal ideology instituted a massive programme of change for Brazilian telecommunications companies, which culminated in their privatization. This programme involved a major effort to change the company's human competencies but combined with employment policies that resulted in a breach of the trust that employees had vested in the company. It was accordingly contested, albeit without much success, as chapters 9 and 10 have shown.

Actors and Institutions

As Lewin and Volberda (1999) argue, the co-evolutionary perspective is an integrative one and therefore draws upon a range of relevant theories. Institutional theory is of particular relevance for understanding Telemig's evolution because of the strong institutional embeddedness that characterized much of the company's life. Recent institutional theories focus on isomorphism among populations of organizations, assuming that this reflects normative, coercive or mimetic pressures to conform to institutional norms (Powell and DiMaggio, 1991). However, it was apparent from examination of the Telemig case that even in a highly institutionalized environment it can be an oversimplification to assume that the influences shaping organizational identity and form are only unidirectional, flowing from higher-level institutions down to organizations. Within the prevailing system, a degree of 'institutional entrepreneurship' (Dacin et al., 2002) was exercised through channels of upward influence by members of the company. This is more consonant with the recognition granted by the so-called 'old institutionalists' to initiatives such as co-optation and lobbying intended to influence the nature and application of institutional norms and policies (Selznick, 1949; Powell and DiMaggio, 1991).

The Telemig case suggests that the two shaded sections of figure 11.1 – institutional regime and political dynamics – identify fields where collective action and adaptation play a particularly significant role in the co-evolutionary process.

The three main phases of Telemig's co-evolution with its context were the periods covered by chapters 4, 5 and 6. These were the foundation period, the period of politicization and the period of reconstruction. During the foundation period collective action by the telecommunications sector founders, acting as a self-aware and cohesive network, created a set of material and institutional conditions for both Telemig and the whole sector. These material and institutional conditions included technological competence, a system of investment financing and a protected market. These founders were guided and motivated by a clear and nationally altruistic ideology. The role they played largely created the institutional regime for the sector and its constituent companies. They were institutional entrepreneurs who were 'makers' of the telecommunications institutional field (Child et al., 2007). They mobilized the support and resources for this project from different levels in the system and secured social legitimacy for it. The network to which they belonged straddled the boundaries between Telemig, Telebrás – the sector holding company – and the federal Ministry of Telecommunications. The network was a clear agency for the co-evolution both of companies and of their environments. The environment in which the new institutional field embedded Telemig and other Brazilian state telecommunications companies was a highly protective one.

During the period of politicization that followed the return to civilian democratic government in 1985, relations between corporate leaders and those in the wider society were no longer mutually supportive. The new politicians were predatory towards state enterprises like Telemig, and while they appointed the company's directorate, the company's management below that level felt increasingly obliged to plan for ways of removing what had become in their eyes harmful political interference. There was a weakening of the relational framework that had previously connected the company and its external bodies as an effective mobilizing force. The corporate identity and organizational culture associated with the tight relational framework that had existed between Telemig and the previous military regime was no longer regarded as socially legitimate. Indeed, it was now subject to active criticism and counter-mobilization by the alliance between telecommunications unions and the Workers Party.

The third period culminated in a large measure of detachment of Telemig from its institutional environment. Strategic movement during this period resulted from a combination of new governmental policies, informed by neoliberalism and aiming to reduce the industrial role of the state, and growing pressure from the company's own management to secure greater freedom from political intervention so as to pursue more competitive policies. While unquestionably globalization and technological advances in the international telecommunications industry were strong drivers towards change, it would be an oversimplification to attribute all of Telemig's evident evolution in this period purely to external forces. By reaching out to multinational companies to transfer technology and to generate support for the company's privatization, Telemig's management took the initiative in creating conditions that would bring the company closer to privatization. It undertook a strong drive to mobilize the resources and competencies that it saw to be necessary to support the company's reconstruction and change, against a backdrop of legitimacy for these actions accorded by the government but not by the bulk of employees or their union.

The collective entrepreneurship of Telemig's leaders was supported by alliances across system levels during the first period and by alliances across corporate borders during the third period. This suggests that if corporate management can mobilize sufficient support through alliances and networks, it may be able to achieve alterations in the rules governing its institutional embeddedness. Strategic change was therefore enabled through the participation of Telemig's leadership in wider circles or 'circuits' of power. Paradoxically, while in a highly institutionalized environment there is greater formal dependence of a company on higher governmental and political authorities, this at the same time affords its leaders greater access to a relational framework through which they can negotiate and exercise influence on higher-level policy and rule-making. Institutional dependence does not necessarily denote that an organization lacks the ability to influence the evolution of the agencies in its environment.

This theoretical position clearly contrasts with the assumption of population ecology that isomorphism will necessarily result from processes of environmental selection. Environmental selection can be modified or nullified by collective entrepreneurship among company leaders, especially if their action is articulated and legitimated by forceful ideologies such as neoliberalism. Rather than the processes of co-evolution leading to homogeneity among the constituent firms within an industry, the degree of latitude their leaders may be able to negotiate collectively with external rule-makers could be an important reason for the empirically observed heterogeneity of strategies and organizational forms among the members of a sector.

This is not to deny that organizations are subject to dependency, but instead to argue that they are likely to enjoy opportunities to modify that dependence and even to take advantage of it. The Telemig case indicates that one aspect of dependency is 'path dependency'. The embeddedness of companies in a highly institutionalized tradition will augment the extent to which their development is historically dependent. As Selznick (1992, p. 232) pointed out, institutions impose constraints on organizations in two main ways: by creating and legitimating a normative order and by 'making it hostage of its own history'. For this reason, the adaptation of a company may reflect the previous conditions of its meso and macro environments rather than current environmental conditions. Thus Telemig's management found it difficult to shake off the authoritarian style of management it had inherited from the military regime even though the culture it claimed to espouse was one of participation and the open door. In the strongly normative climate of many institutions, in which values are strongly internalized, cultural features that were prominent in defining organizational identity in the past are very likely to be maintained and to influence conduct at a later date (Calori et al., 1997). On the other hand, as the Telemig case has also shown, these historically embedded characteristics do not necessarily impose a constraint upon successful evolution.

Indeed, a strong historical legacy can help to enable major change if it is used constructively to provide both competencies and legitimacy to support the change. Previous studies have drawn attention to the positive contributions to successful transformation that can be made by the maintenance of key continuities with the past (Pettigrew, 1985; Child and Smith, 1987). Similarly, the embeddedness of certain beliefs and competencies can provide a continuing source of strength that actually assists evolutionary adaptation.

Adaptation was certainly a necessity for Telemig in the light of the major paradigm shifts that affected the telecommunications industry globally and others that were regional in nature. The paradigmatic global waves were largely economic and technological in nature, and were reviewed in chapter 2. The continental and national waves were primarily political ones, such as the shift from military to civilian regimes that many South American countries experienced during the 1980s and 1990s. In order for an organization like Telemig to adapt to such major shifts, its senior management had to attempt to change its identity, culture and competencies accordingly, as the previous chapters have shown, and to try to change the kind of institutional rules that were considered appropriate to its strategy and operations. These changes were decried and opposed by many employees and by their union, as chapter 9 demonstrates.

The paradigm shifts, and Telemig's adaptation to them, moved it from a protected to a more competitive environment. When this happens, or when the existing competition that firms face increasingly takes on aspects of 'hypercompetition' (D'Aveni, 1994), a third theoretical perspective becomes increasingly relevant to understanding how they co-evolve with those environments. Figure 11.1 draws attention to the development of capabilities as a response to perceived performance deficiencies or threats. It suggests that consequential changes in employment and organizational structures in turn open up possibilities for significant organizational transformations. The resource-based theory of the firm stresses the importance for performance improvement of identifying, selecting, developing and deploying an appropriate bundle of tangible and intangible resources in a way that is superior to and distinct from that of competitors, and cannot readily be copied (Barney, 1991). In the context of environmental change and evolution, it becomes particularly important for firms to be able to adapt, augment and renew those resource bundles, or capabilities, dynamically over time (Teece and Pisano, 1997). In this light, one can view the management-instigated changes in Telemig's culture, identity, practices and competencies as reflecting an attempt to cater to change and evolution in its environment, albeit that their consistency and implementation was variable, especially in the middle period.

In short, the history of Telemig and the processes through which it developed enlighten current discussion of co-evolution in several ways. First, the company operated for much of its life within an environment characterized by structural inertia with a high degree of institutional closure. The expectation is that such closure will limit both the incentive and scope for managerially activated adaptation. Second, under these conditions the focus of evolution shifts to the dynamics of the institutional regime itself, including the networks that support or challenge it. Within such networks, the ability of organizational actors to capitalize on close links with key institutional actors may afford them some initiative in reducing institutional inertia and promoting an evolutionary process. Running throughout is an essentially political process concerned with the exercise and negotiation of influence and power. We now turn to the question of how this political aspect of corporate co-evolution may be analysed.

A Political Interest Theory of Corporate Co-evolution

Chapter 8 introduced some of the components and reasoning of the political interest perspective, including the role of mobilization and legitimacy, in its discussion of Telemig's corporate identity evolution. Without wholly repeating this previous analysis, we now address the main assumptions behind this perspective. We believe that this theoretical perspective can be applied not just to companies like Telemig but to organizations in general.

1 Assumptions

Central to a political interest theory is the concept of interest group, defined as a social collectivity whose members perceive that they have a strong commonality of interests and who therefore tend to act together to negotiate and exert pressure. Political scientists have historically paid most attention to interest groups in the wider society, especially those exerting pressure on government (Bentley, 1908; Berry, 1997). Nevertheless, the role of interest groups within organizations has also been recognized by those scholars who regard organizations as political entities comprised of coalitions of interests (e.g. Cyert and March, 1963). Individuals may belong to more than one interest group; for example, a professional engineer might also be a manager. While their interests are distinct, different interest groups can share a common cause in the case of any given issue that arises.

In this book, an organization has been viewed as a collection of interest groups bound together, but at the same time differentiated, by a set of managerially coordinated *formal and informal contracts*. Formal contracts between interest groups include legally based employment contracts and commercial contracts. Informal contracts are 'psychological contracts' in the sense of being mutual understandings between interest-group members and organizational management that the former take for granted as a normal part of their association with the organization (Rousseau and Parks, 1994). The distribution of power between organizational interest groups is reflected in the terms of the contracts they have with the organization and in their respective abilities to amend those terms.

Organizations are seen to evolve along with changes in the ability of different interest groups to command the *ideational and material resources* necessary for organizational functioning. Although this level of command is liable to change over time in response to changing external conditions as well as to the groups' own bargaining powers, at any one time the group or coalition of groups that controls such resources will in a position to exert a dominating influence over the organization. There may, however, be elements of path dependency in the case of both ideational and material resources. Ideational path dependency is due to adherence to residual ideas and values from the past, such as the family ideal in the case of Telemig. Material path dependency may be due to the legacy of previously successful strategies for obtaining resources (Stinchcombe, 1965).

The ideational resources that organizational interest groups have at their disposal are ideological in nature insofar as they provide them with legitimacy-based influence. Command of an ideology gives an interest group the ability to (a) present its claims in a coherent manner, and (b) secure legitimacy for them by appealing to wider social goals and values. Interest groups do not necessarily develop their own ideologies; they may align themselves to, and import, an existing ideology that holds sway at a higher level of society. An example is the adoption by Telemig's founding management of the military regime's ideology concerning the superiority of rationality over politicking, and the role of telecommunications in promoting national development and integration. Another example was the way in which the triumph of democratic ideals within Brazilian society in the 1980s lent added weight to the labour union's demands for greater participation and openness within Telemig during the 1980.

The ideology that informs political action within a society tends to reinforce the position of some interest groups rather than others. Thus neoliberalism tends to support the rights of business owners rather than those of employees. Sociopolitical ideologies tend to have life cycles – to rise and fall over time. This cyclical pattern impacts upon the power of organizational groups insofar as it is bolstered by their adherence to a particular ideology and thus contributes to the evolution of the priorities expressed in an organization's identity and structure. However, the influence of organizational interest groups is not a function of external ideological support alone. They also have some scope to take the initiative to enhance their legitimacy. Interest-groups can gain additional legitimacy through articulating and publicizing the contributions they make to the organization's well being and how that contribution in turn enables the organization to benefit the wider society. They may also enhance their ability to discredit the standing of other interest groups through effective propaganda, as was the case with the effective use of metaphors critical of management in the Telemig union newspaper.

The power of interest groups rests very importantly on the value to the organization of the resources at their command. The strategic contingencies theory of intra-organizational power developed by Hickson and his colleagues (1971) argues that the power enjoyed by interest groups within an organization will be enhanced when the resources they can offer (such as their skills) are critical to the organization's functioning and when it is difficult for management to obtain those resources from other sources, partly because it is impossible to predict precisely when they are required, as in the case of engineers dealing with system breakdowns. Agencies external to an organization may play a part in defining what its critical resources are. For example, when governments opened national telecommunications markets to competition, they rendered marketing skills a more critical resource for companies in the sector to possess. Similarly, the introduction of environmental pollution regulations can make it critical to employ appropriate experts to avoid the risk of compulsory plant shut-downs. As with ideational resources, interest groups themselves can take actions (mobilize) to enhance their control over critical resources, especially by limiting their availability. This could include limitations on the training and certification of new recruits or, in the case of owners and banks, limitations on the provision of required funding for investment or working capital.

2 Key concepts: mobilization and legitimacy

Mobilization and legitimacy are two concepts that chapter 8 incorporated as the primary drivers of the evolution of corporate identity, and they are discussed in that chapter. Both are key concepts in the political interest perspective. Mobilization is a concept often applied to the development of a collective consciousness and the energizing of action in social and political movements. It can refer to the acquisition of both material and ideational supports. External material supports include the provision of financial resources and institutional support in the form of mandatory freedom to pursue policies and practices consistent with a given identity claim. Internal material support can include the allocation of investment to socialize employees to accept a corporate identity claim through propaganda and training. The political ideology dominant in a society, such as neoliberalism, can provide an important ideational support for a corporate identity claim, feeding into its content and rationale. Mobilization often involves the formation of coalitions and/or the co-optation of support from outside the organization, and these are likely to have particular relevance for an organization providing a public service.

Legitimacy is the second relevant concept. Within the sociological tradition, legitimacy denotes a condition of positive valuation and acceptance enjoyed by persons in positions of power, and by the organizations through which that power is exercised, with particular reference to the policies and actions they undertake. It reflects the extent to which an organization's goals and actions are congruent with wider social values, norms and beliefs. The degree of legitimacy accorded to an organizations's leadership and its policies refers to how far they are positively accepted by other groups or stakeholders within the organization or outside it.

Mobilization and legitimacy reinforce each other in an interest group's bid to secure power within an organization. Both processes cross the boundaries between an organization and its environment. Both are also more effective if they appeal to the interest of other parties to the organization. Management in particular needs to mobilize resources and secure approval for its policies in ways that attract the willing commitment of other groups. The success of an organization depends on the ability of its leading interest group effectively to combine efficient material operations with a set of guiding ideas that command wide appeal. This requires boundary-crossing activities such as convincing financial markets that the organization enjoys good prospects, or lobbying government to change a law or regulation to management's benefit. In a highly institutionalized environment, it is in the interest of both external and organizational groups to establish an active and effective interpersonal relational framework between themselves so as to resolve matters that would in other situations be dealt with through other mechanisms such as state bureaucracy or the market.

The ability of its leading group to maintain its position within an organization will decline if it loses legitimacy and the capacity to mobilize. It will lose legitimacy if it is increasingly unable to satisfy the expectations and interests of other stakeholders. Its capacity to mobilize resources and support will decline if it loses cohesion and standing due to a decline in the power of its sponsors and/or of its supporting ideology. The appointment of less charismatic and poorly qualified leaders can also impair the capacity to mobilize.

3 The political process within co-evolving systems

There is clearly a potential for political processes to enter at various points into the macro, meso and micro co-evolutionary systems portrayed in figure 11.1. Telemig's ideational and material profile was the subject of political debate and contest throughout its evolution, and this became especially evident during periods of major transition such as the move away from the military regime in the first half of the 1980s and the move towards privatization in the mid-1990s. We now explore the dynamics involved in these political processes.

As chapter 8 indicated, the dynamics at play in an organization's co-evolution with its environment centre on its capacity to mobilize support and legitimize its preferred position. In order to prosper and ultimately to survive, an organization's leading group – its 'top management' – needs to enjoy continuing legitimacy in its environment and the capacity to mobilize sufficient resources and other support from external agencies and social groups. Telemig's evolution and transformations during its lifetime clearly illustrate the role of legitimacy and mobilization – for example, as explanatory factors behind the cycles of corporate identity definition and redefinition that were discussed in chapter 8. Legitimacy in effect entails a marshalling of ideational claims that an organization and its management are acting honourably, effectively and in the social interest. It concerns their standing in the eyes of other interest groups – the employees within the organization as well as external groups. Legitimacy is gained primarily through the winning of trust by management; a trust that it is well intentioned towards other groups and capable of delivering on those good intentions. Mobilization entails the securing of

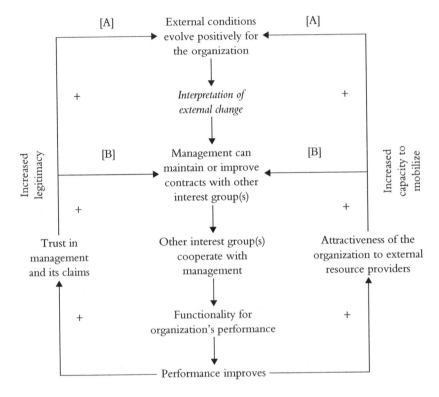

[A]   An increase in management's legitimacy and mobilization capacity strengthens the standing of the organization in its environment and increases its ability to seize opportunities offered by the environment.

[B]   An increase in management's legitimacy and mobilization capacity adds to its intra-organizational power and its ability to institute internal changes if it considers these are required to take advantage of environmental opportunities.

Figure 11.2   The role of interest group power in organizational co-evolution: the case of a virtuous cycle.

requisite resources and other material support for the organization to operate and invest. While most organizations depend upon substantial support from external resource providers, employees are also key human resources and their willing co-operation is essential to success. Legitimacy and mobilization are therefore characteristics both of an organization's internal relations and of its relations with environmental agencies and groups.

Figures 11.2 and 11.3 portray different circumstances concerning legitimacy and mobilization within the processes of change linking an organization to its environment. Figure 11.2 depicts a virtuous cycle in which an organization and its environment are both evolving positively and in which their respective evolutions reinforce one another. In other words, an evolutionary strengthening of the organization feeds positively into the environment – for example, through the

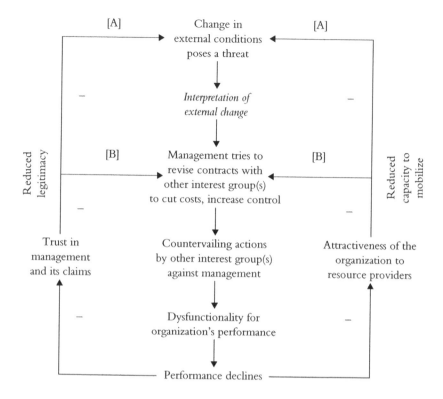

[A] A decline in management's legitimacy and mobilization capacity weakens the standing of the
organization in its environment and further increases environmental pressures on the organization.

[B] A decline in management's legitimacy and mobilization capacity reduces its intra-organizational
power and weakens its ability to institute internal changes in response to the environmental
threat. Management may eventually be replaced.

Figure 11.3 The role of interest group power in organizational co-evolution: the case
of a vicious cycle.

generation of additional employment. Figure 11.3 depicts a vicious cycle in which
the co-evolution is unfavourable to the organization. Its negative feedbacks into
the environment further weaken the organization and they may also have deleteri-
ous effects on environmental evolution unless other competing organizations take
up the slack.

The political process underlying these two contrasting situations involves comparable steps. For convenience, we place environmental change at the top of each
figure as a point of departure, but it should be noted that the process the figures
portray is actually an ongoing one in which movement could be initiated at any
point. If we start with a change in the environment, the next step is that the
environment change is noted and interpreted by an organization's management.
Interpretation involves both making sense of the new situation and drawing

conclusions for action. The interpretation reached may well be conditioned by elements of ideational and material path dependency not shown in the figures. For instance, management may ground its responses to discontinuous external change on old assumptions that past trends are continuing. Or it may consider that its current resource base only permits a given response to the environmental change.

If the environmental change is benign for the organization (figure 11.2), management may feel able to make changes that are positive for the interests of other groups, such as raising rewards and increasing employment. These changes in turn are likely to enhance acceptance of the corporate identity and culture that management is espousing. They may well encourage cooperation with management, even cooperation with the evolutionary introduction of new improved organizational forms and practices that management perceives are necessary to equip the organization to take better advantage of future environmental opportunities. The organization's performance is likely to benefit from a climate of cooperation, and this will enhance management's legitimacy and its capacity to mobilize additional resources. If the organization is a significant player in its environment, these improvements will promote the further benign evolution of that environment through promoting its economic well-being. The goodwill and confidence in the organization that come with enhanced legitimacy facilitate tacit and explicit alliances between its management and interest groups at a higher system level, such as its political sponsors in the Telemig case. In this way, legitimacy contributes to mobilization capacity.

On the other hand, different evolutionary consequences are likely to flow from environmental change that threatens the organization, or at least that is interpreted as such by management (figure 11.3). A common threat is the entry of new competitors into a company's market. In the event of negative environmental change, management is likely to promote internal evolutionary changes that other interest groups perceive to be against their interests. Within the organization these could include structural changes such as downsizing, outsourcing or offshoring, and redrawing employment contracts so as to make them more flexible. Externally, management's reactions might include cutting the dividend paid to shareholders. Actions taken against the interests of internal groups lead to critique and resistance on their part, aimed at challenging management's legitimacy and the corporate identity it is seen as espousing. This was seen in the process of reflective imaging and the use of critical metaphors by Telemig's labour union as the interests of its members came under threat. If resistance to managerially instigated changes fails, the shift in intra-organizational power may encourage a migration of external support from weaker to stronger groups.

An increase in intra-organizational conflict is liable to have immediate dysfunctional consequences for the organization's performance. Actions *vis-à-vis* external groups, such as dividend cuts, may also have eventual negative consequences for the organization's performance if, to continue the example, a downgrading of a company's stock market rating followed and that company consequently found it more costly to raise new funds. It is possible that managerial actions to revise contracts and introduce other changes will turn around the organization's performance, but 'painful medicine' is quite likely to lead to performance decline in the short term at least. If that happens, then management stands to lose both some legitimacy and the capacity to mobilize resources. This may heighten tensions with employee groups who become fearful of their future and it could provoke a further negative change in the environment, with the organization losing support from customers, financiers and owners. The loss of legitimacy can also reduce the capacity of management to persuade external parties to act in the organization's interest by, for example, offering subsidies or tax relief. If the organization is a significant player in its environment, a decline in its performance is likely to create a further negative evolution in that environment, with perhaps losses of employment and demand. Some of the organizational changes undertaken to combat external threats, such as offshoring, would also have negative effects on the community.

The analysis of the evolutionary political process just offered has focused, for reasons of parsimony, on actions taken by an organization's management or leading group. In practice, as the Telemig case has illustrated, non-managerial interest groups can also further their cause within an organization through acting upon both legitimacy and mobilization. Chapter 9 described how the investment of Telemig's union in its newspaper as a propaganda outlet promoted the legitimacy of its cause, especially through the power of critical metaphors. Its alliance with the Workers Party, via the national telecommunications union, enhanced its capacity to countermobilize industrial and other action against the evolution of Telemig's employment policies and organizational practices during the 1980s.

The analysis just offered suggests the following concluding observations on organizational co-evolution:

1   Co-evolution progresses partly in the ideational sphere through the ideas that interest groups articulate and seek to have accepted as socially legitimate.
2   Co-evolution also progresses in the material realm through the process of mobilization to gather resources.
3   Leading organizational actors are likely to form alliances as the basis for collective entrepreneurship. This entrepreneurship aims to develop the capacity to mobilize resources and to gain legitimacy in support of a particular corporate evolutionary 'project'.
4   Collective entrepreneurship may cross system levels and in this way constitute a significant force behind the co-evolution of organizations and environmental agencies.
5   The process of co-evolution can create a heightened consciousness of their interest among the social groups involved, both within an organization and in the environment, especially if there is overt conflict between the satisfaction of different interests.
6   Conflict, in turn, is an important driver of co-evolutionary change.
7   Stages in the co-evolutionary process can be triggered both from the environment and from within an organization.
8   External interventions that trigger evolution may be ideational and/or material.

9   Developments in prevailing business and socio-economic ideologies are particularly important ideational environmental evolutions. Ideologies of national development and integration, democratic pluralism and neoliberalism had an impact on Telemig's evolution at different periods of time. These broad ideologies are also reflected in ideas that have a more immediate impact on organizational evolution, such as lean production and shareholder value. Changes in the value attributed to an organization's occupational interest groups, such as engineers within Telemig, can also encourage changes in the structural position they are granted.

10   Changes in material circumstances include those in market, technological and financial conditions. In Brazilian telecommunications, the opening of markets and technological changes clearly impacted upon individual companies. They were taken to justify the introduction of internal changes. Another material source of evolutionary change is that in an organization's principals, coming about through acquisition and privatization. These have an effect through the changes in corporate control and priorities that ensue. In Telemig's case, the expectation of a change in the nature of ownership, through privatization, triggered a phase of substantial internal evolution, even amounting to a revolution.

11   Internal evolutionary triggers can arise from the Baldwin effect, namely that adaptation can arise from the ability of organizational members to learn. Thus learning can enable management to become more successful in commanding legitimacy and mobilizing necessary resources. Other interest groups can also learn to be more effective in promoting evolutionary change or resisting it.

A political interest theory of co-evolution is rooted in an analysis of the ideational and material factors discussed above that shape the changing distribution of power among organizational interest groups over time: especially the power to define corporate identity, culture, employment and structure. The terms of legal and psychological contracts between interest groups reflect these issues. At root the distribution of power among organizational interest groups therefore comes down to their respective abilities to negotiate those terms and in so doing to shape the evolution of organizations over time.

Note

1   This section draws partly on Rodrigues and Child (2003).

References

Aldrich, H. E. (1999) *Organizations Evolving*. Thousand Oaks, CA: Sage.
Bain, J. S. (1956) *Barriers to New Competition*. Cambridge, MA: Harvard University Press.
Baldwin, J. M. (1896) A new factor in evolution. *The American Naturalist*, 30, 441–51.

Barney, J. B. (1991) Firm resources and sustained competitive advantage. *Journal of Management*, 17, 99–120.

Bentley, A. F. (1908) *The Process of Government*. Chicago: University of Chicago Press.

Berry, J. M. (1997) *The Interest Group Society*, 3rd edn. London: Longman.

Calori, R., Lubatkin, M., Very, P. and Veiga, J. F. (1997) Modeling the origins of nationally bound administrative heritages: theory and field research. *Organization Science*, 8, 681–96.

Chandler, A. D. (1977) *The Visible Hand*. Cambridge, MA: Harvard University Press.

Child, J. (1972) Organizational structure, environment and performance: the role of strategic choice. *Sociology*, 6, 1–22.

Child, J. (1988) On organizations in their sectors. *Organization Studies*, 9, 13–19.

Child, J. (1997) Strategic choice in the analysis of action, structure, organizations and environment: retrospect and prospect. *Organization Studies*, 18, 43–76.

Child, J. and Loveridge, R. (1990) *New Technology in European Services*. Oxford: Blackwell.

Child, J., Lu, Y. and Tsai, S.-H. T. (2007) Institutional entrepreneurship in building an environmental protection system for the People's Republic of China. *Organization Studies* 28: 1013–34.

Child, J. and Smith, C. (1987) The context and process of organizational transformation: Cadbury Limited in its sector. *Journal of Management Studies*, 24, 565–93.

Clegg, S. R. (1989) *Frameworks of Power*. London: Sage.

Cyert, R. M. and March, J. G. (1963) *A Behavioral Theory of the Firm*. Englewood Cliffs, NJ: Prentice Hall.

Dacin, M. T., Goodstein, J. and Scott, W. R. (2002) Institutional theory and institutional change: introduction to the special research forum. *Academy of Management Journal*, 45, 45–57.

D'Aveni, R. A. (1994) *Hypercompetition*. New York: Free Press.

Davies, A. (1994) *Telecommunications and Politics*. New York: Pinter.

Ferraz, J. C. and Lootty, M. (2000) Fusões, aquisições e internacionalização patrimonial no Brasil nos anos 90. In P. da M. Veiga (ed.), *O Brasil e os desafios da globalização*. Rio de Janeiro: Relume-Dumará, pp. 39–63.

Fligstein, N. (1996) Markets as politics: a political-cultural approach to market institutions. *American Sociological Review*, 61, 656–73.

Gersick, C. J. G. (1991) Revolutionary change theories: a multilevel exploration of the punctuated equilibrium paradigm. *Academy of Management Review*, 16, 10–36.

Greenwood, R. and Hinings, C. R. (1987) Editorial introduction: organizational transformations. *Journal of Management Studies*, 24, 561–4.

Greiner, L. E. (1972) Evolution and revolution as organizations grow. *Harvard Business Review*, 76, 37–46.

Hannan, M. T. and Freeman, J. H. (1989) *Organizational Ecology*. Cambridge, MA: Harvard University Press.

Hickson, D. J., Hinings, C. R., Lee, C. A., Schneck, R. G. and Pennings, J. M. (1971) A strategic contingencies theory of intra-organizational power. *Administrative Science Quarterly*, 16, 216–29.

Hirschman, A. O. (1972) *Exit, Voice, and Loyalty*. Cambridge, MA: Harvard University Press.

Huygens, M., Baden-Fuller, C., van den Bosch, F. and Volberda, H. W. (2001) Co-evolution of firm capabilities and industry competition: investigating the music industry 1877–1997. *Organization Studies*, 22, 971–1011.

Journal of Management Studies (2003) Special research symposium. Beyond adaptation vs. selection research: organizing self-renewal in co-evolving environments. 40, 2105–210.

Kull, K. (2000) Organisms can be proud to have been their own designers. *Cybernetics and Human Knowing*, 7, 45–55.

Lewin, A. Y. and Koza, M. P. (2001) Editorial: empirical research in co-evolutionary processes of strategic adaptation and change: the promise and the challenge. *Organization Studies*, 22, v–xii.

Lewin, A. Y., Long, C. P. and Carroll, T. M. (1999) The coevolution of new organizational forms. *Organization Science*, 10, 535–50.

Lewin, A. Y. and Volberda, H. W. (1999) Prolegomena on coevolution: a framework for research on strategy and new organizational forms. *Organization Science*, 10, 519–34.

Lundstedt, S. B. (1990) *Telecommunications, Values and the Public Interest*. Norwood, NJ: Ablex Publishing.

McKelvey, B. (1997) Quasi-natural organization science. *Organization Science*, 8, 352–80.

Oliver, C. (1992) The antecedents of deinstitutionalization. *Organization Studies*, 13, 563–88.

Organization Science (1999) Focused issue: coevolution of strategy and new organizational forms, 10, 519–690.

Organization Studies (2001) Special issue: multi-level analysis and co-evolution, 22, v–xii, 911–1060.

Pettigrew, A. M. (1985) *The Awakening Giant: Continuity and Change in Imperial Chemical Industries*. Oxford: Blackwell.

Pfeffer, J. and Salancik, G. R. (1978) *The External Control of Organizations: A Resource Dependence Perspective*. New York: Harper and Row.

Powell, W. W. and DiMaggio, P. J. (1991) *The New Institutionalism in Organizational Analysis*. Chicago: University of Chicago Press.

Rodrigues, S. B. and Child, J. (2003) Co-evolution and transformation in times of deconstruction: a dynamic multi-level process. *Journal of Management Studies*, 40, 2137–62.

Rousseau, D. M. and Parks, J. M. (1994) The contracts of individuals and organizations. In L. L. Cummings and B. M. Staw (eds), *Research in Organizational Behavior*, volume 15. Greenwich, CT: JAI Press, pp. 1–43.

Saunders, R. J., Warford, J. J. and Wellenius, B. (1994) *Telecommunications and Economic Development*. Baltimore: Johns Hopkins University Press for the World Bank.

Schumpeter, J. A. (1934) *The Theory of Economic Development*. Cambridge, MA: Harvard University Press.

Scott, W. R. and Meyer, J. W. (1983) The organization of society sectors. In J. W. Meyer and W. R. Scott (eds), *Ritual and Rationality*. Beverly Hills, CA: Sage, pp. 129–54.

Selznick, P. (1949) *TVA and the Grass Roots*. Berkeley: University of California Press.

Selznick, P. (1992) *The Moral Commonwealth: Social Theory and the Promise of Community*. Berkeley: University of California Press.

Stinchcombe, A. L. (1965) Social structure and organizations. In J. G. March (ed.), *Handbook of Organizations*. Chicago: Rand McNally, pp. 142–93.

Teece, D. J. and Pisano, G. (1997) Dynamic capabilities and strategic management. *Strategic Management Journal*, 18, 509–33.

Weick, K. E. (1979) *The Social Psychology of Organizing*. Reading, MA: Addison-Wesley.

Weick, K. E. (1995) *Sensemaking in Organizations*. Thousand Oaks, CA: Sage.

Author Index

Subject Index

Printed and bound by CPI Group (UK) Ltd, Croydon, CR0 4YY

16/04/2025

14658828-0001